DANCING WITH DEMONS

DANCING WITH DEMONS

The Authorised Biography
of Dusty Springfield

Penny Valentine
and Vicki Wickham

Hodder & Stoughton

Copyright © 2000 by Penny Valentine and Vicki Wickham

First published in Great Britain in 2000 by Hodder and Stoughton
A division of Hodder Headline

10 9 8 7 6 5 4 3 2 1

A CIP catalogue record for this title is available
from the British Library.

ISBN 0 340 76673 5

Typeset by Palimpsest Book Production Limited,
Polmont, Stirlingshire
Printed and bound in Great Britain by
Clays Ltd, St Ives plc

Hodder and Stoughton
A division of Hodder Headline
338 Euston Road
London NW1 3BH

For Dan and Nona with love

Acknowledgments

A lthough writing is a lonely business there are usually people around who can make the task less onerous. So it was with *Dancing With Demons*. My thanks go to the following people:

To Vicki, my partner in this project, who kept me buoyant and who began, against her better judgement, to believe in the power of re-incarnation. Vicki would like to thank Stevie and Lee for filling in large chunks of her life which she 'had forgotten', and Dusty 'for a long friendship and for introducing me to the sound of American soul singers'. To our editor Rowena Webb and the women at our publishers Hodder. Also to our researcher Kim Bunce for her hard work and enthusiasm.

In memory of my mother Yolanda, and to my father Robert. To Mike Flood Page for his generosity, Mary and Colin, Julie and the American 'family'. To Jenny and Steve Peacock, John Fordham, Alistair Hatchett, Jim Latter and Robert Lee, for their friendship. Julia Francis and Paul, Cath Blackburn and Eddie for the walks. Hermione Harris and Linda Hall who got used to me not ringing back.

To Tris Penna for the tapes and pictures. Nigel Fountain, Polly Pattullo and my colleagues at the Guardian newspaper. Sandra Hall and Phil Stafford in Australia and especially to Susie Whitehead Pope for giving me house room in Sydney.

This book could not have been written without the people across continents who so generously shared their memories of Dusty, only one of whom did not want us to use her real name and so appears as 'Faye Harris': In Britain – Lee Everett-Alkin, Madeline Bell, Simon Bell, Riss Chantelle, Debbie Dannell, Mike Gill, Stevie Holly, Pat Rhodes. In America – Peggy Albrecht, Rosie Casals, Jenny Cohen, Marv Greifinger, Billie Jean King, Barry Krost, Suzanne Lacefield, Nancy Lewis, Helene Sellery, Susan Shroeder, Norma Tanega. In Canada – Carole Pope, Kevan Staples. In Holland – Pieter van der Zwan. In Australia – Doug Reece.

I am also indebted to Merilee Strong's *A Bright Red Scream* and Dominic Davies and Charles Neal's *Pink Therapy*.

Most of all my love and thanks go to the women who have always been there for me: Ros Asquith, Sally Bradbery, Elana Dallas, Michèle Roberts (who shared her knowledge of Catholicism), Diana Simmonds, Val Wilmer, Veronica Norburn and my 'sister from the 60s', Caroline Boucher.

DANCING WITH DEMONS

Prologue

On the evening of 24 November 1999, a month before the dawn of the millennium, over five hundred people are gathered in the ballroom of the Inter-Continental Hotel in London. The event is the annual Women of the Year Awards for the music industry: a night thought up by women working in the business to celebrate the achievements of other women working in the industry. It is a sparkling evening with male 'statues' sprayed gold, deep plushy carpets and champagne flowing. This is not 1975 at the height of the women's movement and so tonight it's a mixed 1990s audience: lovely young women from the press departments; out gay male publicists; rowdy tearaways from promotion; determined women agency bosses; football besotted men who run record labels and live in Surrey with their wives and children.

Amongst the winners this year is Vicki Wickham who is receiving a lifetime achievement award. Privately she jokes that it's 'simply for still being alive', but the truth is that she's pleased she's being recognised for having played such an important role in the rise of music. She edited the seminal 1960s TV show *Ready, Steady, Go!* (the weekend starts here!), went to America and was the *éminence grise* of the revolutionary all-woman black group Labelle and for thirteen fraught and crazy years managed Dusty Springfield.

That week Vicki is interviewed by Caroline Sullivan of the *Guardian* and finally decides, almost accidentally, to come out in print during a conversation about why, although she fancied Brian Jones of the Rolling Stones, nothing ever happened. She laughingly apologises for being such a 'bad lesbian': never went on marches or protests; didn't think much of a 'gay lifestyle'. It has taken Vicki, who is not a star and not in the public eye, until her late fifties finally to say anything publicly about her sexuality. Although she'd been interviewed many times over the years, Vicki never felt it was 'appropriate' to talk about it: 'Mainly I was always talking about someone or something else all the time and anyway, who the hell cares about what I do?' But for Dusty to have come out in the press, she says, would have been a very different matter. 'It would always have been too risky. She would have had everything defined by that.'

Although the music business likes to view itself as a liberal institution, in truth it is after all a business: as conservative, hierarchical and, if not homophobic, certainly as lesbophobic as most. It's a business that has, over the years, learned how to accommodate the sexuality of gay men, both as business people and artists – especially if it doesn't hurt the sales figures: from the careful bisexuality of David Bowie, the more overtly flamboyant Holly Johnson of Frankie Goes To Hollywood, Freddie Mercury, Elton John when he finally came out once he left his longtime manager John Reid and settled with David Furnish, to George Michael, pushed out by the Los Angeles Police Department (an event he even celebrated in his promotional video). But it remains rare, in music, film or television, for one woman to stand up and speak about her relationship with another woman as though it were the 'norm'.

k.d. lang got it out of the way early and looking like young Elvis Presley helped because, well a girl wearing a tuxedo and greased back hair? And she knew we all got it right from the start, so getting a face shave by Cindy Crawford on the front of *Esquire* magazine was only an eye-opener because of the combination of an out lesbian singer and a glamorous model, all legs and dress: butch and femme personified. Even so things went quiet for k.d. for a time.

Count the women musicians who are 'out' on the fingers of one hand – lang, Melissa Etheridge, Janis Ian. They are brave souls. The rise of the religious right in America over the past twenty years has been such that the atmosphere has become closer to that once afforded to McCarthy's witch hunts – with roughly the same effect. TV programmes are boycotted, advertisers withdraw, people get scared for their livelihoods. And of course the really visible lesbian couple becomes an even bigger problem than the single lesbian star. When Ellen DeGeneres and Anne Heche announced they were together and canoodled at the White House, the public world went pear-shaped on them both. Worse for the American right, Heche had, until clapping eyes on DeGeneres across a crowded room, apparently considered herself a heterosexual. In the event she left her husband for Ellen and moved straight in. And in Britain it wasn't until June 2000 that the young Irish singer Sinéad O'Connor finally 'outed' herself during an interview with the lesbian magazine *Curve*, admitting that 'throughout most of my life I've gone out with blokes because I haven't been terribly comfortable about being a lesbian. But I actually am a lesbian.'

It was against this background that Dusty Springfield lived her life. People in the business wondered, the gay and lesbian audience she began to attract had certainly guessed. But Dusty? She didn't want to have to define herself, be pigeonholed: 'I won't play that game.' Truth was she was also terrified that her mainstream audiences would not love her, that the image she had spent so long building up would be shattered and that the industry would cold-shoulder her. And anyway, 'The closet quality of Hollywood and Los Angeles show business is overwhelming,' she once said. 'You can be at a dinner party where you know that at least twelve of the fourteen people there are gay and listen to incredible anti-gay crap. And they play that game because a few industry heads are very anti-gay. It's very tough for most gay people and very difficult to speak out.'

When we decided to work together on this book, with me writing and tussling with Dusty's psychopathology and Vicki opening doors for me that might otherwise have been firmly closed, we spent long days sharing our memories. We knew it would be impossible not to talk about Dusty's sexuality because it went such a long way to explaining one of the enormous pressures she was under – another part of herself she was always having to hide. It was an additional stress to the exhausting work of getting the wigs and dresses and make-up right; of getting the band sounding the way she wanted; of getting each note that would emerge from her voice absolutely spot-on. Emotionally fragile, Dusty was driven to succeed because her often-battered ego needed her audience to assure her that she was loved at all.

Yet the person I interviewed nearly every week in the 1960s as part of my job on a weekly music paper was such a lovely unaffected woman it was, even if it sounds corny now, exactly like meeting up with an old friend each time. If she'd had a boring couple of weeks we'd spend the hour or so embroidering stories round a tiny element of truth so that I had something to write for my paper. Often, she said, these were her favourite pieces. We'd swap information on our latest soul and Motown crushes; after a while I'd be round at her Aubrey Walk house in Kensington or at the parties she and her partner Norma held. By the time Dusty was co-hosting *Ready, Steady, Go!* I'd also met Vicki who was working on the programme.

In May 1968 a revolution broke out first in Paris then London and America. I'd like to say that Dusty, Vicki and I were on the barricades. Sadly, we were not. Instead we were having a rather boozy lunch together in the West End. Dusty had decided that it was time Vicki and I met properly, rather than passing each other at breakneck speed in the corridor of a TV studio. She thought we'd 'get along well'. As usual, when it came to other people, she was completely right. A few months later Vicki and I would be hanging about Vicki's flat in New Cavendish Street waiting for what seemed like hours while Dusty got ready and we could, finally, go out for supper: 'Dusty, that'll do, honestly you look great and it's only us.' None of this was particularly unusual in the 1960s when there was such a unique egalitarian atmosphere in popular music. Musicians, journalists, programme-makers and disc jockeys got drunk together, danced together and caroused together until dawn. If, in her late twenties, Dusty seemed to behave more like a naughty child than a grown woman then she was in good company. We were far from the maturity that would be expected of near-thirty-year-olds at the end of the century. Unpoliced, by society or by ourselves, it was a time when rock stars pretended to be waiters at their own receptions; when they jumped on passers by and rolled them down the stairs of posh hotels; when rock managers often set themselves accidentally on fire. At this children's party adults were banned. We were all in freefall and it never occurred to any of us that we might not land safely.

Dusty once said of that period that drinking was what you did. That if you were nearly unconscious through booze and fell down the stairs nobody tut-tutted or thought you were an immediate candidate for a dry-out: 'They just said, "What a card!"' And it's true that most of us were in a haze and everyone thought everyone else was pretty damn funny.

Who knew Dusty? I thought I did until I started working on this book, but it turned into a journey across the world that unravelled like a detective story. Vicki and I would follow leads that would suddenly go cold then heat up again; one would sometimes lead to another. Gradually a picture began to emerge of a highly talented woman who appeared to be full of life but could suffer from the most debilitating depressions, who could impress you with the most superb singing while suffering the most dreadful psychic panic.

She could often turn herself into the person she thought other people wanted her to be. As a result there were some heterosexual people in her life who believed that she had had her heart 'broken' by a mysterious Italian when she was young; that if songwriter Burt Bacharach had not been happily married to Angie Dickinson Dusty would have been overjoyed. It's likely that Dusty did have a crush on Bacharach because he was one of the few men who understood her, was gentle and just as finicky in the studio as she was. But it was, in fact, to Angie that Dusty ran to pour her heart out when things got tough. She would often say there were footballers she fancied and a string of men in her life that she'd had affairs with. No doubt some footballers' bottoms were a source of great visual pleasure for her and, certainly, she was mad on the game, but if she did occasionally hop into bed with a man it seems it was when she'd had a tiff with a girlfriend and wanted to make her jealous or she was completely out of her head on drugs and drink or downright lonely. The truth was that all Dusty's close long-term relationships, and most of her short-term ones too, were with women, many of whom continued to love her throughout her life.

The story of Dusty is, I think, both sad and uplifting. It's the story of a plain girl who became a lovely woman and a star, who hit the bottom, lost it all and then found success again late in her life – not because audiences felt nostalgic or sorry for her but because they thrilled, as they always had, to her voice. And it's the story of a survivor. However much she was emotionally or physically abused and however much she abused herself Dusty always retained her sense of humour and her old winning ways.

The Dusty of this book is, of course, a composite: only we have the pictures in our heads of who we are and what our life is really like – and we deal with our own demons the best we can. This is a portrait of Dusty made up from other people's memories, other people's stories. But it also comes from Dusty herself and the surprisingly frank things she would often say publicly in interviews. Bit by bit, over an arduous year, Vicki and I recognised many parts of the woman we had known and came to empathise much more with those parts we had never really understood.

Once Dusty went to America in the early 1970s I caught up with her a few times in Los Angeles and it was clear that things were not good. For the first few hours she'd be just as I remembered her – warm, funny and relaxed – but as the night wore on she would get drunk surprisingly quickly, she'd reminisce about the past, and sometimes there would be blood on the pool table because she was so unsteady on pills and booze that she'd fall and gash her face.

Yet my favourite picture of Dusty is not of a tortured soul or a diva in a tight pink sequined dress, but one taken early in her solo career. Her hair looks like it needs a comb, her hands are thrown up in front of her face which is lit with an animated smile. She looks like an excited child at Christmas.

When Dusty was diagnosed with cancer I left a message on her answerphone. Sometimes I'd get home and my own machine would be bleeping. There'd be the sound of that hesitant silence, then of someone putting the phone down at the other end of the line. I like to think that it was Dusty calling back.

Penny Valentine, June 2000

1

New York's emergency services took the 911 call somewhere between midnight and two in the morning. A woman had rung to say she'd had an accident, could they please send an ambulance quickly. The paramedics from Bellevue Hospital on the Lower East Side, who years later would be immortalised in Martin Scorsese's *Bringing Out The Dead*, raced out of the back of Bellevue, their sirens whining, red lights flashing, to a brownstone on the Upper West Side.

Crossing town at this time of night was at least fast. Times Square was lit up and crowded as usual. Yellow cabs bumped over the potholes as ever, but the traffic flowed more freely than during the day and there was room for drivers to get out of the way. The ambulance turned hard right and within five minutes had swung into Amsterdam Avenue and across Columbus. Shrieking into 76th Street, west of Central Park, they screeched to a halt and raced up the stone steps to the door. Why these houses were always called 'walk-ups' made the paramedics smile joylessly – they always hit them on the run. Shit! None of the names on the bells at the front tallied with the one they'd been given. In desperation they pressed them all and after a few seconds the buzzer went and the front door unlocked. Lady, hey maam, maam? They ran up the stairs banging the stretcher into the walls because the space was so narrow. At the top, on the fourth floor, behind the opened apartment door, they found her in her pink tracksuit. Later they wondered how she had managed to open the thick wooden door at all with such badly cut arms. But right now they had a job to do and no time to wonder about anything. And they had seen it before. Often. The NYC paramedics bound her arms and gently carried her down on the stretcher into the back of the life-support unit to Bellevue. They noticed that, despite her tousled hair and the pain she was in, she was a pretty woman with a light, breathy, odd accent that they couldn't quite place.

On a scorching late August day in New York just before the year 2000, with humidity breathtakingly hitting the high nineties, Bellevue is a surprise. New York's oldest public hospital sits towards the end of Manhattan Island on First Avenue at 27th. The main teaching hospital for New York University School of Medicine, those young medics can work in over a hundred speciality clinics, they may even get to treat the President or, given her Senate campaign for the district, Hillary Clinton. But if Bellevue is famous for anything it's because it has the largest psychiatric department on the east coast. Yet far from being a grim institution it looks no different from those around it. In fact it's a happier-looking building than those frowning tower blocks around Central Park with their heavy lidded windows that only shine at night. Today the covered walkway is bustling with people, yet the cathedral-like domed main hall is quiet and cool with a polite woman at the information desk.

Turn left and you're in the main emergency admissions area. Here members of the NYPD stroll, nightsticks hanging threateningly at their sides and tags reading 'Correction Department'. There is an impressive list of services – community support, homeless programmes – but you're warned to keep alert: 'Silence Can Be Deadly' reads a notice on the wall; 'A co-worker who abuses alcohol may put your safety at risk.' With its high Latino intake from the surrounding neighbourhood everything is written out again in Spanish. Bellevue is for ever busy, responding to a city that is constantly fighting against poverty and violence. Human Resources assistant Peter Serrano, who saw his co-worker at the Teachers Insurance and Retirement Funds building shot in front of him, tells the New York Times: 'You have to look over your shoulder all the time. You're never safe, not even at work.'

Out front at Bellevue there's a carnival atmosphere. Hot dog and soda and doughnut stalls, fruit wagons and Angelo's coffee stand, line the avenue outside the gates. People crowd round the garish umbrellas getting a little relief from the heat; some sit on the low wall clutching bags of free clothes and staring dazedly ahead. In the small public garden to one side of the entrance a miniature Italianate fountain splashes gently and there is some welcome shade under the trees. An overweight, pale young woman is talking to three women who have just emerged with their free clothing supplies and are happily going through the contents of their bags, holding things up against each other and dispensing with items they don't feel can be made fashionable even with a small alteration here or there. 'I'm on the programme,' she says. 'Y'know they sit you in a chair with your feet up for so long your legs swell up. Look.' She pulls up her jeans to display her puffy ankles. On her T-shirt it says 'Fix My Head'.

The night in 1985 is the second time Dusty has been on Bellevue's psychiatric wing, the second time she's been booked in under the name Mary O'Brien and just one more time when she's sectioned herself to save her own life. In California her emergency visits to Cedar Sinai and LA County hospitals are so frequent that she says (and she's only half joking) that she knows the first names of all the paramedics who come out to get her.

All her life Dusty had had trouble sleeping. Four hours was her usual tally and from early on friends were used to her calling at one or two in the morning just to talk, even when she was in a relationship. From midnight to two were, everyone knew, her worst times, the times she couldn't bear the loneliness of the dark. When things got bad, as they often did during her fifteen years in America, the worst times became more panic-stricken. Now she would call, not just to talk until the hours went by, but to try and save herself from the unnamed terrors that seemed to overwhelm her. In Los Angeles, says Faye Harris who lived with Dusty for six years, even in the morning Dusty would be depressed. 'She'd wake up and say there was a small dark cloud over her head. Even when things weren't bad she said it. She used to say she never had a moment of joy unless she was on stage. It was the only time she felt confident and happy.' That Dusty could, every morning, constantly tell her partner how unhappy she was says a lot about the depths of the psychological pain she seemed almost permanently to be in. There was nothing Faye could do to make it better and Dusty seemed unable to hold it in to herself. It was so overwhelming it exhausted her. She had to fight to shake it off every day of her life. 'My mother always said I had a very low energy level,' Dusty would recall. 'That I would tire very easily.' Yet nobody who met her out in the world would have guessed: to them Dusty was a bright star, full of life and seductive charm.

Usually at night someone was with her or at the end of the line, but those times when they weren't or when Dusty couldn't get her usual comfort from the sound of a human voice, she would cut herself until she could ring 911 and be taken to safety. And, for her, a psychiatric ward offered a comfort most people found hard to understand.

'If it had been me,' says Vicki who went to visit her at Bellevue, 'after a few hours I'd have rung someone and asked them to "get me out of here", but she never did.' Dusty always loved hotels, it was one of the most consistent things about her. No matter what domestic dramas (the cats couldn't be left, she had flu . . .) held her up from working, the mere mention of being put up in a hotel changed her whole frame of mind. Perhaps it was because a hotel offered her the ultimate freedom: no housework, no responsibility, someone to look after her every need, and she could come and go as she pleased without being answerable to anyone. Who wouldn't love a luxury suite with a marble bathroom that someone else cleaned? And despite its lack of luxury amenities Bellevue became like a hotel to her – somewhere that someone else would take care of her.

In New York that year Dusty, still on the surface smiling and joking, was desperately broke. In town for a one-off single recording, she had borrowed money to try to make some demo records to hawk round. She had booked into a hotel but it was far from luxurious. The building, on 72nd Street, was a 'suite hotel', a series of small dingy bedsits, each with a little kitchenette off at the side. It was overrun with cockroaches and after a week Vicki, by now her manager, decided she had to get Dusty out. Vicki's friend Jeff Cason was leaving for a month in Europe and his apartment at the top of an enviable brownstone on the smart West Side would be empty. Could Dusty move in?

A few days later, with her suitcases and her inevitable purple sparkling shopping bags, Dusty was ensconced away from the 'roaches. But she was still on her own and the nights loomed. She would call her new managers, Vicki and Jenny Cohen, endlessly throughout the day and night on some minor pretext. Cohen would eventually crack under the pressure of it and the endless demands it made on her life, leaving Vicki to cope alone. If there was work in the offing they would tell her about it and be told she'd 'think about it'. Inevitably there would be reasons she couldn't do it, even though by now she was desperately short of money. 'I wouldn't have minded,' says Vicki, 'if she'd just said, "I don't want to," but instead there would be a million excuses: "You don't understand. I don't feel good, I think I'm coming down with flu, I'm too tired." However much you tried to understand, it got terribly frustrating.'

It was as though Dusty was in the grip of a terrible lethargy, a kind of endless depression that nobody knew how to save her from. Earlier, on the night she had dialled the emergency services, she had once again rung Jenny Cohen and Vicki. For a while Dusty only got the answerphone. In growing panic she had run Cohen again, even though she had spoken to her at least twenty times that day. Jenny had talked to her: she and Vicki had decided that Dusty had to seek help to get off the pills she was taking, pills that made her even more anxious and unreasonable and were undermining everything she was trying to do. They suggested a detox centre, which they'd pay for themselves to get her off the drugs and straightened out. In the night Dusty, high on barbiturates, cut her arms up.

The next day Vicki made the trip downtown to Bellevue. Through the main entrance and up in the lift to the psychiatric ward she was 'locked in and out': a door was unlocked which let her into a small anteroom. Here she waited until that door was locked behind her and the other door unlocked in front of her. Although Dusty had her own room to sleep in, during the day she was in the communal area, shuffling around in a hospital gown just like everyone else. To Vicki the sight of Dusty on heavy medication was terrible. It bloated her face and made her function more slowly. When Jenny Cohen turned up the first person she met introduced himself as Colonel Gaddafi which, given Jenny was Jewish, threw her slightly. But Dusty seemed relatively calm however much it upset Jenny to see her on the ward and have to stand behind a yellow line on the floor. Like prison visits, bodily contact on the psychiatric ward was forbidden since it could mean that visitors could pass on drugs brought in from outside.

'She always said the same thing when I asked her if she wanted to come out,' says Vicki. 'That she was manic depressive, that they couldn't get the medication right. But I always got the feeling she didn't really want to leave. For Dust these places really did become like hotels to her.'

Even a psychiatric ward has its advantages: here people are 'looking after you', you have no responsibilities, and someone else cleans and cooks. You can see how Dusty, who seemed to want to be safely held without the emotional commitment that went with relationships, almost found the wards a haven from what she experienced as the harshness of real life and the terrible hours after midnight. It says a lot about Dusty's grim sense of humour that when her friend Helene Sellery collected her from Bellevue and took her back to her ranch in the California hills to recuperate, amongst the items that Dusty produced from her suitcase was the straitjacket she had to wear the first week on the ward at Bellevue.

Yet her life hadn't always been like this. What had happened to one of the greatest women singers in the world, a singer who had enjoyed sixteen hit singles and who had produced *Dusty in Memphis* – an album that was such a classic that, in 1997, thirty years after its release, *Rolling Stone* magazine acclaimed it as part of its essential record collection? Its sound, of 'elegant orchestral soul', one that 'still challenges the listener today'. What had happened to Dusty Springfield, the 1960s icon and erstwhile musicologist; a singer exalted by popular music's leading songwriters Burt Bacharach and Carole King, by the black American singers she herself so admired, and revered by musicians as versatile and productive as Annie Lennox, Elvis Costello, Neil Tennant and Elton John?

2

In the early 1960s London was the place to be and to be Dusty Springfield was to be divine. London had transformed itself from a struggling repressed city of post-war Britain, with its ration books and free sticky-sweet orange juice, into a faintly hedonistic teenage heaven. For both the audiences and the stars they made, it seemed anything and everything was possible – even staying a teenager for ever.

And in the course of five years Dusty had transformed herself: from an overweight, curly-haired ex-convent girl into an attractive blonde with a famously 'whacky' personality and, more importantly, the most stunningly soulful voice ever to emerge from British music.

On the back of the post-war nationalisation of British industry came the growth of technology. The British started to be offered the kind of consumer products enjoyed by their better-off American counterparts: televisions, fridges, record-players. More jobs were created, so many that teenagers now had a much wider choice of occupations. More and more left school – not now to work because they had to and mainly in poorly paid jobs – but to go straight into the market-place where new trades were being created and they could earn high wages. Usually living at home with their families, these post-war 'baby boomers' had record levels of disposable income: advertisers started to aim directly at what they now labelled a 'youth market' with records, magazines and fashion.

In London particularly it was easy to increase your spending power by constantly moving into ever-higher-paid work, and the atmosphere was such that if you had a clever idea or talent and you could run with it you could become rich and, probably, famous no matter whether you came from the working-class areas of Deptford or Hackney, had 'emigrated' to the capital from the slums of Glasgow, or your parents owned most of an island in the Caribbean. You could be a film star like Terry Stamp, you could be a fashion photographer like David Bailey, you could be a small gay Scotsman and make a fortune as a clothes designer, you could be a Sandie Shaw or later a Twiggy, or you could simply hang out with your mates in a pop group.

London became a class and cultural mélange and from it emerged the Mods with their Lambrettas and Vespas, their sharp little suits, the girls with bobbed back-combed hair, tight little jumpers and immaculate make-up. The Mods and, in particular, the Soho area of London had a symbiotic relationship with each other. Sometimes they went down to the Flamingo club to be amongst the black American servicemen on furlough from their airbases and to hear jazz from Georgie Fame and the Blue Flames, or to the cramped dark Marquee which would put on the first of the Mod bands, the Who. But it was the Scene club in Wardour Street, which on Friday nights drew Mods from as far away as Essex and Hertford and where the Who went when they were the High Numbers, that was the one place where you could hear unreleased soul and R&B singles from America (as well as get your mandrax and speed for the weekend).

During the day Carnaby Street, once no more than a side passage parallel to Regent Street, with its boutiques and media blitz, was now the centre of the Mod universe until, with the establishment of 'Swinging London', it became simply a tourist heaven.

So in 1963, if there was another centre of Mod culture, it was a nondescript office building on the edge of the Aldwych in central London. Squeezed between the law courts and the theatre district it was from this basement at Rediffusion TV that the Friday night pop show *Ready, Steady, Go!* went out. The idea behind the show had originally come from Rediffusion's head of light entertainment, Elkan Allan. He wanted to reflect the growing power of the new pop culture through a programme that had a feeling of pop art. The show would feature singers and bands who had singles out, who had got into the charts or who might get into the charts. But it would also have as star guests record producers like Phil Spector, comedians Dudley Moore and Peter Cook or the great young boxing phenomenon Cassius Clay before he became known as Muhammad Ali. The decisions were pretty arbitrary: often people would be in front of the cameras simply because the *RSG!* team liked them. What wasn't arbitrary was the audience. Encouraged to dance throughout the programme, they were as important to the style of the show as the artists who appeared on it.

The week before *RSG!* was aired the programme's editor Vicki Wickham, its young compère Cathy McGowan – whose tresses looked like they had been pressed with an iron – and the Mod-suited Michael Aldred, along with their director Michael Lindsay-Hogg, would scour clubs across the outlying reaches of London, such as Streatham and Chiswick, to find suitable dancers. Tickets for the programme were 'like gold dust' and the young Mods, despite their outward show of cool, were desperate to be on screen. For Vicki, the bustling, young, middle-class girl from Berkshire who raced about the corridors of Rediffusion with her clipboard, there were innumerable embarrassing moments when kids would ambush her, demanding that she dance with them to prove they had the talent to appear before the cameras. Particularly since 'I couldn't dance to save my life'.

If ever 'Swinging London' and the now newly glamorous solo singer Dusty Springfield came together and gelled, it was around *Ready, Steady, Go!*.

Dusty had been born Mary Isobel Catherine Bernadette, the younger of the two children of Gerard and Catherine O'Brien, in the spring of 1939, a few months before the outbreak of the Second World War. The O'Briens, who had married late in life, had certainly assembled an impressive line-up of traditional female saints' names with which to mark their only daughter's entry into the world and the blessed Mary grew up first in Lauderdale Mansions, a solid block of mansion flats near Edgware Road, then in West Hampstead. Since London was being hit with bombing raids by Hitler's Luftwaffe, the O'Briens decided it would be safer to move out. For the next few years the couple brought up little Mary and her older brother Dion in High Wycombe, Buckinghamshire, a market town on the edge of the Chiltern Hills and notable only for furniture manufacture.

Although the children could run fairly freely, the neighbours were always complaining that the family never cut their grass and tax accountant Gerard and Catherine (now known by their friends as OB, after 'O'Brien', and Kay) soon got bored with their life in the country. By 1950 the war had been over for five years, but they were against putting the children back into the heart of an urban environment. Instead they made for Kent Gardens in Ealing.

In the early 1950s Ealing was about the only west London suburb that retained a big, quiet, country charm but was accessible to the city. Its huge rambling Victorian red-brick houses had been built for the then newly expanding white middle classes. It boasted a leafy common and a village green with cake shops, chemists with huge coloured glass jars on dark stained wooden shelves, and the Walpole Picture Theatre on Mattock Lane. Even Ealing film studios, the hub of post-war British film-making, producing what came to be classic British movies like *Passport To Pimlico* and *The Ladykillers*, were discreet. Far from the massive Hollywood lots seen by British audiences on Pathé Newsreels, the Ealing studios reflected the sedate atmosphere of the area. Situated in what were ostensibly the grounds of a private house, the studios were surrounded by flowerbeds, beehives and manicured lawns.

On the surface the O'Briens were perfect for Ealing. Gerard had been brought up in India and so had enjoyed the kind of lifestyle that the British got used to during the days of the Raj; Catherine had come from Ireland, from a Kerry family which boasted a line of journalists amongst its forebears. Mary and Dion attended the respectable local Catholic schools; the family went to the Catholic church every Sunday and on feast days, and they spent holidays at Bognor Regis, a small genteel resort on England's south coast, between the busy docks of Portsmouth and the Regency grandeur of Brighton. On schooldays the children would listen to the large valve radio in the kitchen as they did their homework, or Dion would set up an amateur radio connection and he and Mary would broadcast through to the next room. In Britain most people did not get a television set until the Queen's coronation in 1953 and the O'Briens were no different. Dusty would be in her late teens before TV impinged on her life, the O'Briens' front room boasting a tiny screen set in a large walnut cupboard, designed, with its closing doors, to look like a piece of furniture.

Meanwhile, beneath the surface, the O'Briens' life was not quite like those of their middle-class neighbours. Dusty would recall that it seemed at Kent Gardens as though the local Catholic priest lived semi-permanently in the house. OB, Kay and the priest seemed to have a grand time. So much so that later there would be some conjecture about exactly what was in the teacup Kay always had in her hand. 'It was like living in *Father Ted*,' Dusty once said, referring to the popular 1990s British TV comedy show featuring a trio of crazy Irish priests, not all entirely sober. More oddly, mealtimes would be fraught and bizarrely chaotic. Often a simple request to 'pass the potatoes' would see the contents of the dish hurled on to the floor, sometimes greens would fly across the table. A famous Dusty story was of Kay spending an hour making a perfect trifle and then turning it into mush by hitting it over and over again with a spoon. Years later in Hollywood, Dusty, incensed that a friend had brought cooking brandy instead of five star to put in a stew, threw the entire contents of the pot at the kitchen wall.

On occasion, meals in Ealing would pass surprisingly uneventfully. Nobody can remember quite why these things happened, but it made Mary and Dion grow up thinking that throwing food was the kind of thing people did.

Here then were the O'Briens, superficially quietly conventional. But the accountant father with his passion for neat
columns of precisely balanced figures and his wife who
seldom aired her yearnings for a more colourful life but
tried desperately to create one, managed to produce a son
and a daughter who both grew up with a deep suspicion
of marriage and maintained an uneasy relationship with
each other as adults. What family isn't, in some way or
another, 'dysfunctional'? But the O'Briens would seem to
have manifested this famous label more than most – even
if, in the 1940s and 1950s, the phrase had yet to enter
common parlance. The perfectionism that marked Dusty's
work may well have been inherited from her father, but that
underlying mix of both 'knowing better' and insecurity was
also, in Dusty's case, to be topped off with what she would
later describe as a 'totally addictive personality'. It was a
potentially volatile combination, but it was one that only
emerged when she had left the well-bred Ealing schoolgirl
a long way behind.

If there was anger and frustration expressed in the
O'Briens' food-throwing episodes, it was to be a hobby of
Dusty's ever after and it made her a tensely erratic adult.
It seemed, as the years went by, that somewhere in those
strange years of domestic vandalism Dusty learned some
deep lessons at the school of self-loathing and they would
be impossible to forget. No wonder she came to rely on her
cover of make-up, her wigs and her half-truths. Later came
the other props of drink and drugs. Somewhere along the
line she knew early that confrontation with reality could be
painful.

Mary Isobel Catherine grew up thinking of herself as a

very nondescript sort of girl. Like her brother, she was educated at a series of single-sex Catholic schools and did not seem to nurse any academic aspirations. St Anne's school was populated mainly by the daughters of Second World War immigrants and families from Ireland who had come to London in search of work. Displaced from their own homelands and cultures, a Catholic education for their children made parents feel there was some continuity and stability in their lives. Certainly the nuns set pretty firm parameters on their students and Dusty would later say they were very strict with her, but in the 1950s their habits made them look rather mysterious and thus almost attractive, and they must have come across as, at least, strong, quite powerful women.

For the girls at St Anne's, as in any convent and indeed most single-sex schools in the 1950s, the question of 'sex education' was problematic. Sex outside marriage, girls were told, was bad. Unless you were married to one, men had these uncontrollable sexual urges. Worse, as a Catholic girl you were the custodian of morality. 'If a boy put his hand on your breast,' says a convent-educated friend, 'you'd be the one to go to confession about it. The common image was that boys were terrifying, full of animal lust – until you married one and then, of course, they supposedly became Prince Charming.'

And anyway, Dusty didn't know much about boys. 'Because of parental influence and the segregated school system I had gone through my growing years terrified of boys,' Dusty would tell *Woman* magazine in 1978 in an interview to promote her new album *It Begins Again*. 'To us men were mysterious objects rather than people you love and with whom you feel comfortable. I went in for crushes rather than involvements.' And she would recall that when Mick Jagger and footballer George Best had asked her out in the sixties she had been 'petrified' and declined.

Dusty was not one of the star pupils at St Anne's Convent. She was plump, mousy haired, had a square face and wore glasses. Her sense of humour seemed her only saving grace, making her popular with the other girls but less so with the nuns. Yet for years the one thing she did have was a remarkable singing voice. Her brother recalls that she had been 'a bonny baby with lots of curly hair' and that from quite early on 'she had a special gift'. That gift manifested itself when, at the age of twelve, Mary went into a local record shop and recorded an extraordinarily mature version of Irving Berlin's 'When The Midnight Choo Choo Leaves For Alabam'. Originally written in 1912, the song had featured in the 1940s Fred Astaire/Judy Garland film musical *Easter Parade*. Dusty would always say she had a 'gravelly little voice' as a youngster, but although 'Choo Choo' was a vaudeville number and nearly a parody of black music – with Mary keeping perfect pitch and rhythm – the way she slurried across 'Al-a-ba-aam' gave a hint of what would come.

This ability to reproduce the tone and ambiance of black American vocals would be something that would always set Mary apart once she became Dusty Springfield and it was influenced by the environment that her father created in Kent Gardens. A sometime pianist and jazz aficionado, the paradoxical OB would play his records every evening. Mary and Dion grew up listening, not to Anne Shelton and Vera Lynn like most children in 1950s Britain, but to Jelly Roll Morton, Ella Fitzgerald and Peggy Lee or to classical music on the radio.

When Mary was an adolescent, like all good Catholic girls, she was confirmed into the Catholic Church. Mary had taken first communion at about eight years old when she received the 'blood' and 'body' of Jesus Christ; on the Saturday night she went to confession so that she was suitably 'pure' for Sunday morning mass. Like all the other young local Catholic girls, for her confirmation Mary was bought a new white dress and little white shoes. She might even have worn a frothy white veil and carried a small posy of flowers, although it's unlikely, given her attitude to her 'lumbering self', she would have felt much like a beautiful bride of Christ. Still, it was an occasion. She was the centre of attention and there were photographs taken outside the church and a family party afterwards to celebrate.

During her confirmation Mary was anointed with holy oil by the bishop. She promised to renounce the world, the flesh and the devil: in other words she'd be expected to be a 'good' Catholic, to get married and have Catholic children. Most of all she was expected to put aside any desires that the Church found distasteful. According to the tenets of the Church this anointment is the moment when the Holy Spirit 'enters' the waiting teenager. Did she have her moment of rapture there in the church in Ealing during this highly theatrical ceremony? Did she feel different and know that the Holy Spirit had come to call? Or was it likely that she only had that moment when she got up on stage and sang? For there is surprisingly little distance between the rituals of the Catholic Church and the rituals of going on stage. Certainly, when she was on form, Dusty could move the harshest critic to describe her voice as 'God-given'.

If things were unstable at home Mary grew up with another problem: an older brother who was her parents' 'blue-eyed boy'. A high achiever, he left school with brilliant results and went on to high-powered jobs in the civil service. Mary, on the other hand, was never much interested in what she was being taught. An intelligent girl with a huge curiosity and a magpie attitude to collecting information, she wanted to know about the Blues and to read, not from the canon of English literature, but the Great American Novel. 'I was always very jealous of my brother,' Dusty once said. 'At home he could do nothing wrong.' Her parents doted on him. Mary wouldn't have minded a bit of 'doting' for herself but, as she saw it, she never got the kind of attention and praise he did. Often, it seemed, she got nothing at all. It was as though, as a daughter, she had walked into the wrong movie, with the wrong script, wearing the wrong dress.

Once she was famous, Dusty would fly her parents to opening nights in America and have them around at her parties, partly to give them a treat but partly, it would seem, finally to bask in their admiration. Certainly Kay and OB must have been delighted when their daughter's world filled the vacuum that seemed to exist in their relationship. They were generally known as outgoing people, their home constantly open to Dusty and her friends at any time, day or night. The kind of parents that made Dusty's friends slightly envious. What wouldn't they have given for this seemingly free-for-all environment? Kay would often give 'tea parties' at four in the morning or invite people to dinner which they'd eventually eat at 2 a.m. Yet despite the feeling of 'zaniness' that surrounded the O'Briens, when Dusty spoke, much later in her life, about her childhood it seemed wretched. She would, she said, go and put her hands on the boiler until they burned – the only way she could make anyone in the house concerned or take any notice of her at all.

Everyone who met them, as is often the case, had a different response to the O'Briens. For some the appearance at every party of Kay on Dusty's elbow hinted at a mother who was living a life less ordinary through the success of her glittering daughter. For the eternally reserved Tom they were 'pretty conventional Catholics'. Neither of his parents, according to him, was ambitious either for themselves or for their children. Yet what child doesn't grow up being told things they don't remember and remembering things that everyone else denies?

'I have no recollection of warmness or affection, though my brother says he can remember Mummy bouncing me up and down,' Dusty once told *You* magazine. 'I took whatever criticism there was to heart. Our house was full of raging ambivalence – we none of us wanted to be there.'

Certainly the O'Briens were not a happy couple. If OB had been a child in India during the days of British imperial rule he had also been uprooted and dispatched to boarding school in England very young.

Kay, first generation Irish/English, had also been uprooted – from the south-west of Ireland – had her children in her thirties and disliked both being married and being a housewife. Dusty always remembered how Kay would say, 'Don't get married young. Have all your fun before you do,' as though the union were a life sentence. And for middle-class Catholics in the 1940s and 1950s divorce was certainly out of the question.

Kay and OB were to everyone who met them 'like chalk and cheese, really incompatible'. While Kay was fun-loving and sparky her husband was a solitary, quiet, man, usually with a pipe in his mouth, and something of an intellectual. Like all children, Dusty carried with her always this contradictory mix of personalities: frantic never to be bored and alone she would often delight in her own company; loving fame she longed for times when she could go out and eat on her own without being recognised. Most of the time, it seemed, she never knew what she wanted or what would make her happy.

In many respects, with the frustration and the food-throwing, the family were more like four unhappy children living under the same roof rather than two parents and their offspring. Kay, who loved dancing and was much more gregarious and adventurous than her husband, would sometimes go off to France. She would send OB postcards, said Dusty, not signed 'love' but 'regards'. There would be ferocious rowing between the couple: 'It was top-of-the-stairs stuff,' Dusty once said. 'I'd sit there with my hands over my ears trying not to hear and yet being fascinated at the same time.' She must have learned early that hardly anything was solid and trustworthy. No wonder that as she grew up she always needed to be in control – in the studio, on stage – otherwise, as she was so dramatically to prove, life would descend into chaos.

Meanwhile, in her adolescence, Dusty would become her mother's companion for endless trips to the cinema to alleviate Kay's boredom at home. Equally she would have OB's musical hopes pinned on her: he would nurture her 'special gift' and her sense of rhythm and so her 'ear' for music would be unmatched. When she talked, on the *Dusty – Full Circle* TV programme in 1997, about how OB would beat out the rhythm of a tune on her hand 'and I had to guess what it was', it was not a passing remark. She emphasised the word 'had' in a way that was both forceful, abrupt and surprisingly violent.

'I once talked to my father about the way he used to hit me,' she told *You* magazine many years later. 'I kept it light. I said, "I learned to duck." But he denied it ever happened. He was getting old . . . so why press the point?' Just as she would recall the nuns smacking her hands with a ruler when she got the wrong answer in class, so she would remember her parents' criticisms: 'I would hear my mother say, "Sit up, Mary, sing out, Mary," and a note could die between my larynx and my mouth.'

There was another family attribute that she was to pick up from her childhood. Kay was never one fully to trust other people very much, something she was likely to have passed on to her daughter and although Dusty early in life collected around her a set of people who would be stalwarts, supporting her to the end, there were few people she trusted. One day, much further down the line, in her secretary Pat's kitchen, Dusty was talking, not unusually, about her suspicion of people. Pat turned round from the sink and said, 'Oh, but you trust me don't you?'

'More than I do most people, but only ninety-five per cent,' Dusty replied and Pat couldn't believe, after all the years working for her and looking after her, that she'd said such a thing.

3

By the time she was seventeen Mary was working in Bentalls, the large local department store, but boredom was always hovering. She and Dion had decided to make a real go of their shared music interest and talents, and would get odd bookings at 'posh' clubs in the West End where they would sing and play guitar. By now her brother had left Ealing and so OB would turn up in his car and wait outside the club until they'd finished their set to take Mary home. Mary knew that Bentalls, or the local Boots the Chemist, where she also worked at one time, were not answers to the prayers that she offered up every Sunday morning.

The films that Kay took her daughter off to see so that she could get out of the house had a profound influence on Mary's life: from the age of fourteen she had known that she wanted to sing, to tap-dance with Fred Astaire, to wear those swirling gowns and have long blonde hair. It was an image that she'd started to work on before she left school, although her hair was still curly and brown. It seemed the answer to the deadly tedium of being a stifled shopgirl who played a bit of guitar and who desperately didn't want her parents to think of her as second best.

Each week Dusty would search the small ads in the papers for a job in music. In 1958 she answered an advertisement in the *Stage* for a third member for a newly formed group, the Lana Sisters, and was invited to an audition in London. In those days it wasn't unusual for someone trying to break into show business simply to answer an advert, get an audition and, with luck, be offered the job.

In the late 1950s three perky bubble-cut blondes sang coy, safe, little numbers and were hugely successful as the Beverley Sisters. The audience for a raunchier reprise of the formula was ready and waiting, and booking agents were very keen to present all-female line-ups as 'sister acts', whether the members were related or not. So it was that Riss Chantelle, who had worked with Ivy Benson's unique all-woman big band, and her singer friend Lynne Abrams found themselves sitting in Max Rivers Rehearsal Rooms in Leicester Square listening to a line of girls who came in one by one. Each would go through a number with the pianist Chantelle and Abrams had hired for the day. It was hardly the most convivial atmosphere given that the room was small and you could hear the music coming from the other floors, and the two young women had to concentrate hard, listening and watching not just for a voice that would fit, but a personality too.

When Dusty walked through the door Riss Chantelle thought that her intuition about the letter from Mary O'Brien had been absolutely spot on. With her high heels, her hair in a French pleat, and a black coat, Mary looked okay. When she opened her mouth to sing she sounded great – exactly the lower register that Riss and Lynne needed for the Lanas' harmonies. Riss remembers being very pleased. There was only one moment of doubt: Riss had a habit of pointing a finger when she was talking. Dusty, who had taken her coat off once she knew she'd got the job, hung it on the finger and grinned. 'I did wonder then if I hadn't made a slight mistake,' Riss says with a laugh. It was something she thought more than once. Often, driving to a tour date, there would be a huge bang in the car which nearly made her steer off the road. A bored Dusty didn't chant, 'Are we there yet?' Instead she had blown up a brown paper bag and burst it with her hands. The problem of Dusty's boredom, a constant throughout her life, was overcome once Dusty, at this point a producer-in-waiting, was in charge of the heavy Grundig reel-to-reel tape recorder on which the trio tried out their harmonies during long journeys.

In fact if Dusty Springfield learned lessons that were to serve her well for her entire career it was through being one of the Lana Sisters: how to hold a stage, how to work an audience, how to listen to other musicians with intuition. How to become, not just an entertainer, but – someone else. She had her hair cut so she looked more like Riss and Lynne, got contact lenses to replace her glasses (a short lived experiment since the hard lenses of those days were painful and she was always losing them), wore lurex and satin, and changed her name to 'Shan'. If the beaded dresses and thick black eyeline trademark were to come, Mary Isobel Catherine had taken the first major step towards Dusty.

'Shan' had to be schooled in the art of stagecraft by Riss and Lynne during rehearsals at the Edgware Road Theatre (and endlessly picked up after she kept tripping over the carpet on stage). Although she'd played supper and cabaret clubs with Tom and on her own, Dusty had never ever been 'on stage' properly before and she had to learn how to face an audience without falling into what Riss dreaded: 'looking like an amateur'. As a result the three young women drilled themselves to perfection, keeping their movements small but dramatic; flinging back their tulle overskirts to reveal their tight-fitting pants (highly risqué in the late 1950s!); keeping their harmonies tight. Supporting Adam Faith, Cliff Richard, Nat King Cole and Johnny Ray, appearing regularly on Brian Matthews's morning radio music programme *Saturday Club* or on early television pop shows like *Drumbeat* and *6.5 Special*, touring the US airbases across Europe that, along with the summer seasons at Blackpool were the staple diet of groups in the late fifties, the Lana Sisters provided 'Shan' with two years of invaluable experience and a hit record: 'Seven Little Girls Sitting In The Back Seat' ('Kissin' and a Huggin' With Fred').

While the record gave 'Shan' her first taste of fame it wasn't exactly the kind of song her heart was in. But in those days, says Riss, women performers in Britain tended to get a raw deal from the music publishers' headquarters in Denmark Street or 'Tin Pan Alley' as it got nicknamed. 'Shan' was happier when the Lana Sisters stood on stage, three heads round one microphone, 'internal balance' on their harmonies perfect and sang cover versions of American hits, such as Peggy Lee's 'Okay, You Win'.

If her time with the Lana Sisters gave her a bedrock, it also signalled the way Dusty's career and her family life were somehow inexorably entwined.

It was the meticulous OB who would cut out every reference to the group that appeared in the press or on programmes and file them neatly away; it would be Kay who would suggest to Riss, when they were trying to think of a name for the trio, that they should call themselves the Twister Sisters (Riss says she wishes she had, much more tantalising than Lana, which they found in a telephone book); it would be Tom who would let down all four tyres on Riss's car at one in the morning so that she would have to stay up all night with the O'Briens at their house. Yet Riss, as many people were to think in the future, found it not at all strange but rather endearing, and despite the odd 'Shan' pranks she liked the young woman she worked with at the mike: 'She was such an honest girl. The thing about Dusty was that she was never devious. She never said things behind your back – she'd always say them to your face.' She and Lynne were to stay friends with Dusty for the next two decades – Riss even allowing herself to be mobbed by cameramen at Heathrow airport in the 1960s when, despite her protestations, they accidentally mistook her for Dusty off on a world tour. Meanwhile the artist herself ran chortling and unharried through passport control.

Halfway through her time with the Lana's Dion had started a folk duo with a friend, Tim Feild. When they wanted sister Mary to join she was both flattered and pleased: she was much more drawn to the folksy and Latin-influenced material her brother was writing and to get Tom's approval was an added bonus. By the time she was twenty-one Mary left 'Shan' and the Lana Sisters and joined Dion and Tim.

It was with the Springfields that Dusty would get her first taste of what real fame felt like. Although they always sang 'incredibly fast, incredibly jolly and often out of tune' she would say later, what she experienced for the first time was the warmth that came with success: from audiences and critics alike. And it was with the group that she started to leave some things from her past behind. She had always hated being middle class because it was 'confining' – you weren't rich enough to rule or poor enough to rebel. She didn't think growing up in Ealing and having such a stultifying life there was very romantic either. When the group decided to become more 'American' and chose the name the Springfields – you only had to look at a map of America so see how many towns were called Springfield from Massachusetts to Ohio, New Jersey to Illinois – she and Dion changed their names too. He became Tom. She got out the peroxide bottle and, fighting with the fumes and the burning sensation from her scalp as the ammonia hit, went blonde and became Dusty.

Right from the start the Springfields benefited from the growing power of television in Britain. In 1961 it was apparent that of the group's three-strong line-up it was Dusty who had an immediate rapport with the camera. While Tim looked shy and Tom grinned mirthlessly with his teeth clenched, Dusty was an exuberant presence in her demure pin tucked blouses and full skirts. Although when Dusty announced the title of 'our next song' somewhat breathlessly her voice had the precise, clipped tones of a Sunday school teacher, when she sang her voice, laden with the influences of American soul and R&B, added an extraordinary quality to a Springfields' song. On their hit 'Island Of Dreams', with its now ridiculous-sounding bouncing strings and its pseudo-cowboy pronunciations ('how kin I forgit you'), when Dusty's voice breaks out from the three part harmony it is with the strikingly aching quality that would become instantly recognisable once she went solo: 'High in the sky is a bird on the wing/Please carry me with you'.

The song, written by Tom, held a particularly personal meaning. It was about escape. 'We always wanted to get away,' Tom says. 'I wanted to go to Brazil, Dusty always wanted to go to Hollywood.' For a while Tom had to content himself with drawing Carmen Miranda's shoes. He was fixated by the incredible Latin American all singing, all dancing star and seemed to be obsessed with her absurdly high platform shoes. She wore a pile of fruit on her head, sang 'I Yi Yi Yi Yi I Love You Very Much' and now seems like the height of camp. She was the epitome of everything crazy, glorious and life-enhancing – certainly in comparison to the English suburbs. Dusty, cinema mad, did not go as far as wearing bananas and oranges on her head but she did wear glasses with shocking pink frames and later, when she drove her sports car up and down the Marylebone Road, she may have imagined that she was on Hollywood's Rodeo Drive. If far away was where she would always want to be, for her London right now didn't feel too bad a place to stop by in.

But Dusty was beginning to experience something that was to trouble her for the rest of her life. She had always gone to church for confession (often the Springfields' van would have to wait for her to come out of church before the group could leave for a tour date.) But what was the point of sitting in that box week after week to be told that not only was she a sinner but an affront to God? For early in 1963 she was having her first affair – with a famous singer. First sexual encounters always have a profound effect, good or bad, and Dusty would always say that she never thought she had any real teenage years, doing the things ordinary girls did: hanging out in coffee bars flirting with boys, canoodling in the back row of the cinema stalls. She was either working or spending her nights playing clubs with Tom. It was as though this lack of experience, added to her Catholic schooling, explained why she was so twitchy being around men who found her attractive, when in fact there were likely to be much more complicated reasons. One thing though became clear to her. It was no longer possible to embrace wholeheartedly the religion that she had never really questioned. After all, she was now involved with a woman and her sexual preference went against everything the Catholic Church had taught her. Dusty and the Church parted company, a split that was simply to add to the guilt and the anger she would feel towards herself for the majority of her life.

Although the group started out playing seasons at places as inauspicious as Butlin's Holiday Camp – where Dusty would gamble her week's wages playing cards – the Springfields soon became successful. By 1962 they were selling half a million copies of each single and earning £1,000 a week between them. By 1963 they had toured America with famous solo stars Del Shannon and Johnny Tillotson and had had two more single hits with Tom's 'Silver Threads And Golden Needles' and 'Say I Won't Be There'. The first, with banjo, guitar and tambourine and its overtly country feel, was a huge hit in America and was notable for the way Dusty's voice, suddenly exposed on the break – 'And I dare not drown my sorrow in the warm glow of your wine' – sounded not just like warm honey, but as though it had been recorded in an entirely different studio.

The record marked a historic breakthrough: the Springfields became the first British group ever to enter the American charts, paving the way for the 'British invasion' two years later when the Beatles broke across the Atlantic. The second, 'Say I Won't Be There', was a bizarre straw-and-dungarees country song that was almost a parody of its genre. Yet again Dusty was given the microphone alone for a few lines. This time her voice was double tracked and with a fairly obvious nod at an American black 'girl group' sound. It was an odd mixture, but again it focused the record on Dusty's voice.

In 1962 Tim Feild left to be replaced by Mike Hurst. Tom had always said that he'd give the group three years. Despite their success he was adamant. 'I think that period was always a mixture of argument, compromise and then finally agreement,' he says now about working with his equally stubborn and musically opinionated sister. Tom and Mike Hurst wanted to get away from the cameras and into record production. Neither of them ever felt quite at ease in the spotlight.

Dusty, on the other hand, was thrilled to be up there 'waving my arms around'. She loved the way her voice worked, the way the camera moved with her and the way the audiences responded. She knew that whatever her brother decided, she was going to keep on singing. In September 1963 the group announced it was splitting up and, after a farewell concert at the London Palladium, Dusty signed a deal with Philips as a solo singer. From now on there would be plenty of room on the stage. She would be able to wave her arms about as much as she liked – without the risk of hitting someone else in the face.

4

When the pilot programme for *Ready, Steady, Go!* had gone out at the beginning of 1963 there had been a promise that anyone on it would appear in subsequent shows. The Springfields had been one of the groups to appear on that pilot but, by the time the programme was ready to go on air as a fully fledged series in the autumn of that year, the Springfields had split up. The news about the group did not break in the press until there was an 'official' announcement but before that, in early September, Dusty went into the Rediffusion television offices to tell Vicki that the Springfields couldn't be on the first programme and that she was going solo. It seems extraordinary now to think of an artist wandering into a TV office, but in those days the music world was far more informal and friendly. 'Nobody even really knew how to sell records,' says Vicki, 'never mind how many records it was actually possible to sell. And we really were all mates in those days; it was as though we were all in this thing, whatever it was, together.'

The *RSG!* team, who had all become friendly with this charming, funny and warm twenty-three-year-old decided that, while she was going backwards and forwards to the Philips studios at Marble Arch and cutting her first solo record, Dusty would host the show along with radio DJ

Keith Fordyce. So on early programmes Dusty would chat on screen to the Beatles or the Rolling Stones. It was a few minutes that added to the programme's air of informality and marked Dusty as being an on screen 'natural'. In fact, although she knew most of the people she was talking to as friends, her natural self-consciousness led to her surreptitiously shuffling her feet as she chatted. It was something the cameras never picked up and so nobody viewing the programme would have noticed. But it was indicative of her lack of self-confidence that even in a friendly environment, where there was actually very little real pressure from the studio floor, Dusty was uncomfortable if she wasn't singing. Her 'shuffling' was a habit that, at moments when she felt most awkward and trapped, never left her.

By the time her first solo single 'I Only Want To Be With You' came out in 1964, Dusty's name was so entwined with *RSG!* that it was no surprise she would debut it on the programme. *RSG!* and Dusty were inexorably linked and the Mods, who felt it was their programme, felt she was theirs too. Like them she was besotted by soul and R&B; like them she had The Look.

Dusty's was a look that would come to epitomise sixties Britain. It became part of the iconography of the period – along with Mary Quant's symmetrical hair, Biba's tiny velvet coats, Paco Rabanne's white boots and the rise of *Vogue* and *Nova* magazines. While it was not unusual for female singers to change their names – Marie Laurie became Lulu, Pauline Matthews Kiki Dee, Sandra Goodrich Sandie Shaw and Priscilla White Cilla Black – it was Dusty's 'look', aside from her voice, that set her apart. It was culled from a variety of sources. Although she always said that the thick black lines drawn on her eyelids were the result of her short-sightedness (and certainly she was almost certifiably blind without her glasses) you knew that, once she put those glasses on, if she hadn't liked what she saw she would have done something about her 'panda eyes'.

No, the black lines were very deliberate. Dusty hated what she saw as the 'heaviness' of her face and it's true that she had inherited her father's rounder profile rather than her mother's narrow, birdlike look. Magazine advice in those days was all about detracting from the 'less flattering' parts of your looks by emphasising other parts – usually the eyes. It's likely that Dusty, a voracious reader of everything from history books to glossy fashion mags, took this advice to heart. In the early 1960s there were other influences too. You had to be tiny enough to get into Biba's meanly cut dresses with their skintight sleeves and rows of tiny buttons; blonde enough to catch people's eyes at a hundred yards. Yet while Dusty's contemporaries looked only at *Vogue* models like Twiggy, Jean Shrimpton, Jill Kennington and some of their own peer group for inspiration, Dusty was either in the cinema or devouring film magazines with their full page pictures of alluring film stars.

If you had your finger on the intellectual button, and for much of her life Dusty did, the films coming out of the Continent, from directors such as Antonioni and Jean-Luc Godard were hugely influential – even if you couldn't understand half of them. They went hand in glove with the beatnik fashion of Paris's Left Bank which had already influenced a generation of British teenagers in the late 1950s. Dusty loved Paris and she, her manager Vic Billings and Vicki had gone to the Olympia Theatre in the winter of 1964 to see Dionne Warwick, 'Little' Stevie Wonder and the Shirelles. Dusty had wandered around in a rabbit fur coat that shed everywhere and drove Vic and Vicki mad, but the three had a great weekend shopping, eating, drinking hot chocolate and looking at young Parisians. Here to be cool, Dusty noticed, you wore black, smoked Gitanes and, like the beatnik singer Juliette Gréco, threw enormous amounts of black eyeliner on to dramatise your face. Dusty, a cultural and musical jackdaw, was as transfixed by this European trend as she was by the music rooted in the Black American Baptist churches of the southern states of America, and by the early records from the Stax label. So Gréco (along with the *Vogue* models who often went one step further and painted eyelashes on their faces up to their eyebrows) had a huge influence on her look.

When Dusty was working in the Ealing shops she would save up her two shillings a day lunch money and creep up to the Curzon Cinema in Mayfair to see foreign films. 'I yearned to be an actress but I thought there were far too many actresses, so I became the next best thing.'

What was also true was that Dusty took images that she herself loved and which she thought made women objects of desire: they were all blonde. The American blondeness of Marilyn Monroe, which seemed to go with her sexual attractiveness and vulnerability; the more enigmatic sophistication of a French star such as Catherine Deneuve (whose black velvet bow, catching back her smooth blonde hair, was a look copied directly by Dusty who then influenced a mass of blonde British girls to do the same) or Monica Vitti. If anyone took Dusty's imagination it was the Italian film star Vitti whose face director Antonioni had his camera lusting after so much that in his film *L'Avventura* he slowly panned across an empty landscape until settling for what seemed like minutes on Vitti's profile at the side of the screen. When she read in a film magazine that the Italian travelled the world with a rich countess, Dusty made it known that she was beyond envy. It's likely that ever after Dusty was looking for her own rich countess – even though they were thin on the ground in Dusty's circles.

Along with all these influences Dusty had a range of back-combed or smoothed out wigs to balance her jawline, which she thought was far too heavy, and her nose, which she considered less than perfect. Like all the women singers of *RSG!* Dusty usually wore a variation of her best daily clothes. This would often, in the sixties, include a de rigueur short skirt. Later, having watched herself on television one too many times and even though she encased the offending items in 'slimming' black stockings, she would never appear in front of the cameras in anything other than long dresses or trousers to draw attention away from what she considered as possibly the very worst part of her body – her legs. 'OB's knees,' she would mourn, looking down at what she saw as her inheritance from her father.

By lunchtime on Friday artists would begin to turn up in the dark basement *RSG!* studio. The Rolling Stones would be looking for their dressing-room and fighting with their girlfriends, the Animals would be looking for each other and there would be Dusty, a scarf over her head, her clothes in a plastic wrapping over her arm, her wigs in a box. She had spent the morning applying her make-up ready to have it touched up again after rehearsals under the harsh overhead lights. Now she was ready to entertain everyone who would soon get bored with the endless waiting around. Mainly this was through her *Goon Show* impersonations. It was the one comedy radio programme that middle-class families in the

1950s were obsessed by. Years before *Monty Python*, Peter Sellers, Harry Secombe and Spike Milligan created a string of ludicrous characters (small boy scouts, spies, pensioners) who would involve themselves in surreal open-ended narratives. These would include the transportation of a prison by sea, or two people pushing a grand piano across the Sahara Desert. Dusty had an ear for mimicry that she would carry with her through the rest of her life and those afternoons at *RSG!* would often resound with her tone-perfect copies of Minnie Bannister and Henry Crun, Little Jim, Bluebottle and Count Moriarty.

With nowhere to sit for the next five hours everyone – artists, production team, wandering journalists – would be in windowless darkness, in and out of the dressing-rooms, on the studio floor. In her dressing-room Dusty would while away the time entertaining visiting journalists who always enjoyed her company. One of her favourite tricks was to name her wigs Cilla, Lulu and Sandie, after the other singers on the show. She would pick one up and shake it like a dog with a rat, 'Grrr Cilla!' before hurling it across the room. Since there was little competition between her much more knowing soulful voice and theirs, nobody took this seriously.

If informality marked the Friday night show it was usually accidental. Before Tony Palmer discovered the zoom lens, before the invention of lightweight digital equipment, the heavy *RSG!* cameras trundled across the studio floor like Daleks, moving in for close-ups, slithering awkwardly backwards for long shots. The Mod dancers (too cool to wave at Mum and Dad or grimace for friends) politely moved out of the way. Occasionally an artist would have their legs hit or trip over a thick snaking cable. 'It was chaos,' says Vicki.

'Every week we were trying to get it right.' The fact that they hardly ever did simply added to its charm. And it was, of course, exactly this atmosphere of possible disaster that Dusty enjoyed so much. For her the one thing about being on *RSG!* was not just that she was in a trend-setting inner circle, but that she never got bored.

Two particular highlights in the television calendar, for musicians and audiences alike, were the *RSG!* shows at Christmas and the New Year. Crazily, these went out live, with all the subsequent glitches and near-disasters and with a host of musicians who had entered into the spirit of things by getting the spirit to enter them – usually in copious amounts. For Christmas, amongst the many bizarre items, was the Animals bluesy lead singer Eric Burdon, his Newcastle machismo hardly camouflaged by being dressed as a Christmas tree fairy. For New Year's Eve the show would descend into near-chaos. The studio would be decorated with hundreds of children's party streamers, bright huge balloons would be popped endlessly and the air was filled with the high hoots and honks of feather whistles. Dusty would be one of the many artists who careered on to one of the small 'island' stages and laughingly struggled to perform live through a sea of streamers. The amateurishness of the event, and the anarchic atmosphere, translated itself to the viewers who felt that they were part of the party themselves.

On New Year's Eve, as 1964 dawned, those viewers might well have caught a glimpse of Dusty meeting a young black singer from Newark, New Jersey. If the Lana Sisters had taught Dusty about stagecraft, there's no doubt that the second biggest influence on her career was Madeline Bell. Madeline had come to London as part of the highly

Dusty learned some of her more acute phrasing and the underlying emotion, the mixture of the sacred and the profane, at gospel's roots. From Dusty Madeline, who had grown up listening to the great gospel diva Mahalia Jackson but little else, learned about classical, jazz, opera and the scintillating dance music of Latin America. When Madeline cut her first single in Britain, 'I'm Gonna Make You Love Me', Dusty was delighted to be able to sing back-up on the track; when Dusty went on to cut 'In The Middle Of Nowhere' Madeline returned the compliment. In fact Madeline became a regular back-up singer on Dusty's sessions, along with Lesley Duncan, Kay Garner, Doris Troy and sometimes Kiki Dee. She got six guineas an hour from the record company – but she also got Dusty's hugely enjoyable friendship. A friendship which, as usual with Dusty, lasted for years. If people thought the two made an unlikely alliance – the white middle-class girl from Ealing, the gawky black working-class girl from New Jersey – it's likely that Dusty and Madeline shared more than a love of music. Ironically, just as Dusty equated her 'ear' for sound with OB's fury when she got things 'wrong', so Madeline would often recall that the remarkable volume her voice could conjure up was the result of Alex Bradford punching her on the back during rehearsals to make her sing louder.

While the Springfields were together their tours and TV appearances had been booked by Ellwyn Griffiths, an agent/manager who worked out of an office in Bruton Street in the West End. His secretary was a slim blonde girl called Pat Barnett who stoically fielded phone calls until her boss turned up at midday and after he left for a lunch of pink gins at Quaglino's in Soho. It was Dusty who realised that if the group needed anything done it would be Pat who would do it. They wanted a piano? Pat would book it. They needed transport or train tickets? Pat would fix it. Pat, who until then had only worked with television and radio scriptwriters like Frank Muir and Denis Norden, was at first bemused by this entry into the new pop world, but after a while she began to like it.

The first time she met them, Dusty, Tom and Tim Feild had come bounding up the stairs to the office with Dusty being 'very vivacious and giggly'. Although there were many offices in the building and Pat was used to the sound of people running up and down the stairs all day, this time she had turned round. It wasn't that the group were being noisy: 'I just thought, oh. It was some kind of presence I felt. It was a presence Dusty always had.' And it was one she kept no matter what. Years later, when Pat went shopping with Dusty, even though the singer would wear a scarf and dark glasses and walk into shops quietly, people would turn and stare. 'It wasn't that they could recognise her,' says Pat. 'I don't think they even knew why they looked. It was simply the extraordinary effect she always had.'

Going solo, Dusty realised that Pat Barnett would make her a wonderful secretary. 'Dusty was always the one who'd say, "Look, Pat, we need this and this," when she was with the Springfields. She always knew what they needed. And we got on really well from the start although I was aware that she was always holding back a bit. Like there was something about herself . . . I thought, oh, we'll gradually get to know each other and that will go away. But it never did.'

It probably wasn't only Pat's efficiency that impressed Dusty. Pat, who would be a devoted secretary, fan club organiser and the most tirelessly loyal person Dusty would have around her for the next three decades, was also a champion speed skater. A year later, on her way to a cabaret appearance in Stockton, Dusty would delay her journey and sit in the middle of an industrial estate watching Pat do trials to get her place in the British World Team. It was satisfying to them both when Pat became a British record holder.

It was at Griffiths's office that Dusty finally signed with a new manager. Pat had explained to Griff that now Dusty was going solo she would need someone who knew more about the pop world. Someone had recommended a quiet, fair-haired man called Vic Billings to Dusty. Vic had done some work with the Springfields' agent Tito Burns and after she met him up at Bruton Street she asked Pat what she thought of him.

'Well,' said Pat, 'he seems charming.'

'Good,' replied Dusty, 'because I've just hired him.'

In fact Billings was more than charming. 'He was, without a doubt, a terrific manager for her,' says Vicki. 'He knew exactly what she should be doing and he was spot-on all the time. Plus he wouldn't let her get away with any bullshit.'

Which didn't mean that Dusty, much as she respected him, couldn't also infuriate Billings. By now she had finally moved into the centre of town – into a flat in Baker Street above the post office and the ABC bakery. Its lease was owned by a respectable middle-aged Scottish couple called Murray-Leslie and for a few months Vicki also rented a room there before she moved round the corner to New Cavendish Street. One day, due to do rehearsals for the *Billy Cotton Band Show*, a live light music radio programme, Dusty refused to get out of bed. Although the *Band Show* was good exposure for her to reach a Sunday lunchtime family audience, just the broader base Dusty was beginning to attract along with her young Mods, it wasn't the most exciting programme on earth. 'It's Sunday,' she wailed to Vic when he had rung to remind her, 'and I don't see why I have to go down there now, the rehearsals aren't that important.' She said the same thing when he called round at the flat to pick her up.

Like all managers in such cases Vic knew that his credibility to control his artist was on the line as much as Dusty's reputation as a professional, and he was furious with her. He marched away from the flat up Baker Street with Vicki in tow. It was unusual for Vic to shout, but this time he did. 'What does she mean she won't get out of bed?' he yelled. Vicki, under instructions to take Dusty's dog for a walk, was feeling just as aggrieved, especially as Vic was shouting at her. The pair continued along Baker Street shouting and hurling Dusty's unsuspecting poodle at each other as though it were Dusty herself. Luckily, each time they both adroitly caught it. The dog lived.

Because Dusty went to bed so late and slept in so late, while Vicki's pattern was the exact reverse, Vicki would often have to take the dog for a quick morning stroll. Dusty would always leave her a reminder: one of a trail of notes scattered along the hall of the flat. They would always be in the form of polite mini-letters starting 'Dear Vicki' or, if it was something slightly more difficult than 'please get a pint of milk', 'Darling Vicki'. They would always end 'love Dust'. 'They were always incredibly polite and incredibly mundane,' says Vicki, 'like taking a suit to the cleaners and remembering to ask them to take the buttons off before it went into the machine. Or to say she'd heard something the night before on the radio that I *had* to listen to.'

Dusty's note-leaving became notorious – in one sense they were her aide-mémoire, but they were also her way of non-verbal communication with everyone she knew – and went on throughout her life. 'It was also something to do with her short attention span,' says Vicki. 'It was as though if she didn't write everything down and leave it scattered everywhere she'd simply forget what it was she wanted to tell you about.'

With her new manager and a secretary now in place Dusty only needed one more thing and that was her own back-up band. If Dusty would, over the years, become known for only having gay men around her, the one non-gay man she would rely on for musical and emotional support over the next decade would be her bass player Doug Reece. Reece had been an early member of the Echoes, a band formed by singer Chris Wayne and drummer Laurie Jay. Apart from backing Wayne, they had become the band for top American artists touring Britain, like Gene Vincent and Jerry Lee Lewis, as well as a string of British solo acts. When Jay left the group – he would eventually become the manager for American singer Billy Ocean – Reece took over the business side as well as the music. He had already met Dusty when they had both appeared at the same American airbase together during her days with the Lana Sisters and his with the less well-known Sonny Stewart and the Dynamos.

Reece's mother constantly read the pop papers to keep up with the world her son was moving in and did he know that Dusty was leaving the Springfields and looking for a backing group? Reece hardly paid any attention. 'I thought someone like Dusty would have found a group quickly.' The following week the Echoes' agent George Cooper rang and said the group had to be at the Granada, Kennington in south London by 11 a.m. They would be auditioning for

Dusty and all she had stipulated was that they had to have an organist in the line-up because that was the particular sound she wanted.

When she finally met them that morning Dusty couldn't have known the panic the audition had caused. With constantly changing personnel, the Echoes had that very week lost their organist. Mickey Garrett turned up at the last minute, but neither he nor the new drummer had had any rehearsal time with the rest of the group and neither was great at sight-reading music. None the less Dusty and the group immediately got along and they were signed up, although Reece knew they needed a more versatile drummer to work with Dusty's material and now brought in Bob Wackett. It was in Wackett's front room that the first rehearsal with Dusty took place. Wackett lived in a little two-up, two-down in Friern Barnet, north London. Dusty had driven up in her sports car and immediately asked for a cup of tea, relaxing a bunch of nervous young musicians who were already devoted to her voice but slightly in awe of her.

It was at these rehearsals that the Echoes got to know what Dusty wanted. And she was firm. Wackett's drumming had to be solid, she knew exactly what the guitar and keyboard figures should be like. Most of all she was au fait with the bass 'fills' which had to sound like the soul/R&B records from America that she loved. 'And because she liked full arrangements I had to come up with a way that a four-piece group could sound like a forty-piece orchestra,' says Doug. For the Echoes, rehearsing with Dusty in a tiny sitting-room surrounded by Bob's family photographs was turning into a treat. That's the way it stayed, says Reece, even when the group got bigger – augmented with trombonist Derek

Wadsworth, and trumpeter Derek Andrew, percussion and vocal back-up. With her finely tuned ear for pitch and subtle background arrangements, Dusty got them to 'listen' differently. 'I changed the way I played when I worked with her,' says Reece, 'and she always added a bit of Dusty magic to the songs. She just made them hers.'

Dusty's first solo single 'I Only Want To Be With You' went into the charts with amazing speed both in Britain and America. Written by Mike Hawker and Ivor Raymonde it was a fast track that bore all the trademarks of Dusty's favourite sounds: the rhythm section and horns from her R&B records, the driving double tracking of her voice and the addition of female back-up on the last three words of each line. Up until the early 1960s the American charts had been segregated. R&B records were considered to be for black audiences; white charts were dominated by pop and the odd leftover crooner from the 1950s. With the uptown black groups' reliance on white songwriters and, often, producers, the lines were blurred and the teenage market began to cross over. It was a move that was to benefit Dusty, a white singer with a 'black' sound.

Obviously influenced by the production Phil Spector had created the previous year for the Ronettes' 'Be My Baby', Dusty's first single had another ingredient that showed her musical intelligence. In 1959 producer/arranger Bert Burns had revolutionised R&B by adding an extraordinary counterpoint string arrangement on a Drifters' record, 'There Goes My Baby'. When 'I Only Want To Be With You' broke for a middle section it was filled with strings that swept in to reiterate the melody line. While nowhere near as complex as Burns's arrangement, it 'lifted' the record, holding the audience until Dusty's voice came in again.

On the beach at Bognor:
Mary (*left*) with Dion and their
mother Kay.

Same holiday, same swimming costume:
Mary (*left*) with Dion (*far right*).

A touch of Brazil in Bognor:
Mary and Dion prove you can tango in
sandals.

Jolly hockey sticks! Mary (*front far left*) and the team from St Anne's Convent, Ealing, after a fine round of 'bullying off'.

Family Christmas: Dusty, Tom, Kay and Gerard (note the lack of flying peas).

Days of tulle and high heels: 1958 and Dusty (*far left*) goes professional with the Lana Sisters.

Success with the Springfields and rehearsals for the *Ready Steady Go!* pilot show in 1963. Dusty and Tom with Mike Hurst (*left*).

Making it alone. Dusty premiering her first hit, 'I Only Want to Be With You', on *Ready Steady Go!*

(*Below*) The famous 'Wishin' and Hopin'' duet with Martha Reeves for the Tamla Motown television special that launched the Motown Sound in Britain.

Dusty's first solo appearance with the Echoes was in Liverpool in November 1963. She was the only woman on a 'package' tour with the Searchers, Brian Poole and the Tremeloes, Freddie and the Dreamers, and Dave Berry. The tour was to establish two things about Dusty: one, that she held a stage brilliantly, with an easy, informal relationship to her audience; second, that girls in the audience liked her as much, if not more, than the boys and certainly as much as any of the male groups they'd watched. She always had this endearing quality live – that she'd be a lot of fun to have as a mate – and when the fans went backstage afterwards to get her to sign autographs, that feeling was always cemented. Dusty seemed so unaffected and friendly. Yet she was still speaking in the high, precise tones of her Springfields appearances, using phrases such as 'when one is bound to flop' to the *Daily Mail* reporter after the concert. She was still the polite, middle-class convent girl who had always written her 'thank you' letters. Yet for her fans what counted most was the way she looked, the way she sang and an enthusiasm for a music that matched their own. It was this triumvirate that was to bring her so much success over the next seven years.

5

Touring in the mid-1960s was exciting but it was also unglamorous and exhausting. If she was doing the odd solo date Dusty often drove herself up to the club, while the Echoes and their equipment would be in a Morris van, which they'd customised with aeroplane seats. But Dusty and the band would often go out as part of a 'package' show with groups such as the Swinging Blue Jeans and American singers Bobby Vee and Big Dee Irwin. If they were part of a package Dusty and the Echoes would meet at the back of Madame Tussaud's in Marylebone Road, very close to Baker Street and Dusty's flat, to be picked up by the coach. It was Dusty's lighting man and tour manager Fred Perry's unenviable task to make sure Dusty was there.

Although touring had its compensations in terms of camaraderie, stars would get off stage after 11 p.m., try to unwind and get to bed around two in the morning. At 8 a.m. they had to be ready to get on the coach for the journey, often hundreds of miles, to the next venue. Dusty, of course, found late nights easy to deal with since she didn't know what an early one was, but the dawn wake-up call was a nightmare. To cope, Dusty would, the night before, take off all her make-up but leave her thick mascara, eyeliner and eyeshadow on. She would be staying in bed and breakfast hotels in a small, cold, single room. This was not the era of luxury bathrooms and room service. 'Girl singers' were thin on the ground in those days and the few who were 'on the road', as Dusty was, were not shown any special favours. They were expected to muck in. The only heating came from a tiny gas fire that she had to feed with endless shillings, and she would have to share the bathroom at the end of the hall with the boys in the groups staying on the same floor. In these small hotels there were no evening meals and the towns' cafés closed up by 9 p.m., so Dusty would have to eat enough at the greasy cafés which the coach stopped at during the day to last. The bad food and lack of sleep began to tell on her.

In December 1963 a new revolution had occurred in American music and it had a direct impact on her. Phil Spector had gone into the Gold Star recording studio in Hollywood with four teenage R&B acts from his Philles label – the Ronettes, the Crystals, Bob B. Soxx and the Blue Jeans, and Darlene Love – and recorded an album of Christmas-themed ballads and novelty songs associated with the previous four decades of music. The result of Spector's driving multi-layered studio techniques (there were rumours that he would spend days at LAX airport recording the sound of plane engines) and Jack Nitszche's arrangements revving round these young black voices was to produce the *Phil Spector Christmas Album*. For the next thirty-odd years it was to rank alongside the Beatles' *Sergeant Pepper's Lonely Hearts Club Band*, the Beach Boys' *Pet Sounds* and *Dusty In Memphis* as a groundbreaking moment in popular music.

It says much for Dusty's antennae that she was aware of the *Christmas Album* as soon as it was made. By the time she went back into the studio to cut her second single, the jaunty Hawker/Raymonde track 'Stay Awhile', the production owed more to Spector's influence than anything previously in British music. With an almost identical start to the Ronettes' 'I Saw Mummy Kissing Santa Claus' with bells and strings, 'Stay Awhile' captured both the feverish teen possessiveness of the era's American girl groups and the vocal signature of the Ronettes' lead singer. When Dusty sang the slight sexual innuendo of 'I'll be good to you' it took on the pronunciation of Ronnie Bennett's clipped, slightly nasal stop. It was a subconscious vocal homage that Dusty was to use again, if less obviously, on the 'call and response' structure of 'The Middle Of Nowhere' two years later.

By now Doug Reece had begun to take over rehearsals and direct the Echoes, and Dusty had come to rely on him to understand exactly what sound and feel she wanted behind her on stage, on her TV shows and in the recording studio. And she and Doug got closer. He had met a rather shy girl in Bob's front room who had gradually relaxed and was now her warm self. Out of her wigs with her 'too thin and wispy' blonde hair and her often ill-matched cacophony of trousers and tops, she was still a pretty girl. Yet Doug noticed that she would constantly put herself down and never thought she 'looked right'. Still, when she was living in Baker Street, and before he started going out with Pat Barnett, Doug would be at Dusty's flat listening to soul records and talking music way into the night. Sometimes he'd still be there in the morning and they'd go for breakfast at the Golden Egg in Oxford Street or drive out to London airport where Dusty could dream of escape or at least have scrambled eggs and they could read the Sunday newspapers. Going to sit at airports, even when she wasn't catching a plane, was a habit she would continue for the rest of her life.

If Dusty and Doug Reece's relationship got closer then there's no doubt that one particular shared experience made it happen. In 1964, as part of their touring schedule, Dusty and the Echoes were booked to play seven concerts in South Africa. Arriving in Johannesburg they were met by Dennis Wainer who was promoting their shows, taken to their hotel, and then on to his house for an informal dinner that night.

It was the start of South Africa's summer. The weather was good, the nights were like dark velvet. As far as the dates went 'nothing seemed any different from any of the other tours we'd done,' says Doug. Wainer had deliberately booked them into cinemas and theatres where there were less strict apartheid regulations. South Africa at the time was insulated against opinions aired by the rest of the world, both by its general censorship and its ban on television. The day after they arrived the band went out to the venue to set up the equipment. 'We were,' says Doug, 'due to meet Dusty back at the hotel just as we always did, business as usual.' But when they returned the band were met by Vic Billings and warned there might be a spot of trouble. Someone from the South African government had been in touch about the contract Dusty had signed with Wainer; the government weren't sure that they 'approved' of it. Before she'd left England a clause had been inserted into Dusty's contract at her insistence. It stipulated that she and the band would not, under any circumstances, play to segregated audiences.

Although she could never be considered an activist, Dusty nevertheless read the papers and took her usual fascinated interest in the world. For someone brought up on, thrilled by and admiring of black music, and counting black singers amongst her greatest influences, she was also someone who appreciated the history of slavery and the way black music emerged from the fields and churches that provided slaves with the only voice they had. Combine that with her more liberal feeling that you didn't ban anyone for enjoying themselves because they were a certain colour (any more than if they were a certain sexuality or certain class) and it would have been anathema to fall in with the apartheid rules.

The clause that Dusty inserted was one the performers' union Equity and the Musicians Union had first tried to put forward as a political response to a political problem – the white South African government's apartheid regime. For decades minority white rule had prevented South African blacks from having the vote. Dissent, interracial marriage, the existence of a black face in what was designated a 'white only' area would be enough excuse for imprisonment without trial, sometimes worse. Equity could not force artists to agree to the clause and by the time it was included in its contracts it had been watered down to allow audiences to be segregated, but not theatres. Dusty was having none of it. Before the show Dusty and Vic were approached by two government officials who tried to persuade them to do separate shows for white and black audiences. They refused, and Dusty and the band were delighted, when they got to the concert, to see a packed mixed audience.

Back at the hotel that night, though, there were more men in grey suits with briefcases. They had come to get Dusty to sign some papers saying that her contract was void. That there had been a mistake. But there hadn't, she and Vic protested. Reece remembers that when the government men left it was with the warning that they should all stay inside the hotel since 'there might be people around who won't be very tolerant about all this'. Two police stood on guard at the hotel entrance. 'Whether they were there to protect us or to stop us going out was a bit unclear,' says Reece.

The next morning they were due to leave for a concert in Cape Town, a city Wainer told them was much more easy-going than Johannesburg, which had after all been founded by the Dutch Voortrekkers and retained a very high proportion of right-wing Afrikaners. Wainer wasn't expecting any problems once they moved on. Even so everyone was on edge, particularly since two men had approached Reece over breakfast who had showed a particular interest in the Echoes and told him the band could be stars in South Africa and earn a fortune. 'I got very suspicious,' says Reece, 'especially when I found out from the receptionist that they weren't guests at the hotel and had left in a hurry.' Billings said they were likely to be government people who thought if they could split the Echoes from Dusty by getting them to agree to work under South African law, it would damage her reputation.

Cape Town, on the coast, was a more relaxing city and a few days before Christmas the temperature there was in the eighties. At the Luxurama Theatre in Wittenbome, ten miles out of town, the show was late starting because Reece was anxiously checking the audience out. He knew that if it wasn't a mixed audience there would be no point the Echoes starting their opening act since Dusty would refuse to set foot on the stage. 'I couldn't see any black people in the seats. The stage manager kept making starting motions but it took another ten minutes before I was happy that it was a really mixed audience at the front.' They weren't so happy to see some familiar suits in the audience, but the show was another success and Dusty and the band returned to their hotel for a late supper. The men in suits were there to welcome them with the news that, since Dusty wouldn't sign the papers, she could not leave the hotel – but they would be pleased if she left the country.

She, Vic and the Echoes sat around most of the night drinking tea and eating sandwiches as lawyers in London fought with officialdom. 'I never want to see another tomato sandwich as long as I live!' Dusty said afterwards. From the hotel room Dusty rang through a somewhat coded telegram to Vicki back in Baker Street saying that she had 'faintly hysterical giggles' at the furore she'd caused and, firmly

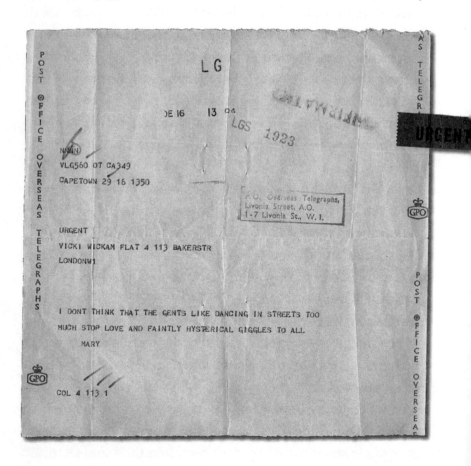

tongue-in-cheek, that she thought the grey suits probably didn't much like 'Dancing In The Street' – a reference to the Martha and the Vandellas number she included in her act.

The next morning they were taken by armed guards to the airport to make sure they left. Yet despite Hendrik Verwoerd and his Ministry of the Interior's best efforts, Dusty's last sight of South Africa was a good one: as they walked across the tarmac to their flight they were greeted by a row of black airport porters. Lined up in their blue boiler suits, their red berets off their heads and held in their hands as a sign of respect, they formed a solemn guard of honour as Dusty climbed the steps to the plane.

Arriving back at Heathrow airport Dusty was surrounded by cameramen and newspaper reporters clamouring for another Dusty controversy. 'I am not political,' Dusty said somewhat disingenuously, vowels nicely rounded. 'I just think people should be allowed to hear me sing irrespective of colour, creed or religion.' Despite her protestations and the antagonism her action raised in some quarters, Dusty's stand was to have interesting reverberations.

First the white South African government hastily started a campaign of disinformation: Dusty had set this problem up explicitly to create publicity for the American tour that would follow her South African concerts. 'I am speechless,' our girl responded, so clearly was not quite, 'I could jump off Tower Bridge if I wanted my name in the papers.' Despite feeling that she'd made matters worse because the South African government would from now on scrutinise every contract made with visiting artists, following her lead a string of British musicians refused to play in South Africa. The first people to obey their consciences were the Zombies, the

Searchers and Eden Kane, all of whom were represented by Tito Burns, now Dusty's agent. In the House of Commons MPs signed a motion applauding Dusty 'standing against the obnoxious doctrine of apartheid'.

Nearly two decades later Dusty would have to be restrained from hitting a white hotel employee near Oakland after he refused to allow Labelle's Nona Hendryx to go on to the hotel tennis court. In the 1990s, at a cocktail party in Buckinghamshire, when the conversation took on what she considered a racist overtone, Dusty announced very loudly that her first lover had been black. Had she also said it had been a woman? 'Oh,' Dusty laughed, 'I didn't think Henley was quite ready for that!'

It was proving to be an eventful year. If anything had kick-started Dusty's career it was the moment when, on her way to Nashville to record with the Springfields in 1962, she had passed the Colony Record Store on Broadway in New York and heard the sound of the Exciters' 'Tell Him'. With Leiber and Stoller's driving back-up, the sharp-edged first line seemed to come from nowhere. Barbara Reid's vocal – 'I know something about love' – sliced the rolling rhythm in two. It was a sound that Dusty was always to say sent a 'tingling sensation' through her body and it was the beginning of what would, over a series of singles, inspire her to try and reproduce that moment, so strong and hard yet vital and joyful, both for herself and for her audience.

In the mid-1960s the New York-based Uptown R&B records, of which the Exciters were emblematic, dominated British pop sensibility from the Mods who called for imports to be played in their clubs to the Beatles who covered Shirelles tracks, and Dusty, whose 'take' on the underlying feeling of those tracks was never surpassed by another white singer.

Uptown was the combination of a slew of small independent black record labels, a range of ferociously talented black and white producers and young black vocal groups, and the dominance of white songwriting teams from New York's Brill Building writing factory which produced some of the most perfect pop songs in the history of music. Aside from the young husband and wife team of Carole King and Gerry Goffin, who had been providing hits for American black groups for years, they included Barry Mann and Cynthia Weil, Ellie Greenwich and Jeff Barry, Burt Bacharach and Hal David. For a musician it was yet another reason to see New York as the centre of their particular universe, an energising, dangerous city that produced an urban R&B centred round teen emotions, less masculine and knowing than its southern cousins. It was Uptown that changed music: it produced Phil Spector's 'wall of sound' and it opened the once white-dominated charts to black labels like Tamla Motown and, later, smoother music from writer/producers Kenny Gamble, Leon Huff and Thom Bell at their studios in Philadelphia.

Now Vic Billings told Dusty that she would be playing the Fox Theatre in New York. More, she would be appearing on the same bill as some of the young acts from Tamla Motown. For Dusty a chance to play in New York and to perform along with some of the leading Motown acts was both extraordinary and exciting. Although flying to New York from London now is so common it's almost thought of as commuting, in 1964 for Dusty it was like a journey on to a film set with a score from the Drifters. Yes, steam really did come up from the grids in the pavement in the winter; the neon lights really were bright on Broadway; Fifth Avenue boasted the glitziest stores in the hemisphere and, in the summer, up on the roof was indeed the only place to be if you wanted to breathe. In September 1964, at Brooklyn's Fox Theatre the other side of the river from Manhattan Island, it was stiflingly hot but nobody had time to go on to the roof. Dusty was part of a first 'British invasion' of groups who were segued with some of the new young Motown acts as well as the Ronettes and the tough-edged Shangri-Las.

In the art deco glory that was the Fox the work was hard. Seven days, six shows a day. With artists packed in tiny dressing rooms it was like working on a sweaty conveyor belt. For Dusty the schedule was a nightmare since the shows started at ten in the morning and finished at ten at night, yet whenever she reminisced about the Fox days later she never complained about the early start but remembered only the thrill. It was here that Dusty could finally stand in the wings and watch Marvin Gaye, the Supremes, Smokey Robinson and the Miracles and the Temptations perform live, cementing the physical impact she had felt when she had first heard their music on import. And it was at the Fox that Dusty was to meet Martha and the Vandellas.

If the Exciters had thrilled her in 1962, a year later Martha and the Vandellas' single 'Heatwave' would have the same effect. Martha Reeves had joined Motown, then known as Gordy Records after its founder, the young black Detroit car mechanic Berry Gordy, as a secretary in 1959. She was in charge of booking studio time for artists, working for the head of A&R Mickey Stevenson. In the way of many of Motown's finest 'accidents', when singer Mary 'My Guy' Wells missed a recording session Martha (who had unsubtly sung in the office corridors at every available opportunity) stepped in and did so well that it was decided she should form her own group with Gloria Williams, Annette Sterling and Rosalind Ashford.

Unlike other softer-stepping Motown acts, Martha and the Vandellas came up with an urgent sound, fast and almost impossible to emulate. Just as Reid's vocal had demanded Dusty's ear, so Martha's first line 'Whenever I'm with him/something inside/starts to burning' and its subsequent landings on being 'filled with desire' with the Vandellas' driving 'oh yeah, oh yeah, yeaaahhh' behind it, cut right through her.

But Dusty was so in awe of the Motown artists and so socially awkward that she didn't know how to make contact with them. Instead of going into the Vandellas' dressing-room and introducing herself, saying how much she liked their music, she did the one thing that she had learned early in Ealing would get people's attention: she chose to smash things. When the first armful of crockery went down the stairs Martha and the group came rushing out of their dressing-room to find out what the noise was about. As indeed did everyone else since they were practically piled on top of each other. In this bizarre way Dusty met her heroes and heroines. Years later Mary of the Shangri-Las, by now a respectable and successful businesswoman working in real estate, would say that she never forgot how Dusty showed her the art of throwing china backstage at the Fox.

Staying in a run-down hotel in Harlem, 'with broken windows and Malcolm X' Dusty was to recall later, she would blithely walk around the area feeling perfectly at home despite the fact that the good people of the neighbourhood were hardly used to a white face on the streets – never mind one with a blonde beehive hairdo. Out in Brooklyn, although Dusty always laughingly blamed the Temptations for introducing her to drink (they apparently gave her a vodka to calm her stage nerves and she liked the feeling it gave her), she became closer and closer to Martha and, if one of the Vandellas didn't make a show or was sick, Dusty would step out on to the Fox stage and sing back-up for the elegant young Marvin Gaye. 'It was,' she would recall, 'one of the great thrills of my life, being a Vandella.'

The next spring when Dusty, Tom, Peppi and Madeline Bell were going to Rio de Janeiro for carnival – a two-day, dawn-to-dusk parade of spectacular samba, music, dancing and parties – Dusty paid for Martha to go with them as a 'thank you' for the Fox. Peppi Borza was an excitable young American dancer whom Dusty and Tom had met when they were in the Springfields touring with Del Shannon. Peppi, delightfully camp, temperamental, but caring (he left Dusty money in his will) was the only person who could ever shake Dusty out of a bad mood – mainly because he refused to indulge her or take anything she said seriously. Dusty always remembered not just the brilliance of carnival but the time she, Martha and Madeline climbed up to the famous statue of Jesus that towers over Rio. Despite the heat, none of the women went 'au naturel' with their hair in Rio. For Martha and Madeline it was part and parcel of being a black singer in the 1960s, before black pride said you didn't have to wear straight wigs like white women's hair. For Dusty it was probably more a case of wanting to look her glamorous best to herself, or indeed to the odd passing fan or photographer. So there they were, a white girl and two black girls under the outstretched arms of the Lord, all wearing scarves so that their wigs wouldn't fly off in the wind.

Although after New York Dusty was supposed to go on to a college tour of America with the Echoes, the all-day concerts at the Fox and a busy after-hours round of socialising with the other singers had exhausted her. She rang Vic in London – she just couldn't cut it. Luckily she was not huge on this particular circuit and Vic managed to get the dates pulled with relatively little problem. The Echoes, who always liked playing out of Britain because their hotels and food were all paid for and fixed up front, came back. It was the first time Dusty had cancelled any dates. If no alarm bells rang in Vic's head at the time, they soon would.

When Dusty returned to London she was even more fixated on the Motown sound. In April 1965 Vicki had convinced Rediffusion to do an hour-long *RSG!* special with the Motown revue, *The Sound of Motown*, and Dusty was the obvious person to front it. 'She always made sure that I played Motown records on the programme for the dancers,' says Vicki, 'because radio didn't play them at the time and she wanted that particular *RSG!* audience to hear them. Anyway she liked dancing to them herself.' The revue had been touring the provinces to half-full houses. Motown was still a label for the cognoscenti, and young ordinary white British audiences were still screaming in the aisles at young ordinary white British groups. Meanwhile there was some discord amongst the Motown artists. By now the Supremes were being heavily pushed by Berry Gordy, who had started to see rather a lot of lead singer Diana Ross, and were overshadowing Martha and her group. The TV show, with Little Stevie Wonder making his first teen appearance, headlined with the Supremes. But it was with Martha that Dusty was to sing her one and only song that day, their version of Bacharach's 'Wishin' and Hopin''. The special, hosted by a woman who was already a huge success in her own right and a fan, and showcasing as it did the verve and artistry of the young black musicians, put the Motown artists firmly in the public consciousness. A year later these artists were often in the British charts.

The *RSG!* special also saw the first of Dusty's more spectacular throwing parties. By now the Murray-Leslies had moved out, leaving Dusty to take over the lease, and she decided to celebrate the arrival in town of Martha and the Vandellas. In her Baker Street flat with the wine flowing, as the party got under way, Dusty grabbed a can of sardines and threw the contents across the room, followed by more fish and the help of Tom, Vicki and Peppi. After a while the floor in Baker Street was awash with fish and oil. As a sardine landed in the handbag of one of the Shangri-Las, Motown's Kim Weston swanned through the door in a full-length mink coat, slipped and went flying. The fish was followed by fireworks on the roof, much to the chagrin of the Vandellas, since many were lit under their legs. It was almost as though life had constantly to be like the cartoons she had watched between the 'A' and 'B' movies with her mother in the cinema in Ealing.

At 5 a.m. everyone had left and Dusty, Vicki, Tom and Peppi were sitting around surveying the wreckage. 'That,' said Dusty, 'was a great party!' After an hour of reliving some of the more farcical episodes from the evening they decided to clean up. Dusty loved her parties but, strangely, she loved cleaning up afterwards too. All her homes were notable for their shining tiles and unstained sinks and she always found cleaning a very therapeutic pastime. It was like making something beautiful and orderly out of a mess. Cleaning on her hands and knees would feature more and more as therapy in Dusty's life, as time went on and things got messier. But in Baker Street in the sixties things were jolly enough. 'Well,' said Dusty grabbing half a leftover chocolate cake, 'let's get rid of this for a start!' and threw it at what she thought was an open window. It wasn't.

A year later Dusty would get another chance to play New York but it would be under very different circumstances and far less joyful. By the autumn of 1966 she was huge in America after the success of a clutch of singles and her first two albums, and was booked to headline at Basin Street East. The white jazz drummer Buddy Rich and his seventeen-piece Big Band were billed to support. It was a tremendous accolade for Dusty to play Basin Street but Rich had a reputation for being difficult, even with his own musicians, and he took it badly that Dusty, a 'pop' singer in his eyes, was billed over him.

That November opening night was a disaster. Rich managed to sabotage Dusty's moment of glory. 'Dusty got chopped up by professional star killers,' wrote the critic Ron Grevatt reviewing the show for *Melody Maker*. Rich, having finished his opening stint, started a stand-up comedy act, then brought on Johnny Carson and Tony Bennett to play a number. Then he introduced a number of famous people in the audience. He went an hour over time. By the time Dusty got on stage the audience, instead of being expectant, were exhausted. And anyway, how do you follow that? She tried with a clutch of Bacharach and David songs, most of her hits and, bravely, a version of Billie Holiday's 'God Bless The Child', but it was not the opening night she had dreamed of.

Her only consolation was that the executives from Philips were furious and complained to Rich in no uncertain terms.

Still very little changed. She had to get up on stage at Basin Street twice nightly and have Rich abuse her, either by not allowing his band, who were backing her with an augmented string section, enough rehearsal time with her, or making derogatory remarks about her singing in his role of compère. One night Madeline Bell was in the audience and was incensed to hear Rich talk about a variety of black singers as 'second rate' before heralding Dusty's entrance with 'and here's a third-rate one'.

'It wouldn't have mattered so much,' Dusty would say later, 'but all the great musicians like Ella Fitzgerald, Duke Ellington and Dionne Warwick make Basin Street East their local pub and you've got to prove something to people like that.'

In fact having Dionne Warwick in the audience was a real test for Dusty. At the same time as she'd heard the Exciters Dusty heard Warwick's 'Don't Make Me Over' 'and I had to sit down very suddenly', she would recall. 'Nobody can sing Bacharach and David music like her. Nobody. It's total gossamer. I knew then that's what I wanted to do. Bacharach and David changed pop music and "Don't Make Me Over" changed my life.' Although she had a string of hits in America with Bacharach and David songs, which they wrote especially for her, Warwick had, early on, found European success harder to attain. This was mainly because British girl singers in the sixties, eager to capture an American sound, had zeroed in on Warwick's recordings. Even though Bacharach and David songs were built round highly sophisticated structures and were difficult to sing, both Cilla Black and Sandie Shaw had had passable hits with 'Anyone Who Had A Heart' and 'Always Something There To Remind Me', initially blocking Warwick's original recordings from the British chart. If Dusty had at first come under the same umbrella, at least, for the classically trained Warwick, who belonged to an exalted line of black singers – sister of Dee Dee, niece of Cissy Houston and the cousin of Whitney – she could admit defeat to someone whose voice she admired. Still, with the arch-exponent of Bacharach and David sitting out front, there was pressure on Dusty to do well.

Dusty, whose nerves were bad enough anyway without such a critical audience, and who never knew what Rich might unleash on her, struggled through the first week in tears every night. Finally she decided to take some control over the situation. First her voice was suffering, as it would every time she felt stressed in the future. With a survival instinct that would become remarkable only because, oddly, she never relied on it again when she needed it, she went to a singing teacher in New York. For two weeks at midday she sang scales, did breathing exercises and learned techniques to de-stress herself mentally. Second she decided to stop being a victim to Rich's whims. She walked into Rich's dressing-room and told him she wanted to put two new numbers into her set and so needed more rehearsal time with the band. When Rich, who had his feet up on the desk, refused, Dusty slapped him across the face in a fury. Rich threatened to sue her for assault.

The three-week season dragged on, although Dusty recovered her equilibrium on stage helped by the singing teacher and the fact that critics, who realised the opening night was not indicative of Dusty's talents, came back to re-review her act and were unanimously flattering. On her last night something happened to Dusty that was to be a repeating pattern throughout her career. Other musicians, the ones who really knew a voice when they heard it, would never fail to think she was wonderful no matter what else was happening. At Basin Street, as she finished her final set, it was Rich's sax player who came out of the line-up, grabbed the mike and said, 'Dear Dusty . . . she's a gas, and I just want to give her a token of how the boys in the band feel about her.' Dusty's goodbye present from the Big Band was a bright red pair of boxing gloves, a tribute to her fighting spirit and the confrontation with Rich that many of them would have liked to have been fearless enough to have done themselves.

Although the Basin Street problems had not been of Dusty's making, and it's unlikely Rich would have been so pugnacious had the top of the bill been a man, the fracas would turn out to be the start of an image that was to haunt Dusty for her whole working life: that she was a difficult performer and that wherever Dusty went, there went trouble. 'And it was because she was a woman,' says Madeline. 'When she'd ask for something nobody would take any notice. So she had to stamp her feet and yell just to get heard and then of course she was a "bitch". I tell you, I learned so much being around her. She got treated like shit by people so many times.'

However unhappy Dusty had been at Basin Street she refused to let it colour her love affair with New York. It was a city she would return to again and again, loving its exhilarating atmosphere, its twenty-four-hour delicatessens, supermarkets and chemists, the way in a city where you couldn't look up without feeling dizzy, the sun would suddenly glint on the golden pineapple that was the Chrysler building. When she was earning better money, some Christmases she would take OB and Kay there for a treat and they would go and visit Vicki who had left London to live in New York in 1970. If she went to stay at the apartment that Vicki shared with singer Nona Hendryx on the Upper West Side it would be a week after she left that, finally, they could remove the traces of her presence: the fine coating of face powder and the thick smell of hair spray that lay all over the spare room.

6

Westbourne Terrace is a wide, sweeping road near Hyde Park, its huge Regency houses with their elegant columns and gleaming windows now amongst some of the most desirable addresses in central London. One end of the street leads to Hyde Park, the other brings you after a ten-minute walk to Queensway. But in 1965, when Dusty moved into number 85, the houses in Westbourne Terrace were a jumble of high-ceilinged rooms broken up into flats and bedsits in an area a little too close to what was then the 'red-light district' of Paddington to be considered salubrious.

By now Dusty was spending a lot of her free time with Vicki. Both middle-class girls in what was turning out to be an exciting and optimistic world, they were roughly the same age, laughed at the same stupid things. Dusty probably envied Vicki's energy level which was certainly higher than her own, nicely rounded vowels that had come from a good education and the fruity chuckle that would burst out of her at the most unexpected moments.

Vicki thinks Dusty probably thought she was 'a sensible sort of girl' and that if she had a job in TV working on a music programme then she must be okay. Whatever the reasons, their friendship was to last for nearly forty years. In her flat in Marylebone Vicki, a girl who had been brought up on Gilbert and Sullivan and *South Pacific*, would listen to Dusty talk about black music without knowing what her points of reference were. 'She was *so* enthusiastic and played me things *so* loudly, as she played everything, that it began to get under my skin. You couldn't be with her for long without getting a musical education and finally, of course, I was as passionately obsessed about that music as she was.'

Even when she wasn't on the programme Dusty would hang out at the *RSG!* studios with Vicki, Cathy, Michael Aldred, Michael Lindsay-Hogg and Vicki's secretary Rosie Simons. Rosie would go on to marry Yardbird's guitarist and Carly Simon producer Paul Samwell-Smith and was the recipient of a tiny orphaned kitten Dusty had decided to rescue – the first of many such felines the singer would scoop up over the years. Dusty was beginning to be recognised as the white queen of soul, effortlessly shifting into her key changes with a vocal delivery that could imbue a song with poignant desperation. Yet however much in her songs she wanted her lover back Dusty never let rip on her records or on stage. She knew that pauses, holding her voice in check and letting it skim across the melody line were much more effective. Even if she'd had the kind of voice that could holler it's doubtful that she would have used it much; her attitude to music was too controlled and sophisticated, her ear too attuned to let her delivery move over a listener like a tank.

In 1965 among her friends were Peppi, Madeline (who would go on to have six hit records as lead singer of Blue Mink and marry first a truck driver, then a musician), and a friend of Vicki's from Liverpool, Stevie Holly. Holly, tall, slim, with dark hair down to her waist, had been the first woman DJ in the country. At eighteen she was seven years younger than Dusty and Vicki, but her work in the clubs and her friendship with the Beatles meant that she had as near an encyclopaedic knowledge about obscure soul records as Dusty did, and the singer was impressed.

Early in the year Stevie Holly had become friends with two members of the flamboyant American all-woman group Goldie and the Gingerbreads, Margo Lewis and Carol MacDonald. The first all-female rock band to be signed to a major label, the foursome had had a hit the year before with 'Can't You Hear My Heartbeat' and toured with the Kinks and the Rolling Stones. Stevie lived opposite Goldie and the group in Bayswater and often met them while she was walking her tiny Yorkshire terrier Peru. When the group split up and lead singer Goldie, whose real name was Genya Ravan, went home to her mother in Brooklyn, Margo and Carol wanted to stay on in London. Looking for a new flat they came across 85 Westbourne Terrace where the singers the Three Bells, three little blondes, twins and a sister, and nicknamed, inevitably, 'ding-dong' by the rest of the house, lived on the top floor.

Carol and Margo discovered that people on the other three floors were beginning to move out. As the flats and rooms became vacant, friends moved in. Margo, Carol and Stevie took on a large two-bedroomed flat with a huge lounge; below them cockney songwriter Leapy Lee shared the rambling basement with a Liverpudlian flatmate Marie Guirron who later went on to marry Justin Hayward of the Moody Blues; Dusty and Madeline Bell took the only other places on offer. Dusty's flat was so small that her bed was a pull-down from the wall but she knew a larger flat on the floor above would soon be coming vacant and despite general bewilderment from friends who say she 'Greta'd it' – preferred to be alone – seemed to get real pleasure from being in this bustling household of songwriters, musicians and would-be stars.

Here, as would be the case when she was happiest in the future, she could either be surrounded by people with whom she shared some enthusiasms or she could be on her own. It was perfect for her. 'She was lovely, there was nothing complicated about her then, although Dusty never wanted to do anything or see anyone,' says Stevie. 'And I think Westbourne Terrace was a sanctuary for her because we had so much fun between ourselves and there was so much going on that she never needed to go out anywhere – she never got bored.'

Dusty may well have seen 85 as a sanctuary. The past two or three years' touring had begun to catch up with her and the South African rumpus had been particularly traumatic. In March she had been out on the road doing two shows a night with another package – this time with the Zombies and, again, Bobby Vee, and was due to open a six-week summer show down on the coast at the Winter Gardens, Bournemouth when she collapsed. It had been an exhausting schedule, but not unusually so for artists in the sixties. Somehow Dusty was always more prone to this sudden depletion of her energy. She always said she loved being on stage and everyone who knew her knew that too, but the effort of getting there and getting it perfect, proving to Kay and OB and Tom that she really was a clever girl to be admired, was draining. It was jazz singer Cleo Laine who deputised for her the first two weeks. By August Dusty had flown off to the Virgin Islands for a month, leaving Vic to cancel all her engagements. Nobody had a hint that this level of exhaustion (Dusty had to get a letter from a Harley Street specialist to prove she could not sing) did not bode well for the future.

In September she seemed back on form and back in the recording studios. Her second solo album *Everything's Coming Up Dusty* was released in November and again gave her two hit singles: the dreamy Carole King/Gerry Goffin 'Some Of Your Lovin'' and the faster 'Little By Little'. By the end of the year things seemed back to normal. Dusty was back on *Ready Steady Go!* and she had been picked to appear in the Royal Variety Show in front of the Queen.

Dusty was now enjoying as much success in America. Such was the sound of her voice, many people who had never seen her assumed she was black, as had happened earlier in Britain even though she had nationwide exposure on *RSG!* She was an international star and her tour schedules were stretching across the world. Of all her records the Goffin and King songs were particularly successful and 'Some Of Your Lovin'' would always be regarded as a Dusty 'classic'. Before Dusty had recorded it Carole King had sent her an acetate of 'Some Of Your Lovin''.

Sending Dusty a demo disc was a habit Carole King continued for years, every time there was a new song she thought would be right for her. Inevitably Dusty would be enthralled, keeping them in a box under her bed as though that way nobody else could record them. Undoubtedly influenced by King's simple uncluttered demo, when she cut 'Some Of Your Lovin'' Dusty did away with her Spector sound and delicately tried her vocal out nearer the front of the track. Slower and more insinuating than her previous records 'Lovin'' proved to be no less popular and it drew out another dimension to Dusty's voice – an entreating, touching vulnerability; a lightly husky quality that brought her in much more intimate contact with her listener. Carole King would always say that Dusty was the only one, of all the singers who covered her and Gerry Goffin's songs, who did it the way it should have sounded.

When she wasn't working, the others at number 85 saw a lot of Dusty. She was simply part of the household. Well, she was until she wanted to get some sleep. Her bed happened to be directly above Stevie's phone and, up early, Vicki would always ring Stevie to tell her about a club she'd been to, or a musician she'd watched, the night before. Dusty, who liked to sleep late, would grumpily come downstairs to complain about the telephone only to be told it had been Vicki. She would stomp back upstairs again muttering about the telephone habits of her friend, but realising that any protests would be futile. Often she would 'borrow' Stevie's dog Peru and take him for a walk in Hyde Park. Although one day she came back from an outing with Madeline and said that she might have to discontinue the walks because 'Madeline says Peru has halitosis', the little dog would often sit happily in Dusty's handbag while she drove him about in her sports car.

That Christmas of 1965 Stevie wanted to go to Liverpool to see her family but could not take Peru with her. She asked Dusty if she'd look after the dog. Of course, Dusty said, but could she borrow Stevie's flat while she was away since her parents, Tom and some friends were coming for Christmas and this way they could stay over. When Stevie came back she went to Dusty's flat to collect her keys and had trouble trying to attract Kay and OB's attention. Listening to a Baby Washington single with their heads pressed to the radio, they were too busy exclaiming that she sounded 'just like our Mary' to pay Stevie any attention. When she finally got into her flat Stevie was even more bemused. It was suspiciously clean, as though nobody had used it. Then she pulled the curtains back. The wall outside and the basement area were covered in food. For the next three months she was clearing brussel sprouts from behind the radiators.

The O'Briens had, as seemed to be their way, celebrated Christmas by hurling their dinner around.

7

If Dusty had a free weekend she, Vicki, Madeline and Stevie might drive off to Vicki's parents in Newbury. Here in the large farmhouse with acres of open space the four women in their twenties would cavort about like schoolgirls playing hide and seek after Sunday lunch. And as dusk fell and Vicki's parents insisted on their 'relaxation' (relative silence while they read the newspapers) the four would settle on the rug in front of the fire, like something out of Louisa May Alcott's *Little Women*, and play a competitive game of pick-a-stick. Like the Alcott sisters, the four inevitably ended up squabbling over whose stick had moved and who had flicked and wobbled the stick underneath.

Although some of the occupants of Westbourne Grove worked during the day and the television would be switched on when any of them were appearing on a programme, evenings would usually be spent as a group, playing records, singing, playing guitar. Margo and Carol, who were now providing back-up vocals, along with Madeline, on Dusty's records, would be practising with her in the flat they shared. Every evening the household would be joined by friends. Amongst these were Lulu and singer Alan David who was going out with one of the Three Bells, and Vicki who, although she was still living round the corner in

New Cavendish Street, almost always came to Westbourne Terrace on her way back from work at Rediffusion.

Then there would be Tom's parties in Chelsea where he lived in 'a proper apartment' unlike the number 85 crowd in their makeshift flats. Despite her brother's retiring personality – even as the host he would be awkward and withdrawn at most social gatherings just as he had been on the Springfields' TV appearances – these would be fabulous affairs compared to the wine and cheese 'do's of the time. Dusty and the crowd from Westbourne Terrace would be augmented by Peppi, Vic Billings and, later, American folk singer Julie Felix. Dusty, with her eclectic musical taste, would spend hours talking to Felix; one of her own favourite songs was the melancholic folk tune 'My Langan Love' which she went on to sing, unaccompanied, on one of her BBC TV series. Lee Everett, wife of the DJ Kenny Everett, would also soon be 'one of the crowd' usually walking about 'like a barefoot hippie'. Kenny was then well on the way to becoming a national treasure and would soon be lured away from pirate radio by the BBC where he was to be a pioneer on Radio One until anarchically disgracing himself and returning to commercial radio. But it was Lee to whom Dusty was particularly drawn and who would remain a friend of Dusty's for her entire life.

This crowd of people would, one way or another, always be consistent in Dusty's life, providing her with a tight circle of friends – almost a bunch of siblings who would laugh, argue, fight and make up again with delightful regularity. They also all shared the same sense of humour, something that seemed incredibly important to Dusty who would get tickled by anything that was slightly, as she saw it, off the wall or caused some kind of disturbance. In 1965 she decided to go on holiday with Madeline, Tom and Vic, renting a large apartment on the Spanish coast at Fuengirola. In the days before mass tourism or lager louts the coastline still retained a little of its wild beauty, the local bars were awash with sangria and the friends spent two weeks lolling around in the heat, eating, drinking and idling away the days. One day, during a round of horseplay, Vic had taken Madeline's bikini bottoms and hoisted them on top of the flagpole on the apartment roof. If Madeline was slightly miffed that half of her one swimsuit was currently unobtainable to her, and Dusty had a giggling fit at the sight of her friend's bright briefs flapping in the hot breeze, the Spanish police were not so happy. Within hours the guardia were at the door protesting that in Franco's Spain only the Spanish flag was allowed to fly and *nothing* was to be added to detract from its noble image. The holidaymakers soon got the message that if Vic didn't get Madeline's bikini down, pronto, they would not be enjoying the rest of their holiday.

Dusty's first album, *A Girl Called Dusty*, had been released in the late spring of 1964 and had proved, with its cover of a relaxed, pretty blonde girl in a blue denim shirt and jeans, to give her not just another huge chart success and critical acclaim but provide her with two more hit singles: Burt Bacharach and Hal David's 'I Just Don't Know What To Do With Myself' and their 'Wishin' and Hopin''. The American songwriters who, until now, had written almost exclusively for Dionne Warwick, produced material that was more complicated than it sounded and was tricky to sing. Of the two numbers 'Wishin'' was the more complex since it moved from a staccato vocal before opening out into much longer notes halfway through each verse, but it was

'I Just Don't Know What To Do With Myself' that was to be the more important. The wrenching ballad, to which Dusty's vocal gave a controlled hint of desperation, was to mark her as a singer who could hold back, open out on the chorus and yet keep an ache in her voice at the same time. It was a remarkably sophisticated attribute in the world of sixties British pop and it made her unique. It also moved her towards slower songs that stretched her voice and towards material where love's longing and losses were highlighted more than the buoyant teen dreams of 'uptown'.

At the end of 1965 Dusty was thrilled when she was invited to the San Remo Festival in Italy. Pat Barnett, as usual intent on making sure everything would be perfect, had offered to take up and iron Dusty's dress for the occasion. Dusty was worried that it was too long and she would catch her heel in the hem on stage. Although Pat put the iron on cool, as soon as the metal touched the green silk it shredded and, panic-stricken, she rang Dusty. The singer proved unexpectedly unconcerned and, with a stand-in dress, she and Vic Billings flew off to Italy.

In the 1960s San Remo, an elegant palm-tree-lined resort on Italy's Adriatic coast, annually hosted the world's biggest song festival – a particularly good showcase for both new songs and some of Europe's greatest singers. Dusty was supposed to be singing 'Face To Face With Love' but, after a perfect rehearsal, her voice kept giving up and eventually she pulled out. It was the first sign of one of Dusty's much later repeating patterns: she would do a wonderful rehearsal but approach it as though it were the performance itself. The combination of an overworked larynx and nerves would then take their toll, and, since everything had to be not just good but perfect, she would not go on.

When she went to concerts of singers she admired, Dusty, brought up by a father who beat out the rhythms of tunes on the back of her hand until she recognised them all, found their music an education. She would sit in the stalls, her glasses firmly on her nose, writing notes to herself about particular phrasings other singers used that she liked. Years later, when she recorded the historic 'Son Of A Preacher Man', although she'd originally been pleased with it and played it three times over the phone to Vicki when it was completed, she was furious with herself when Aretha Franklin covered it the following year. Of course, Aretha had 'done it better'. On the *Dusty – Full Circle* TV programme, nearly thirty years after Dusty's track was released as a single, she gave the perfect masterclass: singing a line from her own version, then rephrasing it so that the vocal emphasis was entirely different, as Aretha had done it. Dusty would never again perform it on stage the same way that she'd recorded it – it would always be with that 'Aretha' emphasis and she disliked the track she'd originally been so pleased with.

For someone with such a finely tuned ear, sitting in the auditorium at San Remo as though she were one of the audience, she was open to a key moment in her career. It was here that she first heard Pino Donnagio's '*Io Che Non Vivo Senza Te*'. Despite her lack of Italian, the drama and sweep of Italian ballads of that period with their strong melody lines and crescendos, the kind of desperate passion the singers imbued them with, was something that hooked her. 'I burst into tears when I heard that song,' she would say later.

Always ahead of the commercial pack, years later she would become enamoured by the edgy, throbbing emotion of Portuguese *fado* in the same way. The hundreds-of-years-old street music was vibrant with emotions of pain, desire and nostalgia. It became most associated with Lisbon and the women there, the *fadista*. For Dusty, although the construction of any song, usually with its chorus opening like petals, was important, what really counted was the emotion that lay just under the surface. She knew, as the orchestra struck up the opening melody line before dropping back for the beginning of Donnagio's song, that she had to record it.

When she got back to England the only problem she had was getting someone to write English lyrics for the song. It was Vicki who blithely said that she was sure she and her friend Simon Napier Bell, manager of the Yardbirds and later to manage George Michael and Andrew Ridgeley's Wham! could do some. 'But the only word of Italian I knew was *ciao* and so it was obvious that neither of us could translate from the original so we had to start from scratch.' The pair decided that since they considered that songs that sold a notion of romantic ever-after love were 'bullshit', it would be interesting to break with the formula. 'You Don't Have To Say You Love Me' was the result. Their lack of Italian was telling. Literally translated, the Donnagio song meant 'I Don't Want To Live Without You'. They had accidentally subverted the entire emotion behind the original which spoke not of 'reasonable' Anglo-Saxon behaviour, but of typically dramatic, clawing Italian intensity: love as life, life without love as not worth a lira. The last lines in the English version were written on the back of an envelope as Vicki sped round to Dusty's flat twenty-four hours later. The writers and the singer agreed that they were 'pretty much rubbish' and on paper they certainly didn't look much:

You don't have to say you love me/ Just be close at hand
You don't have to stay forever/ I will understand
Believe me, believe me, I can't help but love you
But believe me I'll never tie you down

Dusty had already recorded the backing track for the song, arranging it from the original acetate, but at the Philips studio she and her producer Johnny Franz were still dubious about whether the lyrics would actually work. When they did she had something else to worry about: she was concerned about the echo on her voice. With Vicki and Simon in the studio, bewildered that something they had written so quickly was sounding so marvellous, the sound engineer Peter Oliff went to the basement to sort out the sound on Dusty's echo chamber. 'He noticed how good the sound was coming back up the stairwell,' Napier Bell was to remember. Dusty, who had always hated what she heard as the 'dead' sound of the studio in Stanhope Place with its low ceiling and who much preferred to sing in the tiled space of the women's lavatory there, 'went out there and sang into a mike suspended over the stairwell and the sound was perfect'.

'You Don't Have To Say You Love Me' was released in April 1966. It was to prove the song that would become most closely associated with Dusty Springfield. With its edge of self-sacrifice and its climbing chord change, it gave her the biggest hit of her career, selling millions of copies across the world. It became her signature tune on stage and both broadened and deepened her reputation, long before a clutch of other white women 'ballad singers' would wrench a song from its moorings without much intuitive feeling. As a superlative singer of big dramatic ballads she sometimes worried that the song had made her into a singer of 'big ballady things', but it would be that track, whether she liked it or not, that would also turn her into an icon. What girl in the mid and late sixties didn't, after all, stand in front of the mirror with a hairbrush as a microphone and pretend either to be the Supremes on 'Stop In The Name of Love' or to be Dusty, singing along to 'You Don't Have To Say You Love Me' or, later, 'I Close My Eyes And Count To Ten', copying the moment when Dusty's arm moved up and the palm faced outward – as graceful as a temple dancer but as though she were warding off a ghost?

By now Dusty was having her dresses especially made for her by Eric Darnell round the corner in Marylebone High Street. Dusty and Eric would spend hours working out exactly what she needed for which shows – dresses that would come nearly to the ground but which would cling to make a smooth, slim outline; always dresses with sleeves and only unfussy detail. It was as if she wanted, publicly at least, to look thoroughly grown-up, no matter how childlike and vulnerable she may have felt inside. However oddly Dusty dressed when she wasn't on stage – a suede multi-patchwork suit with a strange 'Tommy Tucker' hat; a pair of flares with a lot of jangling jewellery – she knew exactly what worked on stage or television.

On stage for any showcase events or tours, because of the hard spotlights it had to be sequins. For television, because she wanted the attention to concentrate on her face, she got Darnell to put in more detail round the neck – often daisies, repeating the motif in her hair – or the bodice of the dress would be completely covered in bugle beading, an innovation in those days. Sometimes Stevie would go with Vicki and Madeline to the fittings, sitting on little chairs in Darnell's showroom while Dusty swept in and out, modelling one beautiful dress after another. 'And I was so impressed,' says Stevie, 'because of all the singers she was the star and she played the star and looked the star.'

In May Dusty received more plaudits. She was voted both Top British Girl Singer and Top International Female Singer by the readers of the music paper the *New Musical Express* and starred in their huge concert of poll winners at the Empire Pool auditorium, in Wembley, a suburb of north London. It was a great night and Dusty, in one of her glittering dresses, was in top form, happily going down to the front of the stage and making up to the first row who were on their feet (they were the only ones she could see clearly, as she had long since given up wearing contact lenses) and adoring her.

On Friday nights, after the entire household had returned from *Ready, Steady, Go!*, Margo and Madeline Bell would create one of their communal spaghetti suppers in the basement flat where Leapy Lee and Marie lived. In those days there was always dope around and someone had to take on the task of rolling communal joints. Along with this illegal pursuit the most sophisticated wine for the London trendsetters and clubbers was the pink, slightly over-sweet Mateus Rosé, liked not just for its colour but for its rather artistic label and bottle shape (so easy to transform into a lampshade base!). This was the drink much favoured in the basement of Westbourne Terrace. In the convivial atmosphere only one thing marred the proceedings: Marie was over-zealous about clearing plates and glasses during supper. 'It would drive Dusty and Vicki crazy,' says Stevie. 'Margo and Madeline had made huge pots of spaghetti with this great sauce and the idea was always that we'd sit around talking, drinking and singing – Dusty would play guitar –

and then help ourselves to more food. But you'd put your glass or your plate down and it would go swinging past you into the washing up bowl where Marie would start furiously washing everything up and we'd all scream at her.' The sweet, neat Marie apparently took this in her stride and never changed her attitude. Meanwhile the Mateus Rosé took its toll.

One evening Dusty, already given to the dramatic entrance, arrived at the top of the three stairs that led into Stevie's lounge. 'I have,' she said, swaying slightly and for all the world sounding like Lady Bracknell from *The Importance of Being Ernest*, 'decided to commit suicide.' Margo, Carol and Stevie, who had been sitting on the floor playing records, looked up at her bemused. Before anyone could move Dusty had come down the three steps, slipped on a glossy album cover and landed flat on her back. 'There was a dreadful moment of silence,' says Stevie. 'Then we all started to laugh and Dusty giggled so much she cried with laughter, she could see how ridiculous the whole thing was.'

Later they found out that her suicide attempt had consisted of two glasses of wine and half a Valium. Such was Dusty's life in the mid-1960s. Two decades later the stakes would be much higher.

8

By 1966 Dusty had had more hit records than any other female artist in the world. In less than two years 'Stay Awhile', 'I Just Don't Know What To Do With Myself', 'Losing You', 'Some Of Your Lovin'', 'In The Middle Of Nowhere' and 'Little By Little' had all shot into the British top twenty; she had done three month-long sold-out package tours; 'Wishin And Hopin'' and 'I Only Want To Be With You' had been huge American hits while her albums, *A Girl Called Dusty* and *Everything's Coming Up Dusty*, had given her hits on both sides of the Atlantic. Meanwhile, apart from her appearances on *Ready, Steady, Go!*, she had featured in a TV special on Burt Bacharach, at the Royal Variety Show, and garnered a clutch of awards as Britain's best female vocalist. Dusty had even been something of a celebrity pioneer in that she was featured in a national TV advertising campaign for Mother's Pride sliced bread – a product thought to be the height of modernity at the time. Breezily working her way through tongue-twisting lyrics in a cockney voice, Dusty was featured with short blonde hair, a cap and a long striped scarf. She looked for all the world like a cross between the Artful Dodger and Barbara Windsor, delivering the sliced loaf at the end of a long pole to eager customers – who for some reason were leaning out of their upstairs windows.

By April the stir that 'You Don't Have To Say' was causing was extraordinary and had given her an audience way beyond the teenage market. People knew her name, recognised her in the street, felt they had a relationship with her: perfectly ordinary un-Mod people would come up to her and tell her they loved her records and that her voice was the most wonderful thing they'd ever heard. By 1966 anyone in or around the pop world was more likely than not to be drinking too much and taking the odd tablet. Dusty was no exception. Now stories were beginning to circulate: mainly about her eccentric behaviour, how she would throw custard or lemon meringue pies, whole dinner services, glasses, anything that made a noise or a mess.

For journalists, particularly on the daily tabloids, whose bread and butter was to come back to the office with the more outrageous or personal aspects of this new teenage craze called pop – musicians throwing TVs out of hotel windows, long-haired sex fiends out with famous models – Dusty's throwing episodes began to overtake any interest in her voice. These were her 'pranks', things that contributed to her zany image. The voice had got her where she was. Now she was there she was becoming a name to sell newspapers to a public whose interest in the private lives of the famous was beginning to grow. Even so it was fairly harmless stuff compared to what would come later when a much more lethal attitude existed between newspapers desperately clawing for a larger market share of a shrinking readership.

If there was one place that became synonymous with this well-publicised habit of Dusty's it was her first real home and the first house she had been able to afford to buy: 13 Aubrey

Walk, the Kensington house she now shared with Norma Tanega. Norma, with her Mexican/Indian cheekbones and long dark hair, intrigued the English/Irish girl fascinated by intelligent, artistic women. For Dusty, Norma's background of art and politics (Norma had been an early campaigner against America's war in Vietnam; her paintings were huge canvases covered in bold semi-mythological creatures and plants) was an additional bonus to the appeal of a west coast woman whose manic laugh could suddenly erupt from the pit of her stomach.

They had first met in Manchester taping appearances for the lightweight pop TV show *Thank Your Lucky Stars*. For Norma, the whole pop razzmatazz was a new experience. One minute she had been a struggling painter living an unremarkable life in California. The next she had a hit single with a slightly bizarre, semi-folksy track called 'Walking My Cat Named Dog' produced by the Four Seasons' Bob Crewe.

Standing in the studio Norma watched Dusty go through rehearsals. 'I'm standing there with my guitar, like a dork, while this woman, I had no idea who she was, stood on some scaffolding and went over and over this song until it was, of course, perfect.' When suddenly the studio lights went out Norma was confused. 'What's going on?' she asked Dusty, who was sitting with her lighting man Fred Perry. Dusty explained the English tradition of a union tea break for the electricians and cameramen and started to talk to Norma about her work. Norma was enthralled: 'She was witty and flirty, how could you not love her?' Nevertheless Norma had to go back to America and Dusty's phone bill soared. Finally she flew over and met Norma in a hotel in New York. It had been months since they'd actually seen each other and they were both so apprehensive that they stood facing each other like strangers. Even for a woman who found intimacy difficult, Dusty could see this was ridiculous. Eventually she said, 'I've come all this way across the ocean to see you – the least you could do is come across the floor!'

Norma changed continents and for a while they lived together in a mews house in Ennismore Gardens. Norma, who was, beneath her arty exterior, extremely practical, worried about the way Dusty spent money. She convinced her that renting properties was a mistake (Dusty had, since Westbourne Terrace, moved twice – first to Earl's Court and then to Ennismore Gardens in Kensington, both shared with Madeline). Now that she was making real money Norma suggested she should invest in property. It took many more months for her to persuade the woman, who even at twenty-seven years old hated the thought of being tied to any one place, or to have any kind of responsibility, that it made very practical sense to buy Aubrey Walk. Finally one day in 1966 Dusty sat down and wrote out a shopping list. It may be apocryphal but according to everyone who was around at the time the story goes that it read: buy bread, buy milk, buy house.

Aubrey Walk needed a lot of work to turn it into the kind of place Dusty was happy in. She and Norma worked out a kind of deal: Norma, with her artistic eye and knowing what Dusty would want, would be in charge of alterations. Dusty could get on with touring and doing television without having to deal with builders, painters and decorators. Norma encouraged Dusty to go on shopping expeditions to Heals and Harrods to buy beautiful pieces for the house: 'I thought, you have all this money and fame and fortune, let's go and spend it on something beautiful that you can see and have for ever. I didn't care what people thought I was – her secretary, her lackey, whatever. And just going down the street was so amazing. People would just yell out at her, "Hey Dusty – good telly!" She loved it really.' Dusty's shopping expeditions were the stuff of women's magazine articles, especially if she happened to shop with Vic Billings, Norma, Lee Everett and whoever else happened to be around. Then she took the journalist and photographer round the stores and was obliging enough to take off her shoes and bounce on mattresses or emerge with her arms full of stuffed toys.

Given a sacked builder or two, things at Aubrey Walk went smoothly enough. The top floor of the three-storey house was turned into workspace: here was Dusty's trunk of sheet music and acetates which were beginning to be sent by songwriters who admired her voice; along one wall was a huge built-in wardrobe for Dusty's clothes. Norma had a room to use as a studio for her painting, although it would be some years before she had the time to start her own work again. The next floor down was given over to bedrooms with Dusty's king-sized bed and a mirrored wall. Leading off was her make-up space with its wall-length counter and a rail of gowns that she was currently using for her tours and TV appearances. Everything was painted in Dusty's favourite colours, pink or purple. The ground floor was for the more mundane things of life: the kitchen and reception room.

It was on this floor that Dusty's parties took place. They would happen on those occasions when Dusty had a rare few days off or when any American singer friends were in town. Then the house would reverberate with laughter and music from two stadium-sized speakers turned up to Dusty's favoured, thundering, decibel level. Martha and the

Vandellas could be in the front room with larger-than-life soul singer Doris Troy whose delighted bear hugs were enough to take your breath away and who, along with Dionne Warwick and Emily 'Cissy' Houston (whose daughter Whitney would one day be a diva in her own right), had provided back-up for a string of historic Drifters records as well as having three major hits on her own including 'Just One Look'. There'd be Madeline, Vicki, Peppi sometimes Tom, always Dusty's mother and father with a drink in their hands: OB sitting smiling benignly in an armchair; her bright-eyed tiny mother Kay in at every conversation.

In the half-moon designer chair that Dusty had suspended on a chain from the ceiling Julie Felix, her long hair billowing around her face, would twirl silently like a rather elegant statue. This chair was Dusty's great pride and joy. She had generally 'bought big' and Pat, who always helped her move, would despair, since the places Dusty lived in inevitably had small doorways. At Aubrey Walk that chair was first craned up to the first floor through a window. The plan was that it would then easily go down the inside staircase. Unfortunately the door between the first floor and the staircase proved narrower than the chair's ungiving basketwork. With Dusty pulling from the staircase and Fred Perry and Pat pushing from inside the room and with Dusty yelling, 'Push, push,' the chair and door suddenly parted company. The force was so unexpected they all landed on the floor. 'I think we practically built that house round her furniture,' says Pat, 'and moving her was always a nightmare because she'd leave everything until the last minute.'

Now Dusty could afford to shop at Harrods, at Asprey's the Bond Street jewellers, and drink champagne instead of cheap pink wine. Her floor-to-ceiling wardrobes heaved with clothes from expensive shops such as Jaeger (she would buy the same outfit in three or four colours at a time), but she still preferred to stay in with friends than go out to clubs or for expensive meals. After midnight and with the words, 'Oh ho, Dusty's in the kitchen,' any sane person who valued their clothes would leave the celebrations as quickly as they could. Dusty drunk and being in the kitchen meant only one thing: she was about to grab the pies, then the dinner service that she had especially bought from a leading London store for the occasion. Gene Pitney would be seen crouching behind a chair attempting to protect his sharp little Italian-designed suit from harm. The Vandellas might be hitting each other over the head with French bread. Dusty often thought it was hilarious that the quietest people she knew would be the very ones who would most love sploshing around in broken bread, chocolate and meringue, and whose deepest frustrations seemed to be released at Dusty's chaotic events.

What was it about throwing that she loved? Certainly she adored the sound of breaking glass and china as much as she loved the revving of Phil Spector's backings and it's possible to see how, in a strange way, she might 'hear' it as a musical sound. She always remembered that, as a child, she had heard the sound of bombs falling and the dull explosions as they hit, and that, combined with growing up in a home where dishes flew and crashed, must have meant that harsh noises were buried deep in her childhood memories. But the pies? Somehow in Dusty's mind it was a cross between her favourite Marx Brothers movies, old-fashioned slapstick and cartoons. Sometimes it was an utterly spontaneous thing – she would simply throw something when she was irritated.

In September 1966 Stanley Drake, the assistant manager of the restaurant in the GPO Tower in central London would be the recipient of a particularly well-aimed bread roll on the back of his head after Dusty felt he had hassled her waiter enough. The national newspapers the next day decided it had been a pie and quoted Dusty, who had just won an award as Best International Vocalist of the Year from *Melody Maker*, saying, 'This little waiter was trying to do everything he could for us and yet he was being insulted. I hate waiters being pushed around.' Usually the throwing was done with more foresight: 'I get bored very easily,' she would always say. Boredom, any hint of ordinariness, all that space she could fall into if there wasn't something lunatic going on to occupy her mind, was what she had to keep at bay.

By the summer of 1966 Dusty had her own BBC TV series. Given the opportunity to sing anything she wanted and to chose her own guests, Dusty was, perhaps for one of the few times in her life, happy. It showed. With the Echoes, arranger Johnny Pearson and a vast string section, she could chose to do anything. She sang unaccompanied folk songs, a little jazz with Dudley Moore. She sang Bacharach with Burt at the keyboards, hard soul with Tom Jones. She goofed about with Woody Allen and, in a revolutionary move, used one of her stalwart stage numbers, 'Mockingbird', as a duet with Jimi Hendrix. There would be three series and they would all show the breadth of what she could do as a singer. What became obvious was that there was hardly anything she couldn't sing. As Hendrix's guitar wailed and wandered around the song at ear-paining volume, much to the shock of the BBC control room, Dusty held the main vocal line steady for him without losing any of the soulfulness of the original.

Meanwhile her off-stage life was pretty much a continuation of the one she'd enjoyed in Westbourne Terrace.
Dusty seldom involved herself much in the London club
scene so prevalent in the 1960s. Instead there would be
the odd trip to the Sombrero, a Spanish restaurant in
Kensington with a gay bar in the basement, or sometimes
she and Lee Everett would make for the smoky, crowded
public houses of east London where there would be a nightly
parade of drag acts to enjoy. 'Then there'd always be a
drama on stage or in the audience and we'd fall out and
grab a taxi and go. She was adored by all those queens
you know.'

Dusty was always half amused, half fascinated by men
in drag. These female impersonators in their wigs and
dresses and false eyelashes, teetering around on high heels,
masquerading as ultra-feminine. If they were classy and
professional she openly admired them and had a particular
soft spot for Danny La Rue who was, at one time, the
most famous female impersonator in Britain. He had risen
from the clubs to become a top-flight cabaret and television
star. Dusty would go to all his opening nights and they
would regularly have dinner together. When he included an
impersonation of her in his act, alongside Marlene Dietrich,
Bette Davis and Zsa Zsa Gabor, she was thrilled. 'You do
me better than I do myself.'

This was not the attitude she took many years later when
comedian Bobby Davro impersonated her as a drunk, weav-
ing across stage. In 1991 she would win £75,000 in damages
after she sued him for libel. There were other reasons for her
fondness for La Rue, apart from the respect he showed when
all six foot of him would 'become' his favourite women stars.
Irish and a Catholic, he had had a tough childhood, brought

up in poverty by his adored widowed mother, first in Cork, then in London. It had been a hard life and Dusty would have empathised with the vulnerability under the dresses and wigs, as well as being fascinated by his stories of Royal Navy service and being part of the *Forces Show-boat* chorus along with Harry Secombe, one of the *Goon Show* cast.

Aside from visiting American soul and R&B groups, Aubrey Walk also played host to stars on the tennis circuit. Dusty loved sporting occasions even though she herself was useless at anything that required that amount of running and complete concentration. At school she had dabbled in hockey, but it had been a pretty half-hearted affair and bullying-off had not been her particular forte. In the late 1960s, when the game turned professional, tennis players became real stars, equivalent in the eyes of their fan following to anyone in the pop charts. In a period when cultures were colliding and there was a new youthful mobility, it was fashionable to admire, particularly, the young American women players whose power and determination on the circuit was so extreme compared to the rest of the world. Their game was thrillingly aggressive and brought them big prize money.

When the American women's tennis players came to Britain for Wimbledon Dusty and Norma went back to meet them and Billie Jean King and Rosie Casals, in particular, became regular visitors at Aubrey Walk. For Dusty, who was to stay friends with Billie and Rosie throughout her career, the tennis circuit allowed her to be a fan but with none of the competitive concerns she had about music (even though, behind the scenes at a match, most of the players were completely overwhelmed by Dusty's enthusiastic support, given she was so famous herself).

Dusty was now so good on record, so mesmeric on stage, that it was getting easy for Vic Billings to book her anywhere in the world for coast-to-coast tours or the more financially rewarding 'season' at major venues. Yet often it would mean Dusty working with the 'house' band rather than her own musicians and that could sometimes cause problems.

In 1967 Dusty was booked to tour Australia. She wanted to treat Norma and it was the one time Norma stopped protesting about how much it would all cost and actually went with her. The journey to Australia took the best part of an exhausting two and a half days. Two years before they built the glinting, giant clam-shaped opera house on the shoreline, Dusty flew into Sydney for the start of an Australian tour.

Looking out of the plane Dusty saw the city sprawled below, meandering along the coast, its white beaches curling around the city. In the sixties Sydney was yet to enjoy its popularity as the artistic and intellectual heartland of Australia, eventually overwhelming the position of the country's staid parliamentary capital, Canberra. There were no American-style high rises of hotels and apartment blocks which were to spring up in the 1980s. Instead a collection of Victorian two-storey houses with ornate Italian metal balconies strayed just beyond the centre and lines of fishermen's wooden cottages dotted the bays. The glorious sweep of the Harbour Bridge, with its ferries bustling workers backwards and forwards from Manly and the outlying suburbs to the city, straddled a harbour of run down ports and industrial sites. Kings Cross was the centre of prostitution and gambling, and Sydney had a large and vibrant gay quarter.

In September Dusty was booked to do a three-week season at Chequers, a basement nightclub in Goulburn Street, the area which much later would become Sydney's Chinatown. In 1967 the premises were the swankiest in town, host to politicians, gangsters and what passed as the Sydney upper crust. Two hundred people could be accommodated in booths at two sittings each night for supper, coffee, liqueurs and the show. The club's ability to pay well meant that it pulled a constant stream of internationally famous performers such as Eartha Kitt who would appear with a supporting act of a juggler or magician and the Chequers ballet – girls who would swing into their famous routine as 1920s flappers.

Dusty had been to Australia once before, in 1964 as part of a pop package which included Gerry and the Pacemakers, Brian Poole and the Tremeloes, and the American singer Gene Pitney, whose classic '24 Hours From Tulsa' Dusty would later cover, turning the song's effect in the hands of a female narrator. But this was her first visit alone and it had not started well. The moment she landed on a Tuesday she was besieged by John Laws's office at Radio 2UE. Laws had already established himself as the most famous DJ in Australia. Even in 1967 he was not just a man who played records, but someone whose opinions could influence the most powerful politicians in the country.

When his office was told that Dusty could not go to his studios to be interviewed at this very moment because she'd gone to bed, he was incensed. Nobody had ever told Laws he'd have to wait and he certainly wasn't going to take it from this jumped-up pop singer from England. By the afternoon Laws's secretary was ringing Dusty's Australian record company to ask if she would go on Laws's phone-in,

Party Line, that night. No, she was told, but Dusty would be free to do it on Thursday. Laws immediately got on the air and railed against the singer. Thursday would not be convenient with him since by then 'we'd have a star on the show'. He told his assistant to throw Dusty's record in the garbage can.

Australians might have become fascinated by the Laws/Springfield saga which continued over the next forty-eight hours, but it threw Dusty, who had flown in early to rehearse with the Chequers band for the season. In many respects the Laws situation mirrored the Basin Street fiasco. In the sixties women might go off and be stars but they would do what they were told, work hard and know their place. For men like Laws and Buddy Rich, both with obviously massive egos, women who didn't jump had to be brought into line. And Dusty had something else on her mind: the rehearsals were proving problematic and working the musicians, all of whom were solid club players, to have her 'ear', was harder than she'd imagined. Two days after she started rehearsals, in desperation, she phoned England and Doug Reece.

Although their relationship was always platonic – 'I understood her and most of the things she did and she understood me' – Dusty needed Doug around. In Australia in 1967 with a band who weren't hearing her she certainly needed him to save things. Please could he fly over straight away and she'd pay the fare. 'That girl was so intent on getting the same sound live that she got on record,' says Pat Barnett, 'that she'd pay for whatever she needed out of her own pocket. Sometimes, early on, it meant she really wasn't earning much at all and even later, by the time she'd paid for a string section and whatever else she felt the sound needed, there was a huge chunk of her money gone.'

Dusty worried about money all her life. Not that it would be apparent to people outside her circle of close friends: she was renowned for her generosity to people she worked with like producers and musicians. Every Christmas she went on an enormous shopping spree at Harrods to buy expensive, elaborate gifts for everyone she knew.

When he got to Sydney, Reece saw the problem. Dusty had picked the best local singers to do back-up, including the blues/jazz vocalist Kerri Biddell, and had brought in Roland Hanna, a jazz pianist from New York who played for Thad Jones and Mel Lewis, but she just couldn't get the right feel from the other musicians who were more used to backing ballad singers such as Matt Monro, the former bus conductor turned English Frank Sinatra. Once Doug took over rehearsals Dusty relaxed, knowing that despite John Laws she could reclaim her audience. On Dusty's opening night fans for the late show were queuing round the block before the first show had finished. Newspaper critics who opted for calling her, no doubt to her amusement, 'this young English lass' noted an 'indefinable something', that she was 'talented and uninhibited' and that 'she went over big – and I do mean big.'

It was the start of the Australians' love affair with Dusty and hers with Australia and she would have found it ironic that thirty years later Laws was to be hit by the 'Cash for Comments' scandal, when it was revealed that he received payments from several large organisations for mentioning them on air.

'She'd always wear long trousers, never a skirt or shorts, and we'd have a lot of fun, but after fifteen or twenty minutes she'd say her make-up was running and she'd have to stop.'

After tennis there'd usually be a late lunch at Peppi's flat in Chelsea of traditional English roast. Tom would bring his guitar and he and Dusty would sing. 'They seemed like the best times for her,' says Rosie. 'She was so relaxed and having a ball.' Sometimes Dusty would take Billie Jean and Rosie round to Lee Everett's flat in Holland Park Road. Once she arrived with half the players from Wimbledon – including Jimmy Connors. Lee and Kenny Everett lived amongst a vast menagerie: a Great Dane, three Chihuahuas, a litter of kittens, parrots, macaws. Dusty loved the madness of it, all these animals running in and out of the garden.

To stop herself from being pigeonholed, Dusty had taken what some people considered a serious risk. She had followed up the success of 'You Don't Have To Say You Love Me' not with another grand flourishing ballad but with a far more melancholic song: Carole King's 'Going Back'. King's original acetate, despite or maybe because of the emptiness of the sound, had an oddly wistful quality about it that fitted the sentiments of her lyrics about nostalgia for a golden childhood age of innocence. Ironic though it may have been that Dusty identified with the track so much, given her own childhood memories, it was this wistfulness that she would highlight on her own recording, again bringing a light, husky soulfulness to her vocal. Despite its slow pace, the song had a universal appeal. Dusty imbued King's lyrics with a painful sense of hurt, as though, prophetically, living an adult life was just too hard. And the new intimacy in her voice was something that she would use much more in the future. It was this voice that told the listener about her vulnerability and, far from being a disaster, it became yet another reason for her fans to empathise with her.

Still, despite the ease with which she appeared to handle her music, Dusty was getting a reputation for being 'difficult' in the studio. Certainly Dusty's sessions might start much later, take twice as long as anyone else's and be fraught for everyone involved. She would wrench a song apart note by note and reconstruct it again; spend hours on the backing track insisting on getting exactly the 'sound' she could hear in her head. Much of the bad feeling with some of the back-up musicians was caused by Dusty's stop/start routine and the fact that she was determined to get that sound from them, whatever they thought.

'And in those days what were women supposed to know about music?' asks Pat Barnett. 'The people who would say Dust was difficult in the studio were the musicians who had blocked minds. They'd tell her she couldn't get a certain sound and she'd say, "But I've heard it on a record and I know we can get it," and they wouldn't budge until she'd yelled at them, and they're the people who say how awful and difficult she was.'

Unable to sight-read, Dusty relied on Johnny Franz to translate what she wanted into actual notes. Dusty would say that Johnny Franz would sit there reading and she'd never think he was listening then he'd suddenly look up and say, 'No, that should be a B flat.' Like most artists she would cut her vocal track last – another slow process since she was as hard on her own interpretation as she was on her session musicians. Often she would call a halt mid-way through a line because she had 'heard' two notes she didn't think were right. Once she tried to explain to Norma what happened to her when she sang, coming up with the analogy of a river and its two currents: one the notes, one the emotion. And the two currents would make the river flow smoothly.

'She would always know when the emotion would drop off and that's when she'd stop and start again,' says Norma. 'The emotion and the tone had to mesh. People said that she didn't know her own ability, how good she was. She knew her ability all right, that's why it had to be perfect. She knew how to ride that river better than any other raft in the business.'

In 1967 she now had two movie themes to her credit (the forgettable 'The Corrupt Ones' and the hit 'The Look Of Love', written by Bacharach and Hal David) and a successful three-week season at New York's Copacabana nightclub under her belt. Her third album *Where Am I Going?* with its pop-art cover had given her another success, and Clive Westlake's brilliant 'I Close My Eyes And Count To Ten' had given her a single to challenge the impact of 'You Don't Have To Say You Love Me'. Dusty's contract with Philips had expired and she didn't wish to renew it.

When Atlantic Records expressed a desire to sign her Dusty was thrilled. Not only was this the 'house' that Leiber and Stoller had made their home, but it was Aretha Franklin's record label. It also boasted the Drifters, the Coasters and a line-up of the greatest jazz musicians of the century: John Coltrane, the Modern Jazz Quartet, Charlie Mingus and Ornette Coleman. Started in the late 1940s Atlantic had come to epitomise the kind of company that was becoming all too rare twenty years later: one based on real enthusiasm for the music not just the dollar and with a sophisticated bedrock of top-flight session musicians. Now Atlantic's legendary Ahmet Ertegun and Jerry Wexler wanted Dusty to fly over to Memphis where the best of those musicians were based, and record her first album for them.

For a musicologist like Dusty, going to Memphis would initially feel like the most obvious place for her to be in the world. This was the city that had, along with New York, produced the records that had most made her want to sing, to recapture the energy and emotion that she had had an almost physical response to. With white audiences Memphis was the place that had become synonymous with Elvis Presley, who would go on to cover Dusty's 'You Don't Have To Say You Love Me'. But for those in the know, both black and white and for Presley himself, the city was most musically defined by the presence of Satellite, later renamed Stax Records, a label distributed by Atlantic. Estelle Axton and her brother Jim Stewart started Satellite in 1960 and their studio on East McLemore Avenue became the centre for a string of soul/R&B hits: Booker T and the MGs' 'Green Onions', Sam and Dave's 'Hold On I'm Coming', Rufus Thomas's 'Walking The Dog' included.

Stax became synonymous with raw-sounding R&B and Memphis itself grew in musical importance, identified with records by Otis Redding, the Staple Singers, Isaac Hayes, Eddie Floyd, Arthur Conley; by Willie Mitchell's Hi label with Al Green and Ann Peebles and most of all by Aretha Franklin. She cut 'I Never Loved A Man' at the Muscle Shoals studios where the proliferation of superb session musicians, many forming the Muscle Shoals rhythm section and the Memphis Horns and including Steve Cropper, Duck Dunn, Al Jackson, Booker T. Jones, Wayne Jackson and Andrew Love, formed a kind of house band.

Excited though Dusty was, and however 'black' she may

have sounded, she was worried that recording in Memphis would mean she would be expected to 'get down and get with it' in a way that her fragile voice could not cope with. Wexler and co-producers Tom Dowd and Arif Mardin had no such plans. They were smart enough to realise that Dusty should sound like Dusty but be given the chance to stretch herself with the kind of musicians she'd never had the opportunity to work with before, and to give her singing the kind of finesse and status they felt was necessary at this point in her career. But this didn't mean things would be easy for her . . .

For five years at Philips Dusty had been used to going into the studio when the backing tracks were already laid down and then working on her vocal delivery. In Memphis she was to find things didn't work that way. Yes, she could lay her vocal on, but she was expected to work closely with the young musicians on the song's approach, on what might go into the breaks and what overall sound she wanted. For a woman who had always had to fight session musicians, this was an extraordinary way of working. But now she was working with extraordinary musicians: the cool lead bass playing of jazz-influenced Tommy Cogbill, drummer Gene Chrisman and Reggie Young, whose guitar break, dancing round the strings on 'The Windmills Of Your Mind', was to elevate Michel Legrand's pretty filmscore song for Steve McQueen's *The Thomas Crown Affair* to near classical status – even though Dusty always said she hated it because she couldn't identify with the words.

Along with the devastating Sweet Inspirations on backing vocals – Estelle Brown, Myrna Smith, Sylvia Shemwell and the wonderful Cissy Houston – Dusty also had the Memphis Horns behind her. She was working with the cream of the crop and she was stunned to discover that Wexler, Dowd and Mardin, far from wanting the musicians to overcrowd her, had very strong ideas about keeping the backings subtle and leaving huge spaces for her voice.

A year before, when she had recorded Burt Bacharach's 'The Look Of Love' for the *Casino Royale* spoof Bond film, working with Bacharach in the studio, she had used a vocal style of breathtaking intimacy. It had exposed her voice much as 'Going Back' and the equally wistful 'Colouring Book' had done, but because of the lyrics and the way she broke up the words her voice took on a new under-the-covers huskiness which she would use in Memphis, particularly on 'Just A Little Lovin''. Dusty was much more used to burying her voice behind her own 'wall of sound'. It was partly a safety valve against criticism, partly because she always wanted to be part of a sound rather than separate from it, just as the girl groups of the late fifties and early sixties had. She used to say that most of all she wanted her voice to be another instrument in the overall sound of the production. Now Wexler, Dowd and Mardin were telling her the opposite: that her voice would carry the album and the musicians would provide her with a subtle, sophisticated cushion to lean her vocal up against.

But the first thing Dusty had to do was to sort out, with Jerry Wexler, what songs she was going to cut. Wexler had amassed what he thought was a sensitively judged array but he did not know Dusty well. Certainly he did not know that the first word out of Dusty's mouth when she was asked to do anything was always 'no'. It would only be later, when she'd had time to think about it, that she might change her mind. So it was when the first huge batch of material was sifted through. Dusty said 'no' to the entire collection and went back to London. A few weeks later, with time to reconsider, she returned to New York and looked through the same batch again. Now she expressed surprise and delight with the songs – mainly because, she said, they were exactly the ones she would have chosen herself. Perfectly true: a handful from her favourite writers including Carole King and Gerry Goffin, Randy Newman's complex songs and a clutch from Burt Bacharach and Hal David. One of two others she might not have originally chosen was Hinton and Fritts 'Breakfast In Bed', which turned into one of the album's big hits with lesbian listeners and would years later provide a hit for UB40 and the Pretenders' Chrissie Hynde.

The other was John Hurley and Ronnie Watkins's 'Son Of A Preacher Man'. This was a song Aretha had originally been offered but which she had turned down. It was this southern 'grits and greens' number that was finally to overshadow all the other tracks and to project Dusty, temporarily, away from what *Rolling Stone* saw as her potential fate: as a woman singer who would end up on the hotel 'rooms' circuit. And it was the track Aretha would finally record herself a year after hearing Dusty's version.

But it seems that Jerry Wexler, in his enthusiasm for the project, was over-keen to impress Dusty with both Atlantic Records and the Memphis studios. Later she complained that she was intimidated by his constant references to other Atlantic artists who had worked there – 'This is where Aretha stood' – and she was always nervous and hyped up whenever she came to put her vocal tracks down. It's also likely that by the time she'd worked over the songs with the Memphis musicians she was terrified of actually cutting the vocals in front of them, especially since she took so long and was so fussy about the way she sounded.

Whatever, Wexler finally agreed to let her cut her vocals later, in New York. It wasn't so unusual, Aretha had often done the same herself, although as Wexler was to remark later, he'd never had a singer who recorded quite like Dusty did: very late at night, in the dark and with, as usual, the backing track turned up so loudly she could not possibly hear her own voice at all. Wexler, sitting in the studio, knew that there was no way she could hear what she was doing or whether she was in tune or not. He was amazed by the results. Although they often fought (he would later recall, with a chuckle, 'the odd flying ashtray') he was completely overwhelmed by what he described later as her 'miraculous pitch'.

Dusty In Memphis was a huge critical success but it may well have been too advanced for the record-buying public. It only sold 100,000 copies in America, far fewer in Britain and it never made the charts, although 'Son Of A Preacher Man' as a single did reasonably well in both Britain and America. *Dusty In Memphis* was to provide Dusty with her finest accolades but, much later, it was also to be the album that the rest of her work was constantly critically held up against. Ironically, when Atlantic's Ahmet Ertegun finally decided to delete the album from the company catalogue, he discovered it had acquired a huge cult status.

By July 1968 Dusty was opening her first season at the Talk of the Town in Leicester Square, and Aubrey Walk was in uproar. The season was a loud benchmark of Dusty's incredible success. The Talk, a luxurious night- and supper club, was the most prestigious venue in England, usually booking in the top American singers such as Pearl Bailey and Ethel Merman. Despite the mundane menu it was an expensive evening out and the dinner guests for a first night there always included a hefty contingent of other stars. Although Dusty had made two previous appearances at the Talk earlier in her solo career, the first in 1964, neither had exposed her stature as this season would. In

the early days Dusty did not have the confidence that she could hold up a long evening on her own. As a result there would be American-style choreographed dance 'sketches' and routines built round her costume changes, and three dance bands for the clientèle.

These appearances would be much more theatrical affairs – putting on a show – as though, for the audience, Dusty and her voice were not quite enough. By 1968 there were no such qualms. Dusty had not appeared at the nightclub for nearly three years, during which time she had cemented her reputation internationally. She was so admired and respected for her voice, so adored for her image that any extra fluff or dancers were entirely unnecessary. Dusty and an orchestra were quite enough, thank you, and there was a buzz of excitement around months before the box-office was open for bookings.

Once she went solo Dusty had kept on the old Springfields' publicist Keith Goodwin, a solid working-class man of the 'old' music school with offices in Denmark Street. Cramped between shops dealing in music scores and trombones, the office was at the top of narrow, uncarpeted stairs. In many respects Goodwin and Dusty had the kind of relationship that mirrored the one she had with her Philips producer Johnny Franz: 'That poor man, I drive him mad,' she would say. While Dusty respected their musical knowledge, both men learned early on that to argue with Dusty too long was fruitless. Once she had decided something she simply became more entrenched. It was a characteristic that she shared with her brother. 'She may have seemed deliberately difficult,' says Vicki, 'but when it came to knowing what was musically right for her, she was always spot-on.' Franz could accommodate Dusty better but Goodwin, who had the press at his heels, had a more difficult time. He became wearily used to Dusty's refusal to do interviews, turn up on time for photocalls or talk to any journalist she didn't like or trust. In 1968 there were only two she did, which made Goodwin's job almost impossible.

That summer Goodwin was refusing to cancel his annual French holiday in favour of handling Dusty's press for the Talk of the Town season. 'She won't do anything anyway and it will just be a huge pain,' he told his new young assistant Mike Gill before he disappeared. The good-looking teenage Gill, 'with the naïveté that comes with only three weeks in the music business' and with the kind of enthusiasm that came from being an ardent fan, immediately rang Dusty about publicity. When he discovered that one part of the show would feature her dressed and singing as the Hollywood child star Shirley Temple he got carried away with excitement. He was sure he could get her front pages on the nationals if she turned up in her Temple outfit on Monday morning. It was the kind of thing she would have never done for Goodwin, and Goodwin by then wouldn't have even tried, but Dusty was so impressed by Gill's youthful enthusiasm she agreed. Gill had a happy weekend contemplating his successful entry into the heady world of pop publicity.

On the day of the photocall Mike Gill found it hard to work out why his boss had taken a holiday. True, Dusty was a little late facing the nation's pressmen in her Shirley Temple outfit and things were getting tetchy. But when she turned up in her polka dot dress with its puffed sleeves and wide sash, with her red tap shoes, white socks and white bow in her corkscrew curls, even with OB's knees she charmed everybody, Gill included. Yet the relative smoothness of the press call was to prove deceptive. Gill was to enjoy the kind of relationship Dusty had with many young men during her career. Nearly all of them were gay and were bewitched by the singer, but their relationships were usually emotionally exhausting. There would be arguments and tantrums. They'd get drunk together and swear eternal devotion. As time went on, and however much he continued to adore her, Gill had been introduced to his nemesis. Sometimes she'd be reliable, sometimes she wouldn't. Over the years it was a facet of Dusty's behaviour that never changed and

Doug Reece, Pat Rhodes and Dusty on the Bobby Vee tour.

As Mods and Rockers fight at Clacton in 1964, Dusty flies off on her first trip to Australia as part of a package tour with Liverpool's Gerry and the Pacemakers. With Dusty are Gerry Marsden (*far right*), the Beatles' manager Brian Epstein (holding newspapers) and Dusty's manager Vic Billings.

Simply fabulous – Dusty in her famous beaded gown and with the look that marked her place in history.

'Like an excited child at Christmas'

Happy days at Aubrey Walk with (*above*) Norma on drums and (*below*) Dusty only an arm's length away from her guitar.

(*Above*) London 1967: Dusty, Vicki (*right*) and Norma Tanega ham it up for the record.

(*Right*) Norma, Dusty, Peppi, and Madeline Bell.

Norma's favourite picture of Dusty which she signed 'Catherine'.

it often got in the way of the beauty of her voice and the talent of her interpretation.

Having her picture taken was always an ordeal to Dusty. It wasn't just dislike of the lumpy knees she felt she had inherited from her father, it was what she considered her heavy jawline and her 'big bones', even though she was very slim with small breasts and bottom. Like many women, when she looked in the mirror this is not what she saw: she still saw the overweight schoolgirl she'd once been. Like many women without self-confidence, having her image 'stolen' by the flashbulb and then not being in control of the pictures terrified her. Would she look the way she wanted to be seen with an almost cinematic image? Or would she look like a dumpy frump with too much make-up on?

Dusty's opening night at Talk of the Town was a triumph with, among others, Shirley Bassey on her feet leading the encores. So triumphant a sell-out was it that Mike Gill got slightly carried away. One night that week he made the mistake of smuggling in a photographer from the *Sunday Times*. Because Dusty had banned all photographs while she was on stage, the man spent a large part of the evening under the table but did manage to get some shots. When Gill went backstage after the performance he was met with 'MIKE!!' 'I knew that voice,' he says. 'I knew she'd found out.' Dusty was furious and yelled at the unfortunate Gill for five gruelling minutes. Leaving the dressing-room in tears he was chased by Dusty's hairdresser, the little blond Australian John Adams. 'Dusty's really angry and she won't talk to you, but she's given me fifty pounds to get you drunk,' said Adams. It was typical of Dusty that after an outburst she would be mortified that she had upset someone, and fifty pounds in those days was no small potatoes. Gill and Adams fell out of the theatre and took the West End bars by storm. Gill kept his job.

By the 1980s and 1990s Dusty would be known as a diva. It was always a loaded term. Although it strictly means a famous woman singer, in common usage it tends to suggest a difficult, neurotic temperament as well as a glamorous, dramatic quality. In the music business it has also become used as a derogatory term, coming to mean that such women are deliberately erratic, often making people around them jump to their every whim. Then there was the music business itself which, as the years went by, grew in popular and financial importance. Stars began to inhabit a kind of glorified playpen. For solo artists this was particularly problematic.

Whilst groups united against the world and their acolytes and could pull each other up on their behaviour if they chose to, solo stars, like small spoiled children, tended to be allowed to have tantrums. The bigger the star, it seemed, the bigger the tantrum and once they had tantrums the behaviour became addictive. Just as no spoiled child is used to the word 'no', so no star would put up with it, unless the reason was so rock solid that even they couldn't argue.

It was and remains the most insecure and vulnerable artists, the less grounded people, who fare worst in such an environment. As they get more famous the pressures mount to outdo themselves and their last appearance. And as their egos get larger, their obsessions become more obsessive. How many times, for instance, was Elton John's Lear jet stalled on an American runway, while his staff frantically ran around trying to 'get him out of a sulk', because someone had forgotten to check his chart placing that morning? This is the behaviour, not of a multi-million selling album artist, more of the small, overweight Reg Dwight who felt his father had never cared about him and who, like Dusty, invented a new character to inhabit: this bejewelled, outrageous extrovert who was not small, fat and unloved.

Dusty may have been a diva but she never had a Lear jet, in fact she never made the millions that her audiences might have imagined. Her homes were not always her own. There were no Lalique lamps or original works of art on the walls. Instead it was her voice, her personality and her slightly eccentric behaviour that people liked. After her first night triumph at the Talk of the Town she took all her friends, including her chauffeur, to breakfast at the Cavendish Hotel. There, at two in the morning, they drank red wine out of a bone china teapot to celebrate the joy of encores. Only Dusty could have convinced the hotel that breaking their licensing laws was a good idea. At the table Gill was on tenterhooks. Dusty knew the first editions of the daily papers were on the streets and had sent out for them to see if her Shirley Temple photocall had indeed produced the front-page pictures Gill had promised. Luckily nobody had been murdered, the Bank of England hadn't collapsed and there were no new wars in the world, so Dusty's full length picture adorned every tabloid front page. She was delighted, Gill was ecstatic. In the future he would try to rekindle that moment with her, but it was often a steep uphill struggle.

Yet while trying to please Dusty could be difficult, what attracted people to her as much as her talent was the vulnerability she exuded. Certainly her nerves got so bad before she went on stage that she would break out in an angry red rash across her chest. Meanwhile, as she became more and more tense, she would hurl things out of her bag and across the room and start shouting. Sometimes people would say to Pat Barnett, 'Good God, why is she shouting at you like that?' But the secretary would be unruffled: 'Oh, she's not shouting *at* me, she's just shouting. It's to relieve the tension. I don't take any notice.'

And for Dusty there was an additional problem: despite her wit, her talent and her intellect, what everyone noticed about her was her almost pathological urge to muddy up good things. Was it just the terror of being bored and thus boring, or of being orderly and thus ordinary? It may have been both but it was overlaid with something else – a lack of actually being able to get pleasure from the world she inhabited and its demands. So it's not surprising that, as time went on, she kept people waiting or couldn't go on stage. It was another form of self-destruction. Dusty had grown up, but the only thing she thought anyone liked about her was her voice.

It was a voice that would give her sixteen hit singles and get her voted the best female singer, not just in Britain but in the world, by the people she respected most – the music fans who bought records and read the four British music weeklies. Of the four she was always most thrilled by her polling success in *Melody Maker*, given that its readership tended to be more sophisticated than the others and more likely to buy jazz records than pop. And Dusty was a particular favourite of the paper, not just for her singing but for her musical knowledge. In the mid-sixties she would appear regularly in their 'Blind Date' column. Here, singers would listen and comment on a selection of newly released singles by other artists without seeing the labels. Where most artists would correctly identify one or two singles, Dusty always knew who and what record it was immediately the vocal started, and she would go on to give a knowledgeable critique of the production and the record's pedigree. Dusty might have been short-sighted, but her ears certainly always compensated.

10

In 1969 Dusty was more successful than she could have ever imagined. Touring northern clubs in silver dresses, she was now being paid £1,000 a night to 'house full' signs. Dusty was being acclaimed as 'a singer's singer' and music critics were satisfied that all the things they had thought Dusty's voice capable of had been borne out on the *Memphis* album. But back in London her personal life was beginning to lurch. She and Norma were starting to have more than the odd snap at each other. Norma would try hard, however much she was goaded, not to fight 'Cat' as she called Dusty in reference to the Catherine in her name and her penchant for collecting strays from the streets of Kensington.

But in fact it was often Norma's attempts to laugh things off, or to adopt a fairly passive stance, that infuriated Dusty the most. When Dusty found out that Norma had been having a short-lived affair during her absence recording in America she was furious. It didn't seem to help that Dusty was not averse to the odd one-night stand herself. As she told the *Evening Standard* the following year: 'I'm promiscuous . . . I don't leap into bed with someone new every night but I can be very unfaithful. It's fun while it's happening, but it's not fun afterwards because I'm filled with self-recrimination.'

Although eventually Dusty said to Norma that she 'didn't blame' her, it was likely that it was her natural jealousy mixed with those self-recriminations that would start the ashtrays and ornaments being hurled through the air.

Since Dusty's arguments would invariably start after midnight, friends would be kept up until two in the morning having to act as telephone referees. With Norma on one line and Dusty, usually in tears, on an extension, they would get an almost literal blow-by-blow account of events in the Kensington house until, realising that the participants had worn themselves out and were now giggling, the weary arbitrator would point out that she had to get to work in five hours' time.

Billie Jean King recalls how she would often try and step in between Norma and Dusty: 'That was the kind of person I was, I thought I could help, solve things, make things okay. Rescue people. Now I know better.' Still the Kensington parties kept on rolling when Dusty was back in town.

That autumn Dusty went to Sigma Sound, the Philadelphia studios of Kenny Gamble and Leon Huff, to record her second album for Atlantic. Home of Bessie Smith and playground to Charlie Parker, Philadelphia had a long tradition of being a centre for music: not just for jazz but as the base for the teen idols on the Cameo Parkway record label. It put out the coast-to-coast pop TV programme *American Bandstand* and was the city in which Chubby Checker recorded his million-selling dance record 'The Twist'. Yet Sigma was the only building that had a four-track recording studio and it would be another two years before, along with producer Thom Bell, songwriters Gamble and Huff would produce a smooth sound that became the basis of what was identifiably 'Philly' soul:

lighter than Motown with lush string arrangements, the records on Philadelphia International from Harold Melvin, the Detroit Spinners and the Stylistics would electrify the early seventies dance floors.

But in 1969 that sound had not been refined, although Gamble and Huff had a good track record with Wilson Pickett and the sweet-voiced Jerry Butler. Because of her background Dusty was familiar with Gamble and Huff's work long before she met them; because of her vocal aptitude she could imbue a variety of very similar songwriting packages with a very broad selection of vocal interpretations. What could have been an album where one song ran boringly into another became a more evocative and shaded collection, what writer Rob Hoerburger later came to describe as sounding as though Dusty was 'a couple of drinks past midnight, shoes off, hair down, make-up smudged'.

Dusty was ahead of her time and *A Brand New Me*, released in Britain as *From Dusty . . . With Love* (the British end of Atlantic no doubt assuming that her fans would not want a new Dusty at this point), only did moderately well. Although the title single got into the American charts, it hardly made a dent in Britain. No matter how much she was improving as a singer, no matter how much praise she was receiving from other musicians and artists, the lack of chart success for her albums was what affected and depressed Dusty most. She needed to please her audience. She was highly unusual in the music world for always spending hours after a concert signing autographs for fans. Whereas most musicians would jump in a car and make a dash for it, Dusty would sit in her dressing-room with her audience crowding round her – 'the women staring admiringly' noted one critic, 'the men straightening their ties and looking sheepish' – talking to people, putting her signature on photographs and programmes and charming them all.

It was the approval of her audience that she needed, their love made manifest in the amount of records they bought was the only thing that would console her. If they didn't love her who the hell would? It was something that would continue to haunt her and it was her desperate need for an audience's constant reassurance that would bring about a disastrous period in her life.

At the end of 1969 the arguments in Kensington were getting much worse. One day early in the New Year Tom pushed a note under the door for Norma. 'Since you two are fighting all the time,' Norma remembers it saying, 'don't you think it would be better if you went back to America?' It seems now an extraordinary intervention for Dusty's brother to make, but although Norma was upset at the time, she decided that perhaps it would be better if she and Dusty did have a break after nearly four years. It would not, this time, be by Dusty going away to record or tour, but by Norma going back to Los Angeles. By the middle of 1970 she packed her bags and flew home to the west coast, leaving Dusty alone.

For the next two years Dusty planned her exodus to America. The lack of commercial success of the Memphis and Philadelphia albums had been devastating and 'You Don't Have To Say You Love Me' had turned into a musical albatross around her neck. Although Vicki and Simon Napier Bell had thought they were subverting the normal sentiments of the popular love song, the result was actually a self-sacrificial ballad where the singer took the role of a pathetically noble lover who had no needs of their own. Given its flourishing, chord-climbing melody line, the song was turning into a kind of communal sob-in for Dusty's audiences. And the audiences themselves had changed – from Dusty's sixties peer group to a much larger, more wide-ranging, cross-section of people.

On one level it meant that Dusty was constantly in demand and could expect large pay cheques from the big northern club circuit. On another, not really helped by her choice of Clive Westlake's take on another 'Italian-style' ballad 'All I See Is You', it pushed Dusty away from the black soul music of her youth where her heart lay into the cabaret circuit dominated by Shirley Bassey. A circuit where glitter and drama and huge orchestral sweeps were far more popular than a tight rhythm section and a gospel-influenced vocal cut-across. One night in the kitchen at Aubrey Walk, with her shoes kicked off and a bottle of Chablis close at hand, Dusty confided to Mike Gill that she'd love to stop it all and just go out on stage as lead singer of a small group, singing the eclectic mix of soul, R&B, *fado* and indigenous songs she loved so much 'But I can't now, I've trapped myself.'

But it wasn't just the problems of direction that worried Dusty – after all some of Motown's finest women singers were having to take the same path, leaving their home audiences at the Apollo in Harlem to succeed on the white nightclub round – it was also that England was so small and she was haunted by the spectre of endlessly playing the same clubs to the appreciative chicken-in-a-basket crowd, doing summer seasons at holiday resorts on the coast and – heaven help us – pantomime at Christmas.

At the beginning of 1969 Dusty was telling journalists that she could work every club on the circuit 'but they wouldn't want me back next year. I have to spread myself out, make myself desirable. I don't think I want to go on doing what I am doing for another five years – I'd be standing still.'

By the end of 1970 she was flying regularly to Los Angeles, partly to see Norma and partly to talk to agents and managers there. She and her manager Vic Billings had decided to call it a day. There was no antagonism, they simply agreed that if Dusty really wanted to go to America it was obvious that she needed Americans to take care of business for her. Vic didn't particularly want to leave England and didn't know America well enough to guide Dusty the way he had for the past six years. While the British music critics and her audiences reeled from the news that Dusty would leave England for good, Pat Barnett, who had been the efficient organiser of everything from dresses to Steinway pianos, had to tell Dusty that she couldn't go with her. She knew Tony, her husband, would not be able to get a work permit and anyway she was now pregnant. Later Pat always felt that if she could have gone with Dusty what happened to her in Los Angeles might have been averted. 'I don't know . . . maybe I couldn't have stopped it even if I'd been there all the time. All I know is I was hearing things over the years that I just couldn't believe – not my Dust – I don't know what happened to her over there.'

On 13 June 1970 Dusty had gone to Pat and Tony Rhodes's wedding with Norma and Madeline. It had been a jolly occasion on a scorching day in London but, in an odd way, it marked the conundrum Dusty found herself in. She was no longer a woman who could just go to a friend's wedding as any old member of the crowd. So that she didn't outshine Pat, Dusty had been to Oxford Street and bought a cotton dress from a chain store. Long and smothered in tiny flowers it made Dusty look incredibly pretty, like a shy teenager, but it was Pat in her tiny tight-fitting suit who looked stunning in the photographs and it was Pat who had to admit she and her friends were the tiniest bit disappointed that Dusty didn't look more glamorous and 'starry'. 'Poor girl,' Pat sighs, 'it was so sweet of her to dress down so she wouldn't outdo me – she just couldn't win.'

For the next two years Dusty continued to work sporadically in Britain, but more and more of her time was being spent on the west coast. She and Norma tried to live together again but it wasn't working and they both agreed that it probably wouldn't ever again. Dusty had now signed to new American managers and was mainly doing TV appearances: in America on coast-to-coast music shows, in Britain she appeared with Tom Jones on his own TV specials. She was being managed by Alan Bernard, Mace Newfeld and Sherwin Bash, the 'kings' of seventies management in America who had put the Carpenters and the Captain and Tenille into the public consciousness and the top ten. She also did two things that were to haunt her for the rest of her career.

In September 1970 she was interviewed by Ray Connolly for the London *Evening Standard*. Basically it was all part of the promotion she was doing for her version of the old Rascals hit 'How Can I Be Sure?' and, like all her interviews, it displayed Dusty's usual mixture of near-truths and jokey evasions. Here she is at thirty 'off down the corridor in a Minihaha embroidered suit wearing a great chunk of iron and brass work round her neck like something she pinched off a Russian orthodox altar'. It's an odd interview given that Connolly doesn't mention her music at all and although he says, 'I like her very much,' he describes her as having a 'pretty, lumpy little face' and 'she says she's thirty, she might be more but she certainly isn't less.' Dusty gave Connolly a quote which was, much later, to make the interview notorious: 'I couldn't stand to be thought to be a big butch lady,' she said, 'but I know that I'm as perfectly capable of being swayed by a girl as by a boy.' It was pure Dusty – always candid, never telling an outright lie, but never telling the complete truth either.

Years after, people would wonder if Dusty hadn't said as much as she did because she was off to America and off-guard. Mike Gill thinks it was 'just her bit of mischief'. Although it was to be quoted time and again when the question of Dusty's sexuality came up – and in the British press during the 1980s and 1990s that subject became quite a fixation – in fact the year the piece came out hardly anyone took any notice and the Standard didn't even use it in their headline. 'I don't remember being worried by it at all,' says Gill. 'It didn't backfire on her and there weren't a million phone calls. It was a very different environment in those days and the press was different.'

The second event that was to have repercussions was what transpired to be her last appearance at the Talk of the Town. In December 1972, after spending months in Los Angeles, Dusty was booked to do one of her seasons at the now familiar venue. These had always proved to be her most successful appearances – a triumph for artist and audience alike. Usually she received standing ovations every night and any star in London would fight to get a table to be able to say they 'saw Dusty at the Talk'.

By 11.30 on her opening night in 1972 Dusty was forty

minutes late going on stage and Mike Gill was getting worried. For years Dusty, despite her protestations that she always asked her voice to do things it wasn't naturally capable of, had never had an evening when she actually couldn't sing. Now she had a problem with her throat. It was so tense before she started a show that even her usual cure of port and lemon failed to work. By the time Gill arrived backstage a Harley Street specialist had been called out. He sprayed Dusty's larynx with cortisone, a rather unpleasant treatment like being force fed, and he warned her that he couldn't do it a lot or she would lose her singing voice once and for all.

After midnight Dusty finally at last greeted a restless but enthusiastic audience. From the opening number it was clear to everyone that she was really struggling. Elton John and Rod Stewart were amongst the star-sprinkled audience that Dusty always attracted to her London dates and now they rushed down to the front of the stage. 'Come on, Dust,' they encouraged her from the footlights. 'Come on, you can do it, girl.' Dusty seemed to relax and, despite the coughs and apologies, managed to finish her set with the audience on its feet demanding encores even though she, and they, knew she had certainly not been at her finest.

The next day the Talk of the Town management were stunned to get a phone call saying that Dusty had been advised by her doctor to have three days' complete rest. It was unheard of for an artist to pull dates so early in a sold-out season. The Talk took it badly and ostensibly sacked her. Dusty was due to have collected £6,000 for her four weeks' work, no small sum in the early 1970s; now she'd lose most of it and on top of that there was the enormous dent to her reputation and self-esteem as an artist. Her lawyers sued for damages and a spokesperson for the Talk of the Town was quoted as saying, 'We do not wish to comment except to say that we would still like to book Dusty some time next year.' Dusty's American management told the *Sun*, taking the moral high ground: 'As far as we're concerned she will never play the Talk of the Town again.' She never did.

It was the first time Dusty had looked less than perfect and it was a major disappointment to her fans. The press latched on to the story and made her suddenly seem very unreliable, and people working in the music business in Britain began to get a whiff that their golden girl might let them down.

Despite this Dusty, who had always dreamed of going to Hollywood just as all those hopeful young women in the 1950s had fantasised about being discovered while working at Schwab's soda fountain, her talks with her new American management had suddenly fired her up. Dusty, this good-looking blonde with a fantastic voice? Wow, she could be huge, she could get into films, nothing was impossible. It was exactly what Dusty wanted to hear, that she could expand into other areas, that they would seriously consider her in a movie. She had dreams of Fred Astaire and Ginger Rogers dancing their way across the screen and of all the great American film musicals she had seen as a child. At crisis point in her private and professional life she began, in her early thirties, to indulge in daydreams that might now seem unrealistic. But the optimism of the sixties was still in the air, and the feeling that anything was possible didn't go away overnight when the seventies dawned. So, to think podgy, short-sighted old Mary Isobel Catherine might be a movie star! Incredible. She forgot about the failure of the

Talk of the Town season – now she had a new fantasy in her sights.

Meanwhile there were British dates to meet that she'd agreed a year earlier, most of them seasons in the out-of-London clubs that were the provinces' answer to the Talk of the Town. These went relatively smoothly, although in January, when the *Daily Express* reporter turned up to Batley in Yorkshire where Dusty was doing five nights with Lulu, he noticed that she had three magnums of champagne and a bottle of vodka in the dressing-room. 'It's been one of my down days,' she told him. 'I seem to be having more of them lately.' The days of a quick nip of port and lemon for her throat before the show were clearly over.

When Mike Gill and Elton John arrived at Batley for the first night Gill also noticed she was drinking more. 'I'd never really thought of her as having a problem. I mean we all got blasted in those days so I don't suppose I really noticed how much she was drinking. But I do remember being surprised when she asked me to mix her a vodka and Coke before she went on stage. That was very unusual for her, she'd have them afterwards but never before a show. I just hid the glass from her, filled it with Coke and waved the vodka bottle over it just so it smelled right.'

For Dusty the northern nightclub circuit was one she usually enjoyed, mainly because her audiences were so appreciative. They had saved their money, come along for their one night out, had their chicken dinner and a glass or two of wine and were warmed by her smile, her voice and the on-stage chat. Sometimes, though, she would fume at the odd club owner who, as she became more and more popular, would cram the tables in to make more money. It infuriated her that her audience might be uncomfortable, that they might not be able to move easily if they wanted to and that the owner was ignoring their needs in favour of what Dusty saw as his own greed. She took an enormous delight when one night, at a club she considered had a particularly avaricious owner, the grand piano slowly slid off the stage during rehearsal and crashed into the orchestra pit. Since her contract stipulated that she would have the use of a grand he was forced to pay for a replacement.

It was at one of these seasons, at the Cranberry Fold Inn outside Blackburn, on the edge of the Lancashire moors, that the journalist Marcelle Bernstein spoke to Dusty. Bernstein's fine piece perfectly captured not just Dusty's intelligent musicianship and insecurities, but her magical quality as a performer. Bernstein noticed that Dusty couldn't bear to be photographed from the left-hand side because that was her 'bad profile'; that she tried to hide the two 'heavy lines' running from her nose to the corners of her mouth by putting thick make up over them even though, 'they're the very lines which, on stage, widen her face into laughter'.

In Lancashire she is 'so electric that waiters slop beer into the scampi and chips' watching her as they serve the audience; she seems to 'grow taller, slimmer before the footlights. It's not just the long false nails that extend her fingers but the almost-love, the rapport between watchers and watched, audience and star.' It was exactly this emotion, this frisson of 'almost-love' that Dusty would always acknowledge as the adrenaline that would course through her and make her feel alive. It was what kept Dusty singing.

By the end of 1972 the northern club circuit was behind her. Dusty had sold Aubrey Walk. She'd said goodbye to

11

'Good afternoon, ladies and gentlemen. We are currently passing over San Bernadino. It's a lovely seventy-eight degrees with a light breeze on the coast, warmer inland. We will be touching down at three thirty-five local time.'

LAX is one of the busiest airports in the world and it's always a relief to leave the frenetically charged atmosphere to step through the glass sliding doors on to the pavement and be wrapped in a sultry afternoon, a bright blue sky broken only by the languid waving leaves on the palm trees. Despite the thin smog line, it would lift anyone's spirits. For Dusty it would have been the most exciting moment in her life for a long time. This was it, the place she would finally become the biggest star in the world. She was famous in America, the Americans admired her voice and they had a tradition of knowing how to groom their women stars, letting them cross over musical genres, as Peggy Lee had from jazz to hits like 'Fever'. To Dusty it seemed that the Americans knew how to plot career moves with precision; the place was much more open to different kinds of music and anyway, it was so huge – the possibilities were, it seemed to Dusty, endless.

Dusty's car went past the bougainvillea-clad houses on the freeway into the centre of Los Angeles; past chain motels and Carl Jnr's burger bar and Brenda's Talk of the Town hair salon; past oil ricks and pastel houses. However many times she went to LA she kept expecting to see the sea and had to remind herself that to start with LA seems to be all freeways. Up La Tjera Boulevard, then La Cienega: the names alone were thrilling, conjouring up as they did Los Angeles's past and its proximity to the Mexican border (however debatable California's relationship is to that now impoverished country). Beverly Hills loomed with its much larger more ornate Spanish styled houses and modern glass office blocks. You could stop off at the Beverly Hills Hotel where a young Warren Beatty strolled through the lobby ('Call for Mr Beatty. Mr Beatty please!') and an old Groucho Marx took lunch amidst the palms and fountains; you could check in to the more low-key Sunset Marquis on West Hollywood's Alta Loma Road, where the staff were kind even if you weren't famous and huge yellow hibiscus, like smiling dinner plates, entertained humming birds by the turquoise swimming pool in the gardens.

But when Dusty's car finally drew up that day in 1972 it was at an apartment block in Westwood on Hilgard. The flats had been converted from dormitories that had belonged to the University of California and despite their new spaciousness they were painted a depressing uniform mustard yellow throughout. Still Dusty was excited. Her agent was a rotund and popular gay man, Howard Portugais, who made her laugh, and she had 'the circuit' coming up.

This circuit consisted of top class hotels across America where artists would entertain customers in a showcase environment. These were not customers hungry for the music. They had, for one thing, just eaten a large expensive meal. These were gruelling, but ultimately financially successful tours, and in terms of promoting artists to a wider public had paid off over the years. For artists used to the friendly but slightly tacky beer and chicken circuit back in Britain, the 'rooms' were rather seductive glossy venues when you'd never done them before.

Dusty would be booked into a huge suite at each hotel. There was twenty-four-hour room service, huge TVs in every room – everything Dusty loved about hotel life was here. The problem was that because of sound checks, rehearsals and appearances she could never leave the environs. One city led to the next, one hotel to another. By the time she came off stage she was exhausted, with only enough energy to order a cheeseburger and fries in her room. If you're a solo performer it can be a very lonely life.

Inevitably, too, she would spend the minutes before going on stage in the hotel kitchen surrounded by waiters shouting out food orders and next to the garbage pails. The kitchens were always next to the stage and here she would strain to hear the opening bars of her music. The way she would get revved up enough to go on was to stand as close to the stage and the band as she could and let the music wash over her, move her body in time to the sound. Although that was easy enough in a concert hall, in a hotel kitchen, with the noise and the crashing of pans, it was nearly impossible.

Still, she'd managed it at the West Side Room at the Century Plaza, where she'd opened in those early days of 1972 and it was here that she met Faye Harris, the small, smart, film journalist she would live with for the next six turbulent years. Faye had gone to Dusty's Plaza opening party. It was one of Hollywood's most exciting nights; Dusty's reputation in America was huge and her fans included film stars and music business moguls. Two hours after the party began Dusty turned up. By then Faye had left. 'She had kept the press waiting and a whole bunch of famous people. We didn't know that this wasn't unusual for her. In America everyone in the business assumed that part of your responsibility on your opening night is that you turn up and greet your guests.' It took some time for Faye to realise that whatever else, reliability was not exactly Dusty's forte.

Undeterred, Faye went back the next night to see the show and meet the singer. 'Tom was there and Dusty was very emotional. She was talking about Ireland and the IRA and crying. I wasn't impressed with her because she was famous; I'd been raised with famous people all my life. I was impressed because she was so articulate and passionate about the subject and when she started to cry . . . I thought she was the most extraordinary person I'd ever met and I fell in love with her right there.'

Over the next few months, while she was out on the road, Dusty and Faye would talk over the phone. Already Dusty was starting to worry about the direction her managers had mapped out for her and thought they had simply slotted her into a previously successful pattern without paying attention to who she really was and what she could do. Dusty, used to the empathetic management of Vic, became more prone to nerves than ever. It was like getting on an assembly line, popping out at the other end 'Americanised' and despite the *Memphis* album it was beginning to look like *Rolling Stone* magazine's worse fears that Dusty would end up as a lounge singer were being realised.

By the summer Dusty had left the mustard apartment and moved to a two-storey house on Kings Road, West Hollywood, an area known as 'boys town' because of its large male gay population. Even though she loved it there with its modernity and beige carpet, she still never unpacked. Faye was living in an apartment three blocks away and Dusty was now spending most of her time there. Finally they decided to rent together and moved into the hills of Studio City. They'd only been there for a few months, with a mattress on the bedroom floor, when one night Faye said to her '"Wouldn't it be nice if we had a pool." I really like swimming and it was just one of those things you kind of say without thinking about it.' The next day Dusty went and bought a modern glass and wood house in Laurel Canyon – with a pool.

The house on Dona Teresa Drive had Dusty's favourite kind of room: a living-room with a two-storey vaulted ceiling. It also had marble floors, a huge 'recreation' room overlooking the living room with an entertainment centre running along one vast expanse of wall. Although Faye's bedroom was full of furniture from her home, Dusty's had just one thing: a massive bed with white drapes falling from the ceiling. It was her Hollywood film-star bed and she would lie in it looking out through the plate-glass windows to her large swimming pool and to the lights of Hollywood itself. There was very little else in the house: a sofa and coffee table in the lounge; a dinette set for the times that Dusty would cook her and Faye's favourite dinner – lamb chops and broccoli.

One day Dusty joked that the recreation room was really as big as a bowling alley. Taken with the thought, the next day she had a bowling lane installed. It was the kind of impulsive gesture that fascinated the people around her. For Faye, who had been raised in a rather reserved family and considered herself 'square', it just added to the joy.

Before they had moved to Laurel Canyon Dusty had gone back to England for a flying visit. She phoned Faye: since it was coming up for Christmas why didn't she come over and spend the season with the O'Briens?

Christmas Eve would, even when she was famous, be the one time Dusty would return to the Church that had, in so many respects, let her down. She had celebrated the pre-Christmas midnight mass in many cities across the world over the years; this year she took Faye to Brompton Oratory in Knightsbridge. Christmas Day was spent at Tom's house in Chelsea. Massive amounts of drink were consumed by everyone, including the O'Brien family. Peppi impersonated Dusty, dressed in a wig and one of her stage gowns, and mimed to 'All I See Is You' much to the delight of his subject. By six the next morning, of everyone, it was Dusty's mother Kay who was still going strong. Dusty meanwhile was suddenly taken with the idea of flying Faye to Rome for the New Year.

In the Excelsior Hotel close to Rome's Via Veneto, on New Year's Eve, Dusty, having drunk a lot on the plane, fell into a deep sleep. In an Italian city famed for its food Faye, who had never been to Europe, was left to order cannelloni on room service and wonder if being in Rome with a snoring pop star was really such a good idea. Just before midnight Dusty sobered up and decided they would go to Doney's on the Via Veneto. Doney's in the 1970s was one of the most famous restaurants for well-off Italians to meet on New Year's Eve, and it was filled with men in dinner jackets and women in long gowns amongst the old cut glass mirrors and lights. Outside, at tables on the pavement, in the surprisingly mild night air, you could sit and have your coffee and drinks and watch the film stars and extras from the Rome studios strolling to and fro. On a clear, crisp morning on New Year's Day 1973, Dusty and Faye went to the Vatican City and watched dawn break over St Peter's Basilica. 'It was so typical. First it looked like a completely ruined New Year's Eve and then we have this wonderful time. That kind of joie de vivre that she sometimes had is hard to find. That style and generosity. Of course that sudden impulse expense – it was also one of the reasons she always had terrible financial problems.'

Back in Los Angeles and with the move to Laurel Canyon complete and by now with five cats installed – most rescued from the streets of Los Angeles – she and Faye decided to have a party to celebrate their new home. They would invite people to bring spray cans of paint and write messages of good luck on the large white empty walls. Later they would paint over them. Singers Anne Murray and Cass Elliot from the Mamas and Papas, and Hollywood film friends such as the dancer and actress Ann-Margret and the comedienne Lily Tomlin, duly arrived and sprayed. The messages stayed until the couple moved out a few years later, no redecorating having been managed. Meanwhile life had an ordinary domestic quality about it. Dusty and Faye didn't go out much, cooked together quite a bit, watched movies and housed passing tennis players, including Billie Jean and Rosie, who would crash on mattresses in the recreation room.

She and Faye would travel to all the major American cities to support the women players, particularly Billie Jean who had revolutionised women's tennis and fought for equal purses with the male players. She and Gladys Heldman had finally founded the women's tennis circuit in 1970 and worked ceaselessly to promote it and make it financially successful. Apart from knowing that King was not openly out, Dusty and Faye also knew that she was for ever being hounded by the press who seemed to want to bring this woman's champion down. 'It was a very important time for the women's movement in America and we needed to be right there for Billie,' says Faye. 'Dusty would sweat with anxiety and hardly be able to speak when she was watching and she'd scream if something went the right way. At the end of every match she was exhausted. "I don't know why I do this to myself," she'd say.' But of course she did. There was a gay woman on the centre court. In a way Dusty could see that Billie, both on and off the court, was involved in a battle that could easily have been her own.

By the mid-seventies the hotel 'circuit' was beginning to dry up. Music was changing and the west coast was the first place to experience the rise of rock and then its inexorable move out of concert halls and into baseball and sports stadiums. Now young American audiences, bored with the domination of British groups in their charts, wanted young American bands to idolise: bands like the Eagles, the Doobie Brothers and heavy drug users Aerosmith, who played a potent hard-edged rock, began to enjoy fantastic success and use larger and larger amplifiers until the sound became excruciating.

In the middle of this Dusty was stuck. She was not alone. Her great idol, Aretha Franklin, having made what transpired to be a disastrous move away from Atlantic Records, was also having a lean time and would not have another hit record until the mid-1980s when she joined up with Annie Lennox for 'Sisters Are Doing It For Themselves'. Meanwhile, although Dusty had bought herself a Jensen Intercepta, with less and less live work she was spending more and more time in the house. Faye's full-time job meant she was out all day and Dusty would mooch about indoors, bored and frustrated.

She was likely to spend too much time sitting about talking to the cats – Grover had been named after the character in *Sesame Street* and, when Fred Perry would later look after the cats for Dusty, Rosie Casals would recall that this one in particular 'hated him, would claw him to death'; Rupert Bear was named after the children's storybook character. When he finally disappeared Dusty ran all over the canyon in the middle of the night desperately calling his name out loud for hours. Sister Mary Catherine was the one female in the batch and Fortnum and Mason were called after one of Dusty's favourite expensive food shops in Piccadilly, which, she liked to point out in America, also served the Queen. If the felines didn't need her, she'd watch a bit of tennis or a ball game on TV and listlessly thumb through film magazines.

She couldn't swim (the pool was her concession to both Faye and Hollywood – how, after all, could you be a star if you didn't have a pool?) and with the time difference between LA and England there weren't a lot of people she could call. So for much of the day she would either sleep off a hangover or mooch about. For a woman who distrusted most people, LA, with its overblown sense of glamour and its veneer of adoration, presented a particular problem for Dusty. When you were on the 'up' not enough people could be your friends. Once there was a whiff of failure you were dropped in favour of someone else.

Hollywood, where the streets are hosed down daily, was also the place where agents told their stars, 'There are only two film directors you should work for: the one who wants to get your dress off and fuck you and the one who wants to get your dress off and wear it.' It had been that way since the big studio bosses of the 1930s, and the music industry, which in many ways now modelled itself on the studio system, was to prove only slightly more forgiving.

Sometimes an old friend would turn up in town such as Vicki or Lee Everett, but in the main Dusty was bored. Occasionally she would get dressed in her inevitable pink tracksuit and visit one of the only two women in the city she liked and admired – Ann-Margret or the earthy blonde film star wife of Burt Bacharach, Angie Dickinson. Once or twice, in the middle of the day, Faye would persuade her to wear a smart jacket and scarf and go to one of the restaurants that were the 'watering holes' of Hollywood's well-off lesbians, famously the Green Café on San Vincenti and Melrose. But Dusty was not really a lady who lunched. 'It was an attempt to fit in but . . . I'm not that kind of person,' she'd say later.

She began to get angry with Faye: 'You have such a purposeful walk,' she'd say balefully, or be infuriated at the way Faye tied her dressing-gown in the same perfect knot every morning. Not a woman to be intimidated, Faye rode it out and refused to alter either her walk or the knot.

Dusty might take a few mandrax as the day wore on to make the world look less sharp at the edges, go out and buy a bottle of vodka and drink the lot. When Madeline Bell opened a season with Blue Mink at the Troubador, the Los Angeles club famous for launching more great musicians than any other, there were two people she was surprised to see. One was Elton John who was in town buying up the Tower Records store and who decided to introduce Blue Mink on stage on their opening night; the other was Dusty.

Madeline remembers backstage being chaos after the group had finished their set. 'Then I heard this voice behind me. "Hey, you not going to speak to me then?" There was this woman in a big pull-on hat. I didn't know who it was.' It was only when Madeline pulled up the brim that she recognised Dusty: 'But it took a minute. She didn't look good and she was very pale, like a sort of pale country girl. And she had none of her usual heavy make-up on.'

For Dusty not to wear make-up was extraordinary, but when she talked about the drink and the drugs later in her life she would say that what she loved was the occasional feeling that she could go out without caring what she looked like. They were her Dutch courage – even if they often made her fall over.

Once, when a friend from England came to supper Dusty decided to order in giant sized boxes of Kentucky fried chicken as a cultural treat (in those days the good smiling colonel had barely crossed the Atlantic). After supper Lee, who was staying at the house, went to put the bones in the rubbish bin. 'No,' said Dusty. 'Don't put them in there – the cats will get them and choke.' Lee went to put them on top of a cupboard and was told the same thing; even the microwave didn't suit. Finally Lee opened the garden doors and hurled the lot into the swimming pool.

Over the next few days of her visit the pool took on a surreal life of its own: chairs, chicken bones, even some mannequins' legs were all submerged, the latter having been stolen by Dusty and Lee on one of their less salubrious outings. 'When I left the house you couldn't see the pool for things which were floating in it.' During the fortnight of Lee's visit a New York agent turned up to talk to Dusty about work. It was a hot day and Lee and Dusty were lounging

12

'Cooeee, shit! Cooeee, Elton John . . . shit!' In the grounds of the Beverly Hills Hotel Dusty was trying to negotiate the path to the bungalow Elton and his manager John Reid were sharing. It was a purple LA night and despite the lights that discreetly dotted the palm trees, partly because of her short-sightedness, partly because she was slightly the worse for wear, she kept tripping over the stones. By the time Elton finally opened the door and hauled her in, worried that the whole of Beverly Hills would wake up and realise that the singer he most admired was not her old self, she was giggling uncontrollably.

Over the next two hours, with Dusty veering from laughter to sobbing, Elton tried to convince her to get back to the recording studio. Dusty had already worked with him in better days when, for a laugh and for friendship's sake, she'd provided back-up on some of the tracks for his *Tumbleweed Connection* LP. Why didn't she do a number with him for his new album? 'I can't,' Dusty wailed. 'I can't do it, my voice has gone.' Used to her reticence and negativity and putting her attitude down to a mix of drink and dramas, Elton eventually convinced her to come in for a backing track on *Caribou*, 'The Bitch Is Back'. She'd be working with people she knew, nobody was expecting anything and at least it might give her some confidence back. He also talked to her about the possibility of going into the studio and producing an album for her. Seemingly buoyed up by meeting her old friend she promised to turn up for the session.

Luckily the session was late at night, when historically Dusty had always worked the best – but not this night. It became clear after the first half-hour that her voice had nearly gone and that she was squirming with embarrassment. Despite the gentle encouragement of Cissy Houston from the *Memphis* album days, the smiles and the nervous giggles, Dusty was struggling to hit the higher notes and kept stopping and starting. It was gruelling to watch and everyone in the studio felt for her. They knew it could happen to them any time. And in a way it was made worse by the fact that this was a voice they had respected for most of their lives – which, of course, was one of the reasons why Dusty was seizing up. 'Listen,' Dusty said finally, 'I really can't do this.'

Since she was a little girl her voice, a voice that could sing anything from jazz to blues to ballad without effort, had been her great gift. Now something she always thought she'd have, no matter what else happened, was beginning to suffer under the weight of drink and the drugs. Yet perversely it would often function perfectly. Later in the week she would go back and, miraculously, complete the track. She was furious with herself, when, some time later, Elton signed another British woman singer, her old back-up singer Kiki Dee, to his record label and duetted with her on 'Don't Go Breaking My Heart' which became a huge hit, even though it was not one of his most memorable songs.

Although she was not making albums Dusty was getting some recording work, mainly on back-up or helping writers cut demonstration tapes of their songs. Cass Elliot was also on this circuit and they both had a habit of over-compensating for the place they now found themselves in. One night, after a late session, Dusty and Lee Everett gave Cass a lift home via the English pub on Sunset Strip. By the time they arrived at her house the big ebullient singer had passed out on the back seat of the car. It was not going to be an easy job to remove her and after some weak heaving from Dusty and Lee, who were not entirely sober themselves, they stood on the pavement as dawn was breaking and contem-plated their predicament. After unsteadily walking up and down the street for a while Lee spotted a wheelbarrow and liberated it from the owner's garden. Dusty and she finally managed a push-heave haul that extricated the dead weight of Cass into the barrow. They managed to navigate Cass to the front door, whereupon they rang the bell and drove away, still laughing.

After the Elton saga Anne Murray had pulled Dusty in to do some work with her on 'Blue Finger Lou' and she was feeling a little better. Cheerful enough to take off to be with Vicki and Nona Hendryx in Paris where they went out to the 'girl bar' Katmandu, and Dusty and Faye danced the *merengue* in the middle of the floor. It caused such a stir that the crowd that night – chic young women who looked like fashion models – suddenly realised who was in their midst. Dusty was in demand: talked to, followed to the ladies' room. She left in good spirits and with her ego seriously lifted.

In the spring of 1975 Dusty and Faye were in New York for a few days to watch the women's tennis. One evening she and Faye went out to dinner with Billie Jean King, Rosie Casals and a young Czechoslovakian player Martina Navratilova. The twenty-year-old Martina, who at seventeen had become the Czech champion, was already a sensation on the US tennis circuit, playing the kind of tough women's tennis even the Americans were not used to watching or expecting from their own female players. Everyone in the women's team had become fond of Martina and she seemed enamoured not just of America but also of Billie Jean King. But she was due to return to Czechoslovakia in a few weeks' time.

In the Horn of Plenty restaurant in Greenwich Village Dusty and Faye spent most of the evening teasing Martina about running away from the communist government and the repression back home. What they didn't know – only Billie and Martina did – was that she had already decided to defect. The next day she called a press conference and announced her intention not to return to Czechoslovakia.

By the summer of 1975 things at Dona Teresa were going downhill. Dusty was so desperate at her lack of success and the constant emptiness of her days that she began to cut herself with alarming regularity. The first time anyone realised that Dusty would take such drastic steps to deal with her overwhelming feelings was at the time of her ill-fated Talk of the Town season. When Madeline had gone to see her at the flat that had been rented for her London stay, Dusty had taken her away from the cluster of record company people into a side room. Here she showed her old friend her lacerated arms and legs. Both women broke down in tears. 'It was those Dusty demons,' Madeline says. 'She could never really explain them to you but you knew they were there. All she knew was that she could never wear short sleeves any more and it made her really sad.' Madeline had tried to convince Dusty not to go back to LA but, 'She'd hit that point in her career here that can often happen, when you just feel you're treading in mud, and she couldn't see any way round without going back to America.'

Three years later Faye was endlessly trying to talk to Dusty about getting sober and coming off her pills, they were both exhausted and decided to have a few months' break from each other. Faye, who had always kept a small bag of overnight clothes in the bathroom cupboard so she could run out of the house when things became too much for her, rented an apartment close by. The royalty cheques Pat faithfully sent from London every six months were getting smaller; things were financially tight. Dusty decided to sell the house at Dona Teresa and rent something smaller in Beverly Hills – and she and Faye decided to move back in together.

The rental in Sierra Alta Way was close to Lily Tomlin and Jane Wagner and next door to Dusty's great musical hero Phil Spector. Unfortunately this was the notorious period when Spector was living with his singer wife Ronnie. At three in the morning the neighbours – including Dusty – would be woken up by the sound of random gunfire. It was Phil in his garden. 'All us women were terrified,' says Faye. 'Lily and Jane were practically crawling around the floor all night.'

The record companies, realising that Dusty was in no shape to get into the studio, had spent the past few years releasing compilation albums of her back catalogue. They sold well and it brought in a bit of extra money when the royalty cheques arrived. But Dusty felt that the re-release of her old material, often cut from the wrong mixes or with the wrong vocal track, kept her firmly in the past. And if that was the past – where was her future? When she had no company she'd sometimes hang around in her nightdress, comfort eating, gaining weight, listening to her own records and crying. Often she'd clean the kitchen floor even though there wasn't a speck of dirt on it, just to make it shine – as though it could make her shine too. Now a size or two larger, she refused to go into shops in case she was recognised. Instead she ordered clothes from high-quality mail-order catalogues: soon her closets were even more full of fabulous dresses she couldn't get into, or expensive suits she never wore. Those days were the worst – for everyone, including Dusty.

By the time Faye got back in the evening if Dusty had had a reasonable day, ironing shirts and folding them as she'd learned at the Bentalls store in Ealing as a sales assistant when she first left school, Faye would be met by what she called 'the good Dusty', the woman who had first moved her, the shy, funny and talented woman who could brilliantly mimic any voice from Ethel Merman to the characters in *Sesame Street*. But the good Dusty did not want to be a housewife all day or be left alone.

For most people it would have been a difficult situation. For Dusty, who was used to fame and applause and whose whole life had been geared towards success, it was excruciating. Dusty began to take other pills on top of the mandrax and booze while she watched baseball on TV. It wasn't that she was interested in the game as such, says Faye, just that it was slow and hypnotic. Often the general cocktail of drugs made things worse. 'It was terrible. It wasn't as though the drink and the drugs made her happy. It was like a bad trip for her.'

And if nobody was around? This was the time the

paramedics would have to be called out because Dusty would cut her arms.

Coming home from work Faye says she never knew what to expect. 'I couldn't believe she couldn't fix all this and I couldn't believe I couldn't fix it either. This kind sweet girl, brighter than anyone I've ever met and she just couldn't put it all together.' When she was calmer and sober there would be good evenings in when Faye would cook and they'd watch the British series *Upstairs, Downstairs* on public service TV. One day they invited friends to a very proper tea party with cucumber sandwiches and a harp player, in the manner of an English upper-class afternoon that may have no longer existed but certainly charmed the Americans.

Although when Dusty got out of control she became desperate, she only ever injured herself. She never attacked another person, although many of her friends knew they could easily be hurt if they got in the way. 'I would just run,' says Faye. 'In those years I think I stayed a night in every hotel in Los Angeles.' And these days throwing, once a joke, was serious. No longer simply a question of enjoying the sound of breaking glass, when Dusty was in another place, full of chemicals and alcohol, rooms were destroyed and possessions ruined. Billie Jean King remembers being woken in the night – it was an emergency. Dusty was out smashing car windows and she and her husband Larry did what they could to sort it out. When Rosie Casals had Dusty to stay at her house in San Francisco for three days, just before one of her periods of hospitalisation, she trashed the place and Rosie had to move out. When she stayed at Jeff Cason's in New York before she went into Bellevue she smashed his crockery and his window. It was as though all she wanted was to be restrained in a place away from it all, and if this was the way to get it, so be it.

'When I saw her in all those hospitals,' says Vicki, 'even though she was contented there I felt so sorry for her. You just wanted to put your arms round her and take her home – but you knew you wouldn't have any glass left in your windows. I'd pay for things, try and help any way I could as her friend, but I suppose I don't think I would have been keen to give her the keys to my apartment.'

13

In a world that values you for what you do, and in a music business that values success above all else, a career vacuum throws you back on your old self – the complex multi-dimensional person you are. For Dusty this meant being thrown back to the child she had spent her life trying to forget – and she was totally unprepared to deal with it.

'Her life was no more difficult than that of millions of others. Presumably as a result of her sensitivity she suffered more intensely than most people from the frustrations of childhood, but she experienced joy more intensely also. Yet the reason for her despair was not her suffering but the impossibility of communicating her suffering to another person.'

So wrote the eminent psychoanalyst Alice Miller about Sylvia Plath. For Plath the main person to whom she could not communicate her suffering was her mother and when that suffering became too great, when the hiding of who she really was under the bright smiling clever girl became too much, the poet killed herself.

If Dusty's suffering went a long way back to her childhood and was also uncommunicable, nobody who knew her ever believed that Dusty would take her own life. In fact once, when a friend, exasperated with the repetitive cutting, the night-time hospital emergencies and the frantic phone calls, asked her why she just didn't go ahead and kill herself she replied, 'Don't you think I'd know how to if I wanted to?' Yet Dusty's addiction to cutting her arms, which so horrified and upset her friends and lovers in the seventies and eighties, and which people not so close to her saw as merely a violent form of attention-seeking, was really a continuation of the hand burning she had undertaken as a child in Ealing. By the end of the century self-mutilation and particularly 'cutting' would be recognised as being far more prevalent in Western society than anyone had imagined (over two million people in America alone) and in the 1990s the ill-fated Diana, Princess of Wales would talk in her television interview about cutting herself because 'you have so much pain inside yourself'. But in the 1970s, when Dusty was doing it over and over again, nobody was talking.

For Dusty, cutting was a way of dealing with exactly this chaotic psychic pain. She may never have known why she sliced her arms with such dreadful regularity when she was in Los Angeles. She once told her friend Helene Sellery it was a way of getting people's attention: 'When they see blood – it's the only time they listen to you.' But therapists are only too familiar with this 'acting out'. Creating a visible outer pain that somehow she could control, make happen herself, when everything else in her life seemed to be so out of her control, was the route Dusty took more and more as she became less and less successful. And for many 'cutters' the very act of drawing and seeing their own blood and the pain it creates makes them feel alive. For Dusty who may well have grown up feeling rejected and unwanted, not good enough and finally self-hating; who carried a great well of depression around with her from early in her life and who did not seem to know what good 'mothering' was, there was a terrible emptiness inside. No wonder she always had a terror, right from the start of her adolescence, of being bored – with no external stimuli she was forced to look inside herself. 'I think she wanted to feel something, anything,' says Faye. And cutting herself was a way of getting that feeling very directly.

Cutting seems to have another benefit to the 'cutter': it often deals with a very high level of anxiety and panic, the kind of manic quality that Dusty often exhibited by her throwing and breaking.

By the time things started to go wrong for her professionally in Los Angeles and Dusty started to cut her arms and legs regularly, very little was known publicly about why people took to cutting – often over a period that would last for twenty years. Cutters were simply seen as mentally disturbed. As early as the 1940s psychiatrists, psychotherapists and the medical profession had been publishing papers on self-mutilation and why people would want to harm themselves like this. In the 1960s the theory was that such people were possibly hysterics, psychotics or psychopaths; certainly they were always diagnosed as schizophrenic. By the late 1980s things had advanced. Neurologists had begun to think that cutting had more to do with a specific chemical imbalance in the brain. It was a theory that some friends of Dusty's clung to – that if only the hospitals could get her serotonin level straight she would stop cutting. At the same time psychologists began to find that, like Dusty, most cutters were particularly gifted people who might well have an overdevelopment of certain parts of their ego and an underdevelopment of others, so that the act of cutting was a way of not becoming overwhelmed; psychiatrists and psychotherapists continued to believe that cutting was a non-verbal way of dealing with feelings of childhood neglect, abandonment or abuse.

Yet all these debates were going on 'behind the scenes', within and between the professions themselves. It was not until 1993 that the American public became aware of why people scarred themselves in this terrible way, when journalist Marilee Strong wrote a groundbreaking article in the *San Francisco Focus*. Strong, who became a respected researcher into cutters, found that they hurt themselves not to inflict pain but to relieve it: 'to soothe themselves and purge their inner demons through a kind of ritual mortification of the flesh. Rather than a suicidal gesture, cutting is a symbol of the fight to stay alive.'

Dusty was finally diagnosed as being manic depressive, but she would never ever look very closely at where the roots of that lay. Although once her parents died she talked more freely in interviews about her family, she would never lay open her childhood to really serious analysis. However bad her life in LA became and however worried her friends were about her, Dusty refused to get any steady professional help. She saw countless psychiatrists and therapists as the result of being hospitalised – but she never saw them more than once. 'Ha, I beat them again,' she'd say with an edge of something like triumph in her voice when she returned from the psychiatric ward. The only one she ever seemed to have any time for was a child psychiatrist whom she said 'seemed to know what he was talking about'. But such was her resistance to looking at that child, even when things were at their worst, that she never went back to see him.

And if she had, what would she have looked at? A family life where her parents were likely to be so wrapped up in their own problems and emotions that she thought they had no time for her but just that little bit necessary for her clever brother; a home full of noisy crashing and erratic behaviour; a family acting out their individual traumas in a sort of sign language – physically removing themselves, throwing dishes, maybe even having a little too much to drink. With so much going on under the surface, and sometimes above it, Dusty once chillingly remarked in an interview, trying to make a joke of it, that she reckoned if, when she'd been young, she'd slashed her wrists, 'It would have been my luck to have died quietly in the corner unnoticed.' It was a bleak analogy.

'I think she felt emotionally abused that's for sure,' says Billie Jean King. 'All she had when she was growing up was all that access to music.'

And it was a family that seemed to have a problem being verbally or physically affectionate. Instead things were hidden behind a joke, batted away. No wonder films meant so much to young Mary Isobel Catherine. Hollywood musicals had always been constructed as a form of escape from the harsh realities of the America of the Depression, and Dusty would have found it enchanting and emotionally satisfying that all that dancing and singing could overcome any problems the characters suffered along the way; that the films would leave her feeling positive and that success and fame as an entertainer was, surely, a glorious thing that made you happy. More, going to the cinema with Kay must have been the only time she felt really close to her mother. There in the dark, sharing their sweets, Dusty could feel the warmth of her mother's body next to her, the warmth she so longed for. And for three hours, through the cartoons and second feature and main film, she would have had Kay to herself. Her mother, usually so busy fighting with her father or praising Tom, was finally hers and she had her attention in that way for a whole wonderful afternoon – until they got back home.

Growing up, Dusty, who envied Tom, would follow his lead. And Tom was not needy the way she was and had probably learned early from his father that closing off physically was as good a way as any to survive. As a result, even when they were older, there would be no presents, no cards at Christmas between Dusty and Tom. Instead they would write each other a cheque made out for five million pounds which they would exchange and then tear up in front of each other. It was their 'little joke'. From this background, surprisingly, emerged Dusty, a hugely affectionate and often generous woman. But she would still freeze physically when people hugged her. It was as though, desperate for affection, she seemed never to have learned how to receive it and take it in. Even when Kay was dying of cancer and Dusty went to see her in hospital, her mother did not hug or kiss her. Instead, Dusty recalled, that through her morphine-induced haze, Kay reached up and 'with this claw' pinched her daughter's nose. It was the only time Dusty remembered her mother being physically demonstrative to her, yet the death of her mother left her bereft, feeling that she shouldn't have got on a plane back to America. When OB died in 1979, some years after his wife, Dusty may not have been so overwhelmed but she felt extraordinarily guilty again. Her life was by then in such a mess she had not seen him for some time and, although she had the same kind of ambivalent relationship with her father as she did with her brother, the fact that OB had died alone, with a batch of full milk bottles on the doorstep, was an image that haunted her.

It's doubtful that the O'Briens had any idea of the unconscious effect of their behaviour on their daughter, and despite their 'neglect', or perhaps because of it, Dusty desperately wanted them to be proud of her and adore her. She was thrilled that they seemed so proud of her career. 'Poor things,' she would say to journalists much later on when talking about her upbringing, 'they did the best they could.' She not only had them at her parties but at all her opening nights, took them to New York with Norma to spend Christmas with Vicki and Nona, to Pat's for other Christmases where 'Dusty could be herself'. She could kick off her shoes, sit on the floor and enjoy Pat's world – her husband, son and her parents Carol and George whom Dusty had known since Pat started to work for her and whom she tellingly called her 'second mum and dad'.

There's no doubt that if Dusty had been 'special' as a child, she had certainly never felt loved, or lovable, until she stood on stage. Shimmering under a spotlight, she could look out into the darkened arena and Kay's voice could not reach her, nor her father's sudden bursts of temper, nor Tom telling her she didn't know what emotion was or that he had found a 'new Dusty' with Judith Durham, the lead singer of his Australian group the Seekers who could do everything his sister could (a fact that must have mortified the jolly Durham as much as it did Dusty).

Instead, with her rhythm section pounding behind her and like an athlete leaving the blocks, on a good night she was off, her voice easing through a song, filling it with such a particular universal emotion that it was often hard to remember she hadn't written it herself. These were the only times when she knew she was special and it was her need to feel it over and over again that would often trigger her wilder behaviour when nobody was asking her to get in front of her audience.

And when she didn't have that as her release and her comfort? There was just guilt and self-hatred. Whatever Kay and OB secretly thought about the number of 'girlfriends' Dusty seemed to share her homes with, or the bevy of gay men in her life, they never enquired and were not told. 'Sexuality was never discussed in our house. It didn't exist,' Dusty once said. 'Don't ask, don't tell', which in 1999 became the key point in the argument about gays in the US military, was an adage that Dusty, born when she was, grew up with. In Britain, even in the libertarian sixties, nobody in the music world talked about their sexuality anyway. 'Everyone was going to bed with everyone else,' says Vicki, 'but nobody thought it was important – it was just another source of gossip. In those days people might have said who they went to bed with, but never what they did once they got there.'

Throughout her life and especially when she was at her lowest ebb in Los Angeles, Dusty would spend hours talking to Billie Jean about the way she felt. 'Billie always understood her better than me,' says Rosie Casals. 'They were both perfectionists and Billie would listen and advise and try to help. Me, I'm not a perfectionist and I couldn't understand why she was doing these things to herself, why she felt the way she did. If I could have sung the way she did . . . I'd have just been pumping those albums out! I said to her once, "As a tennis player when you're old you're done but as a musician you're still capable of having that voice, you don't have to worry about being in shape." But she did worry, she worried about everything and she had a dark, dark side and with all that slicing and dicing that she did? She should have been dead ten times over.'

When they talked in later years Billie Jean would gently point out the stress involved in Dusty hiding who she really was. 'And I understood. It hadn't been easy for me, a fireman's daughter, to tell my parents,' says Billie Jean. 'But in the end you have to take that risk. You have to say, "This is who I am," and hope they will love you as that person.'

'She was always hiding behind something,' says Rosie. 'She hid behind the make-up, hid behind the clothes, hid behind the music.'

Although Dusty respected Billie Jean and found her comforting, motherly attitude a relief, it must have seemed to her that not hiding was too great a risk. In 1981 Billie Jean was sued for palimony by her former secretary Marilyn Barnett after a four-year affair. It caused a scandal and the American and British press went to town. The tennis star and her manager husband at the time, Larry King, put a brave face on things in the face of such intense press coverage and Barnett lost the case, but the publicity lost Billie Jean nearly a million dollars in sponsorship. Once she and King broke up and she lived more openly as a lesbian she eventually recouped much of her respect and popularity with spectators.

If that ordeal had tried Billie Jean what would happen to her, someone less emotionally strong, if she came out? What would happen to her fans, to her stardom, to her own self-image? When, finally, in the mid-seventies, Dusty did tell her parents she was gay, there was no road to Damascus. 'They didn't really take her seriously,' says Lee Everett. 'They sort of ignored it, like, "Oh, that's just something our Mary would say." It was terrible for her really.' And it must have been: Dusty had 'saved up' this confession for a decade or more, only to have it dismissed as unimportant.

The O'Briens were a solid Catholic family, yet as late as 1986 the Vatican, in line with many other religions, was issuing statements that homosexuals were 'disordered in their nature and evil in their love'. But the rigidity of religion is an insidious thing and friends say that even if she stopped being a practising Catholic, and if she had her faith in God shaken, Dusty none the less continued all her life to believe in some kind of 'higher being'. But to believe in something powerful and good you also had to believe in the reverse. Just as for many people the existence of God only works if they believe in the existence of the devil, so Dusty would be overwhelmed by the notion of demons: real or imaginary. When the drugs and drinking were at their worst, Faye remembers, Dusty would curl up in a ball on the floor completely lost in a world of panic and paranoia saying that the demons were coming. 'They're coming, they're coming and they're telling me to do bad things . . .' For Dusty that meant that the cutting would start again.

And it was this pain that Dusty dragged along with her and made her exhaustingly protective of Kay and OB. She kept the drugs and one-nighters from them too, just as Pat Barnett always felt Dusty protected her from the worst excesses of her life. 'She once said to me, "You're so naïve, you don't really know about me do you?"' says Pat. 'I said to her, "I know what I need to know," and she was quite thoughtful for a moment. Then she laughed and told me I was probably quite right!'

If they did guess, OB and Kay tucked it away out of sight. Certainly they never made any attempt to 'rescue' their daughter during her years in LA and friends say that Tom, who had been rung up one too many times one night, closed down on Dusty too – for the next twenty years. It was a relationship that would only unsteadily reassert itself in the mid-1990s.

Most of all Dusty's huge fear wasn't just of the disapproval of God, even though the friend she made during her darkest years, Helene Sellery, like many other people, believed that 'thou shalt not' from the scriptures hung heavily on her conscience. It was her own self-image. Brought up in a homophobic world in which to be camp was forgivable but to be gay was a crime, and having worked so hard to turn herself from a dumpy adolescent to a soft blonde icon, Dusty was practically phobic about being seen as 'un-feminine'. She had grown up at a time in which the popular image of what a lesbian 'looked like' was the stereotype ersatz butch male: cropped-haired, wearing a man's suit, taking on so-called 'masculine' social attributes. (She may or may not have been surprised that even in 1999 this stereotype was exactly the image used by the hit US television show *Ally McBeal*.)

She internalised the attitude of the Church towards lesbianism as a sin and the prevailing external homophobia into disapproval of herself. It added to her depression, so that her energy level was often so low it would take all her strength to get on stage at all. Nobody could criticise Dusty as well as Dusty could, and it drove her. How many times over the years, for instance, was she told she was unique:

in reviews, by fans, the accolades showered down on her all her early recording life. Yet unique wasn't good enough. She had to be better: better than Aretha Franklin, than Marvin Gaye – the great black soul voices of a generation. In her own eyes she could never be just 'good enough' and it was this feeling that drove her and made her hard to work with. 'She wanted to be straight, she wanted to be a good Catholic and she wanted to be black,' says Norma Tanega. Instead, as she saw it, she was the opposite of them all.

And if she saw her childhood played out against the backdrop of endless criticism then she learned early that, for her, there was no such thing as 'good enough'. Dusty was so demanding of her recordings that even the most easy-going producers and musicians would be gnawing their fingers down. In the studio, isolated from the applause, although she could normally cut a vocal track in a first take, she would spend hours re-recording what she thought was a faulty phrase, the wrong breath, the incorrect note. For Burt Bacharach, himself a perfectionist, Dusty's insistence on going over and over what even he considered an irreproach-able track became almost wilful self-destruction: a search for unobtainable perfection that comes up time and again in the profile of people who regularly cut themselves.

Perhaps it's not surprising then, given her childhood and the way she viewed herself, that people who knew her well surmised that, finally, while she came across like an adult on the surface, most of the time she was a child. In the late sixties she would often turn up to interviews clutching a small teddy bear called Einstein. Male reviewers of her early solo appearances would find no fault in the music she made, the consummate power of her voice, but her 'between songs' breathy chat, in what they called a 'little girl' voice, would irritate them. Dusty responded that she put this voice on because she was so nervous once the music stopped and she had to make verbal contact with her audience standing there, spotlit, exposed. Yet she would also admit that she would react to criticism or a hurtful remark like a small child and that she had never really grown up.

Once she was famous, and later when she looked back on her life, Dusty always said that she had created 'a monster' with Dusty Springfield. Certainly she was trapped in her image, but it's more likely that the real 'monster', the one who had tantrums and sliced her arms, was poor little needy Mary Isobel Catherine: unloved, unlovable and abandoned by the only woman who could mother her – Dusty herself. Yet Dusty couldn't do it. Longing for that mothering, first from her own mother then through a succession of relationships with women, she had somehow never learned how.

'It was the interplay between the child and the woman that was so remarkable about her,' says Helene Sellery. 'And in many ways it was so charming, and in many ways it was damn near fatal.'

14

'Somewhere,' said Dusty once, 'I crossed the line between heavy drinking into problem drinking.' In fact it had happened very early in the LA period and only six months in to her relationship with Faye.

In the autumn of 1972 Dusty had been recording her *Cameo* album with producers Dennis Lambert and Brian Potter. Although she had been signed to do a second Atlantic album to follow *Memphis* she disliked the material they had chosen for her and only cut a few tracks before she managed to get out of her contract. Songwriters Lambert and Potter were also ABC/Dunhill's 'house producers' who had a string of 'white hits' in the early seventies, although they usually recorded black artists. The Four Tops, who had left Motown, were in the studio with Lambert and Potter during the day, and Dusty would come in at night along with a third producer, Steve Barri – a peculiar choice given that he was more associated with white west coast records.

Levi Stubbs, Renaldo Benson, Lawrence Payton and 'Duke' Fakir were in and out of the studio in three hours, well trained from their Detroit days and functioning as a mutually supportive, almost cliquey group. Dusty would have dinner with Faye just round the corner from the studio, then go in for the evening, nervous and feeling very alone.

There was no Pat, no Echoes, no Johnny Franz to give the musicians the nod and there was a management company trying to push her towards appearing in Las Vegas. One night, halfway through the sessions in December, Dusty had taken too many pills and drunk far too much. She fell on the floor and, says Faye, 'rolled up like a rug' before passing out. Faye, furious that Dusty would look like this in front of the recording engineer, had to have help to pick her up and take her to a hospital in Long Beach that had an alcoholic ward. 'It was awful there, but there was a part of her that believed it was where she belonged. She went to some terrible places over the years but it seemed that the lower she went the more comfortable she felt.'

And for Dusty there was a kind of comfort to be drawn in existing day to day alongside other people who clearly could not cope with the pressures of life. Here, on these wards, there was nobody better than her, nobody to point out what a failure she was, nobody to wag a finger in disapproval.

Certainly the strain of her recording sessions showed when *Cameo* came out. Most of the Lambert and Potter songs would have been ideal for a group like the Tops where Stubbs's desperate growling voice would have jumped out from the springboard the rest of the group provided him with, but for Dusty, whose voice sounds thin and uncomfortable, the material was difficult and did not have the wonderful rise and blossoming on the chorus that she was used to. None of this was helped by a production that tended to be over-fussy and included a very harsh-sounding female back-up. Although Lambert and Potter were hot at the time and although Dusty included a tantalising version of Van Morrison's 'Tupelo Honey', the album, like the Gamble and Huff one, didn't gel. It also boasted the worst cover in the history of popular music. It looked like a hastily drawn tiny portrait of Dusty inside what appeared to be a Christmas cracker brooch, but it's likely that Dusty didn't want to do a photoshoot for the cover given the condition she was in most of that time. *Cameo* was her third flop in a row.

Just after *Cameo* was released *Rolling Stone* magazine writer Ben Fong Torres interviewed Dusty for two hours. She was, he recalls, feeling 'down in the dumps, unhappy with the album and uncertain about her musical direction'. Like everyone he found her charming, 'but that day she was oddly dressed: wearing a floppy hat, Moroccan necklaces and what she called "apologetic platforms".' During the course of the interview it's pretty clear that Dusty is not exactly sober as a judge. She often meanders vaguely about what she should be doing, says she hates her *Memphis* album and that she sang flat through 'The Look Of Love'. The interview was never published by *Rolling Stone*, mainly because *Cameo* sank without trace, but right at the end Dusty pulls off her usual coup de théâtre: Fong Torres quotes back at her a remark that her favourite actor is Daffy Duck. 'Well,' says Dusty, 'I still like Daffy Duck. Can't think of anyone I like better. Actually that's who I'm having an affair with. Difficult, but rewarding!'

Dusty could have good days, even weeks, but the down days were getting closer together. After *Cameo* she was to do a second album for Dunhill, in 1973, this time with Brooks Arthur. She was not exactly in good form and the sessions at Arthur's house in Nyack New Jersey, over the Tappanzee Bridge, quickly descended into a depressing chaos. It was at one of these sessions that, as writer Lucy O'Brien reported, a young local singer, Bruce Springsteen, was hanging around waiting to go into the studios. Luckily, since he was so impressed with Dusty's voice, it must have been one of the very few moments when she could actually sing. Brooks Arthur had been the producer behind Janis Ian's first three successful albums and had experience dealing with women artists' often-fragile egos, but even he was not prepared for Dusty's apparent self-destruction.

'Everyone in New York wanted to be on those sessions – Janis Ian, Melissa Manchester – everyone,' says Faye, but in the two-storey clapboard house in Nyack Dusty's voice was in bad shape again, she was lonely, and, more importantly, back in London, her mother Kay was dying and Dusty had just come back from seeing her. Vicki and Nona Hendryx would often invite her into Manhattan for the evening in an attempt to cheer her up and that October she got excited by the idea of going to Labelle's show at the Metropolitan Opera House – the first time a black vocal group had ever appeared there. On the 6th Dusty was driven across the bridge for a television appearance before the Metropolitan concert. Channel 13, the public broadcast service, were about to start screening the *Monty Python* TV series and their manager for America, Nancy Lewis, had thought Dusty would be the ideal person to be interviewed by the station by way of introducing the Pythons' sense of humour to an American audience.

For Dusty, who had been doing so little publicly, the combination of events seemed a happy one. Nancy, the gentle mid-Westerner who had worked in London with the Who so knew exactly how erratic most pop stars could be, was pleased to see that when she went to pick her up from Nyack to take her to the television studio Dusty seemed reasonably okay. On the way into town they talked about how Dusty would do the TV then change into her Metropolitan clothes at Nancy's flat on Central Park, but by the time they got to Channel 13 Nancy noticed that Dusty had begun to repeat what she was saying and was going off at tangents mid-way through the conversation.

The interview with the station was going out 'live' and by the time Dusty was on air she was making absolutely no sense at all. Luckily the interviewer thought this was all part of some zany plot, concocted by Nancy and Dusty in *Monty Python* style, and so battled on through a series of questions to which Dusty gave incomprehensible answers. Back at Nancy's flat, Dusty, with her hairdresser John Adams in tow, started to get ready to go to the concert, but it got so late that Nancy had to leave without her – dashing across the street so that she wouldn't miss Labelle's historic occasion. It wasn't until gone midnight and halfway through the triumphant after-concert party that Dusty finally turned up, 'in great spirits' Nancy recalls. Her spirits got even greater as the night wore on, so much so that when John Adams took her back to Nancy's flat to collect her things she promptly passed out on the sofa.

That night Nancy got no sleep at all. Although she'd originally thought Dusty would simply sleep it off for an hour, as the night wore on she became increasingly concerned that there was no sound or movement from her front room. Nancy, knowing that things weren't that rosy for the singer and that she would often take more pills than she could remember, kept getting up like the worried mother of a new baby to check that she could still hear Dusty breathing.

For the next few weeks, and back in Nyack, Dusty sat drinking vodka and Coke and watching baseball on TV.

The one thing she wasn't doing, for long stretches at a time, was singing. Finally she was yet again rushed to hospital – Rockland State – after she sliced up her arms. The sessions for *Longing* produced only three releasable tracks.

Dusty was not to record another album for five years.

By the end of the year Dusty finally realised that she was unable to control her drinking and that the only way she might cope was to join Alcoholics Anonymous. There were plenty of AA meetings to go to in Los Angeles, God knows, sometimes a hundred a week. She started out attending a group at Cedar Sinai full of film stars and musicians until people began to go on national television talking about their experiences there. 'She had a childlike belief that if it was called Alcoholics Anonymous it was the anonymity that was so important,' says her friend Helene Sellery. Yet it wasn't just childlike, it was central to Dusty's thinking.

In the mid-sixties she and Vic had threatened to sue an artist who was selling a painting he'd done of Dusty naked from the waist up which she'd certainly never posed for. In the event it was sold for seventy-five pounds and Dusty probably found it hilarious that the man who bought it was a pig farmer. 'But,' said Vic to the press at the time, 'Dusty has a huge teenage and family following. She cannot afford to have people thinking she would pose semi-nude.' All through her life she used up so much of her energy trying to protect her image, terrified her private life would come out in public – any aspect of it at all. And if people promised not to tell? They should keep their promise. From then on Dusty, who went to AA under the name Mary O'Brien, would seek out smaller local groups where the risk was far less.

'There was a happy part of her that could get happy

drunk,' says Rosie Casals. 'But then the mood would just snap and she'd get ugly drunk and not remember what she did or what she said. Sometimes the next day she'd ask, "Was I bad last night?" and you'd have to tell her, "Yup, you were pretty abusive." She wasn't easy to be friends with. I think she loved people but had trouble showing it. But if you needed something she'd be there for you. And there were people for her, even when she was in a stupor she was wise enough to go back to the people she knew would take care of her.'

Become a member of AA and you can go to a meeting anywhere in the Western world at most times of the day and night. In church halls and rooms attached to hospitals people gather in the only really safe place they know – amongst other people who are equally addicted and finding life too tough to cope with unless they're 'using'. These aren't the poor old guys who shuffle along the street hurling abuse at the traffic. At any AA meeting there will be an enormous cross-section of people, depending where it's held: from women at home with the children all day to real-estate operators in their expensive designer suits; from company executives to painters; from young abused girls to elderly literary figures.

If Dusty was initially attracted by the anonymity she would also have liked the feeling that she was in a large supportive therapy group but with no pressure to speak if she didn't want to. Equally there would be no disapproval if she said she'd only been sober for a few days, a few hours possibly, between meetings – or that she hadn't. Despite no longer being a practising Catholic she might also have been attracted to the notion that there was some 'higher being', someone or something more responsible than she was. Over the years the organisation, run by its members, had lost much of its original religious zeal. Although a meeting of any group still finishes holding hands and saying the Serenity Prayer, 'God grant me the serenity to accept the things that I cannot change/Courage to change the things that I can/And the wisdom to know the difference', there is often a debate about what the word 'God' actually means to the people in the room. Most people are on and off the wagon or on or off something most of the time they're in AA. While, after many years, Dusty finally conquered her reliance on the bottle, all the time she lived in America she never managed to give up the variety of pills that she took – from diuretics to barbiturates.

Dusty met three women during her long period in and out of AA – Helene Sellery, Suzanne Lacefield and Peggy Albrecht – and one way or another, they each saved her life.

In 1976 during the coffee break at an AA meeting in Los Angeles Dusty noticed a tall blonde woman who looked like Lauren Bacall standing on her own. 'Hello,' said one of the shyest people on earth. 'My name's Mary. Here's my phone number. If you want these meetings to help then you have to talk to people, otherwise you'll be back drinking.' Dusty, with a few meetings under her belt, felt that Helene, a newcomer, needed support and it was part of the AA coda that it was a mutually supportive organisation. It was also likely that Dusty liked the look of the willowy woman. Helene remembers feeling offended that Dusty immediately took her for an alcoholic. 'I could have been an observer for God's sake but of course she knew, they all knew, alcoholics always recognise each other.' For the next few weeks Helene would get phone calls from Dusty anywhere between midnight and two in the morning. It was the old Dusty habit of not being able to sleep and those two hours were the ones that had always, and would always, haunt her all her life. One night Helene's room-mate Andy picked up the phone. 'There's something about that voice and that accent,' he said to her afterwards. 'I know I recognise that voice from somewhere.'

'I didn't know what he was talking about,' says Helene. 'I just knew that the Mary O'Brien I met was a very caring, discerning person. It was only because of her that I stayed in AA. I didn't like participation events and I didn't like people knowing about my private life. I was an adult woman. I was a problem solver, not giver. Dusty broke through that veneer. If she hadn't I would have been dead years ago.'

After the first thirty days without a drink an AA member receives their first 'chip' and is applauded by the rest of the group for their effort. When Helene's thirty days were up she took Andy along with her and they met Dusty. After a few minutes of talking, Andy, who worked as a musical director, said, 'You're the woman on the phone, aren't you? You're not Mary O'Brien, you're Dusty Springfield.' Helene was 'musically illiterate outside a touch of classical' and had no idea who the singer was. It must have pleased Dusty that this intelligent, elegant woman was her friend even though she'd never heard one of her records; equally she would have found common ground with Helene outside their shared drinking. Like Dusty, Helene had another identity. Her birth name was Kate Titus, but she had been adopted at the age of seven and her name changed.

Over the many years and many times that Dusty would be rushed to hospital it would always be Helene who would pick 'Mary O'Brien' up after her treatment on the psychiatric ward. Dusty would always book herself in as Mary and everyone around her knew they had to do the same if they rang for the paramedics. It usually worked in terms of keeping her anonymity. Only once, after the Nyack disaster, did an English nurse recognise her and tip off the newspapers. Sometimes reverting back to her original name worked rather too well. Once Helene went to collect Dusty from a hospital on the coast. When she got there the nurse said she was very sorry but Helene certainly could not take Mary O'Brien home. This had never happened before and Helene was amazed: why on earth couldn't she take her friend? Well, said the nurse, they still thought she was a very disturbed woman. Someone had overheard her talking in the phone box about picking up an award. 'I'm afraid she appears to be suffering under the delusion that she's a very famous singer.'

Each time Helene collected Dusty, from hospitals all over New York and Los Angeles, the only place Dusty ever wanted to go for a while, even when she was living with Faye, was to Helene's home in the countryside outside Los Angeles – Tarzana.

The house, often referred to as the chicken ranch, was actually something of a sanctuary for animals. Because of Helene's good heart it had also turned into something of a sanctuary for injured people. For Dusty it was the perfect place to escape to, miles out of town, with cats and goats and chickens roaming about. More importantly nobody could reach her there. It was here that Dusty and Helene would start a friendship that would last for a quarter of a century and it was here, some years later, that they would become more than friends.

Sometimes Dusty would get Helene to drive her to the

coast near LAX so she could watch the planes taking off and hear their deafening roar; sometimes they went to eat at Dusty's favourite places – truckers' diners on the motorway. Dusty, with her six-egg omelette in front of her, was always happier when she was somewhere she didn't feel she had to 'perform' and the noisy camaraderie of these diners full of men who constantly travelled the road and had no idea who she was, made her feel comfortable. Once, though, she did decide she'd like to try something more upmarket and she got Helene to take her to Prima's, one of Los Angeles's most exclusive restaurants, where they had to leave halfway through the meal. During a particularly interesting part of her conversation and with hands flying, Helene's prawn became disengaged from her fork and hurtled down the cleavage of a woman seated in the next booth, much to Dusty's hysteria: 'She was beside herself laughing and had slipped right down in her seat so that this dowager, or whatever she was, couldn't see her. The thing was that I didn't know what I'd done, the woman didn't know where the prawn came from, and only Dusty saw what had happened.'

In the summer the Californian countryside can turn as dry and hot as the desert but Dusty would still sometimes call from one of her stays in detox or psychiatric units and want to spend some time at Tarzana. Despite hating the sun and the heat and unable to swim, she would put on a huge hat and purposefully stride out to the pool to prove that's what she really wanted to do. There was, in fact, only one time she actually got in the water, an occasion missed by Helene who was feeding the goats, but witnessed by one of Helene's other 'rescued' guests, a woman doctor whom Dusty had taken a dislike to. Even so, when she blithely informed Helene that she had just swum seven lengths of the pool, the doctor came in handy . 'Ask her,' Dusty said. 'She was here, she knows.'

'But Dusty,' Helene protested. 'You don't swim, you never have.'

'I know,' said Dusty. 'It's amazing what Quaaludes will do'.

It was only the second time that Helene was aware that Dusty was on a variety of pills and in the intervening period she had forgotten the euphoric effects that Quaaludes had on her friend. The first time she had experienced it Helene had been sitting in the living-room of Dusty's house in the Canyon and heard a crash and a thump. Dusty had fallen down the stairs and hit her head.

'Let that be an example to you,' she said when she got up.

'Of what, falling downstairs?'

'No,' said Dusty sternly, 'Of Quaaludes – you're never to take them or this will happen.'

Helene said she'd thought the incident so funny that, although she told Dusty she'd write the name of the pills down, she didn't think she was really serious. 'She never took anything like that in front of me, so I had no idea when she was on them. She was very defensive but she was also very protective.'

Helene wasn't the only one not to realise how high Dusty would often be. When Barry Krost, Dusty's new manager, took her to concerts at Frank Lloyd Wright's Hollywood Bowl in the mid-1970s they had some great evenings. They went to see Bette Midler, they went out to dinner. 'It would be months later that she'd turn round and say, '"Remember that night? Well I was out of my mind." And I'm not naïve but I really didn't guess. She said to me once, "The trouble with addiction is that people become such breathtaking liars."' Dusty's 'lying' was of a familiar variety. Although Faye, Helene and Vicki knew what she was on most of the time, even with them she would hedge around the amounts. So it would be a vague 'a few' mandrax when they asked, as opposed to the real amount she'd thrown down throughout the day; only 'a couple' of her diuretic tablets. Not even her closest friends could get a complete list of what she actually took and if they had they would have doubtless been amazed that she was still alive or, at least, in any way coherent.

Krost was the man who finally managed to get her a record contract after the Brooks Arthur débâcle. A small man with a large office in Beverly Hills, he seemed exactly right for Dusty. Acerbic enough to deal with Hollywood, behind his tough, unsentimental exterior there was an Englishman who shared her sense of humour and knew the *Goon Show*. Not only that but Krost had originally managed Cat Stevens in London and, when he left the Springfields, Mike Hurst had produced some of Stevens's early records, so there was a real connection between the singer and her new manager.

Krost remembers that while Dusty was occasionally 'prone to hysteria if something was hurting her' he was usually utterly charmed by her. 'She behaved immaculately ninety per cent of the time, but then there'd be occasions. Look, I don't care if artists do drugs or don't do drugs, but if they're supposed to be in the studio or on stage and they ring and say, "I've collapsed, I'm in hospital, in rehab" . . . well, we would have a row.' Dusty and Krost had very quiet rows. 'You couldn't win if you started screaming at her and I learned that from experience.'

(*Above left*) Best of friends. Dusty with Helene Sellery in Los Angeles.

(*Above right*) Los Angeles 1972: Dusty shows off her snare skills to *Hollywood Reporter*'s Sue Cameron.

(*Right*) Dusty with Vicki and Nona Hendryx on New York's Upper West Side.

Dusty back in London with old friend Elton John and Lulu in 1975.

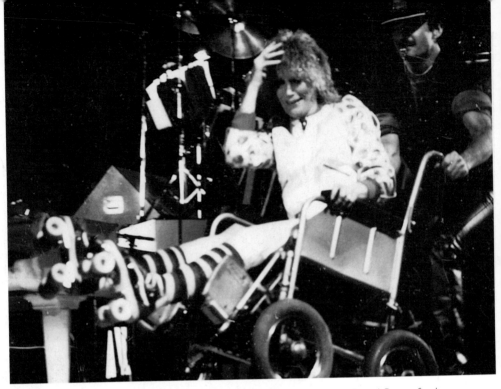

'Champagne and mandrax please.' Dusty gets a helping hand from Peppi Borza for her breathtaking roller-skating debut at the sell-out concerts at London's Theatre Royal.

At New York's Grand Finale, 1980, Rock Hudson visits Dusty backstage.

Also at the Grand Finale, Dusty greets Carole Pope (*far left*) and Nona Hendryx (*far right*).

Daffy Duck eat your heart out! Dusty in Toronto switches her allegiance to Mickey Mouse.

Running on empty: 1984 and a wraith-like Dusty is snapped by Helene in Los Angeles.

Photo session for flier to publicise Dusty's appearances on LosAngeles gay club circuit.

In fact Krost represented Dusty for four years, nursing her through the odd TV appearance, a few concerts and the album *It Begins Again.* It was always heavy-going. 'But she brought out the paternal in you and she did have that incredible talent. I'd been to see her when she first started working in America, at the Plaza, and I remember being thrilled, just like a fan.'

At dinner, when Krost says either Dusty would dress up or 'look like shit' but either way 'had style without a doubt', they would often talk about religion. He remembers that neither of them could work out why the Catholic Church protected gay priests but were so hard on gays outside the Church and how, even in the mid-1970s, Dusty would confide that she was still haunted by the Church's image of death and damnation. 'You know, the "am I going to burn in hell because of what I've done?" stuff.'

Throughout the Krost period Dusty would spend weeks at a time at Tarzana. The first time she had gone to the ranch she had insisted on taking the back roads and had arrived not for lunch, as Helene and she had planned, but when it was dark. She had put a bag on the table. 'I'm sorry I'm late but here's dinner,' she said to Helene. Inside were two dozen doughnuts. Dusty was tired and said she'd look around the ranch later and see the animals, but that right now she would love a bath. Some time later Helene heard a dreadful scream from the bathroom. Rushing in and fearing the worst she was confronted by the sight of Dusty, up to her neck in bubbles, with one of Helene's large black and white goats staring at her. The goats could wander anywhere they wanted and this one had a particular affection for bubbles.

'Dusty, it's only a goat for God's sake.'

'I know,' shrieked Dusty, 'but it's as big as a Buick!'

After a while she got used to animals ranging through the house at will, tearing the stuffing out of cushions and generally causing chaos. It might have reminded her of Lee Everett's flat in Holland Park. She particularly loved it that, in her wonderfully eccentric way, Helene drove a station wagon full of straw and had once turned up to an AA meeting with a goat 'because I couldn't get her out of the damn car'. It was, naturally, 'Dusty's goat'.

15

In the autumn of 1976 the hugely successful Labelle were
booked to do a concert at Oakland near San Francisco
as part of a west coast tour. Vicki, who was the group's
manager, knew Dusty needed to get back on stage. She
suggested that Dusty came up from Los Angeles and did
one number with Patti, Nona and Sarah Dash. She'd done
a little session work on other people's recordings but it had
been nearly four years since Dusty had undertaken any live
appearances in America. Now back with Faye at the house
in Sierra Alta Way, Dusty was in a short period of sobriety
and she thought, why not? Anyway, if nothing else, they'd
have such a good time with Vicki and 'the girls'.

At the Paramount Theatre in Oakland none of the
audience that night had an inkling that Dusty might appear.
Labelle were riding on the wave of their number one record
'Lady Marmalade' (Voulez Vous Couchez Avec Moi Ce
Soir?). At the old movie hall with its gold and red velvet
seats the promoter Bill Graham, who had been responsible
for the historic Grateful Dead, Janis Joplin and Sly and the
Family Stone concerts at San Francisco's Fillmore Theatre,
had gone out and bought a silver tea set especially for Dusty.
He arrived backstage with it on a tray and with a dish of
cucumber sandwiches. Dusty was so happy to be there that

for the first time Vicki remembered she never complained about anything. Instead she quietly got out a towel and spread her make-up out on it, allowing plenty of time for her transformation as in the old days.

Faye says it was always the same – even at home Dusty got a towel out to put her make-up on. 'I could see her go into this kind of "trance" that happened before she went on stage, putting her make up on very slowly and getting this look in her eyes like a deer in headlights.'

Dusty had always tried to stand as close to the stage as she could before going on and with Labelle halfway through their set she could hear the crowd screaming and the rhythm section pounding and was so excited that she was jumping in the wings. When she ran out to join the group on their 'What Can I Do For You?' the Paramount, not to mention Sylvester – he of the 'You Make Me Feel Mighty Real' disco classic – who was in the audience that night, went wild. For Dusty it must have been the best feeling. She had spent the past two years in and out of rehab. Now, buoyed up by her black 'sisters' on stage, the only responsibility she had was to sing in tune and have a good time. She did both wonderfully, finally coming off after Labelle's great hit 'Lady Marmalade'.

It was past midnight when the show finished. Back at the hotel Patti Labelle, as usual, rustled up ribs and greens on a hotplate in her room. With Vicki having gone off to bed as soon as she could, Dusty, Faye, Patti, Nona and Sarah talked all night and, as dawn broke, Dusty and the group sang an acappella version of 'Isn't It A Shame'. It was the end of a perfect evening and Dusty could count those on one finger these days.

Back in Los Angeles Barry Krost had managed to get

Dusty a new contract with Artie Mogul at United Artists and she was lined up for her album sessions with the British producer Roy Thomas Baker who had worked on the Queen albums with Freddie Mercury. Dusty was to say that she enjoyed working with Baker because he understood her. It was also likely that because Baker was so busy with other projects, he more or less left her alone when it came to cutting her vocals.

Dusty liked to have company around her in the studio and Helene would often go and sit there for hours, with her nose stuck in *American Geographic* to counter her boredom. Indeed recording sessions, with their endless stopping and starting, are tedious places unless you happen to be one of the musicians – rather like film sets if you're not an actor or director – and with Dusty's penchant for only singing a phrase at a time sessions would drag on all night. Not everyone had Helene's patience. Rosie Casals would drop by if she was in town but found it too tense: 'In pins and needles hoping she'd get through it and the orchestration was always too loud hiding that great voice, but that was the way she liked it.'

Despite the advance of modern technology Dusty still had problems working out the time difference between the west coast and London and catching that one 'window' when she could call people in England and know they'd be there and be conscious. So she still relied on her hastily scrawled notes to make contact; as ever she neither had the patience nor the incentive to write anything longer than a dozen or so lines to anyone. She often dropped a note to Pat, desperate to keep contact with one of the few people she thought cared about her, and indeed her secretary would often ring her during her time in Los Angeles, usually on the pretext of

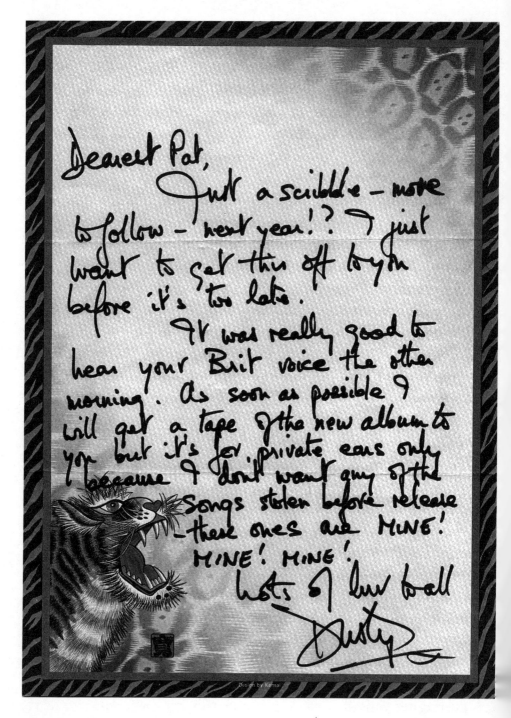

Dearest Pat,
          Just a scribble — more
to follow — next year!? I just
want to get this off to you
before it's too late.

          It was really good to
hear your Brit voice the other
morning. As soon as possible I
will get a tape of the new album to
you but it's for private ears only
because I don't want any of the
          songs stolen before release
          — these ones are MINE!
          MINE! MINE!
               Lots of luv to all
                    Dusty

Design by Kansai

188

making sure Dusty had received her royalty cheques but in truth more likely to calm herself that the rumours she was hearing about Dusty hadn't led to something more dreadful than simply falling off a stool in the recording studio.

On the day that Dusty was cutting her final tracks for *It Begins Again* in West Hollywood she learned that Faye was leaving her. Despite AA, Dusty seemed only able to manage to spend a few weeks at a time sober and she was still on a variety of pills, including slimming tablets to deal with her fluctuating weight. Faye, who had kept on an apartment of her own, went down to the studio and in an alley outside told Dusty that she was going to move back to her own place permanently. Functioning on some kind of emotional 'remote', Dusty managed to finish her tracks and then went home.

'I think all her big relationships tried to help her,' says Rosie Casals. 'But they suffered. It gets to the point that however much you love this person and care, it doesn't help them and it doesn't help you. And when, however hard you try, you can't do anything – the next step is to move away.'

For twenty-two years Dusty would ring her friend Helene every night, but for the twenty-four hours after these recording sessions there was no call from LA to the ranch. By the next day Helene was beginning to feel uneasy. She rang Suzanne Lacefield in town. Suzanne, a pretty blonde woman who had worked in real estate, had, for many years, been one of Dusty's sponsors in AA – one of the people an AA member relies on to help them through and who has usually been there before them. Suzanne agreed, it was unlike Dusty not to call and she hadn't heard from her either. She'd go round to the house and just check everything was all right.

It wasn't.

At first Suzanne thought Dusty had got drunk and passed out. When she couldn't get an answer she had looked through the glass doors of the house. 'You could see the kitchen and I could see Dusty on the floor and started to pound the doors to wake her up.' When Dusty did not move Suzanne frantically broke the glass and rushed in. She could not see Dusty breathing nor could she feel a pulse. 'I was shaking her and screaming at her and trying to phone an ambulance at the same time. There were aspirins everywhere and an empty bottle of vodka and all this earth where she'd fallen into a plant pot. I was screaming, "Don't you dare bury yourself, you're not dead yet. Get back into this body – don't you do this."'

At Cedar Sinai Hospital 'Mary O'Brien' was in emergency for six hours. At the start it was, said doctors, touch and go as to whether she'd pull through. Helene had driven in from the ranch, Suzanne's partner Barbara had turned up. Barry Krost and his brother Jackie were pacing up and down the corridor outside Dusty's room. Finally she was transferred to the psychiatric lock-up. She was in a bed with metal sides and Suzanne sat with her, waiting for her to wake up. Finally her eyes flickered and focused on Suzanne: 'Oh shit!' she said.

If she was fearful of her sponsor's fury she was right to be. Like the mother of a lost child that's suddenly been found, Suzanne was so relieved that Dusty was alive she started to yell at her. 'I really let her have it, called her a bitch, told her that she didn't get to die unless I said so. She got very lively then and told me to get out of "my fucking room" and we had a great row.' Nobody who knew her thinks Dusty really intended to kill herself. 'I don't think she did,' says Suzanne. 'It was her usual thing about not having any coping skills when things went wrong.'

Once, when she was explaining to a journalist from *Woman* magazine how she could always put emotion into the French ballad 'If You Go Away', Dusty said it was because it was about the fear of rejection and abandonment. 'And that's something a lot of people can identify with. It's that first-day-at-school feeling: "Don't go away and leave me, Mama ..." But it's the kind of feeling that can stay with you through life and become obsessive. It's what happened to me.'

Certainly Faye leaving had knocked Dusty off her feet. When her single from *It Begins Again*, 'Let Me Love You Once' came out in June Barry Krost had decided that he'd keep Dusty away from the press. Two weeks earlier the *Daily Mail* had reported that the 'exiled British singer is fighting off rumours of ill-health'. By now Dusty had added another weapon to her arsenal of addiction: cocaine. It was easy to come by in Hollywood and there was no shortage of people to help you consume it either. Dusty's circle had extended to what Helene would later call 'some highly unsuitable people' and whom Lee Everett saw as 'the kind of people that make you hold tightly on to your handbag'.

Years later, when she talked about the effect of taking cocaine in her interviews Dusty said it 'brought me to my knees faster than anything'. It was also the only experience in her whole life she remained bitter about. Dusty had always hated being alone and the new friends who turned up along with the coke made her, with Faye gone, feel less unloved and unwanted. She believed they really did like her – 'I was so naïve' – until the money and the coke ran out a year later, and so did they.

It was months before Dusty was able to go to London to do promotion for the album and in all her interviews she talked about the end of a special long-term relationship with enormous sadness: 'I always knew that one day I'd be rejected and I had rehearsed my entire life for that moment. But the rehearsal didn't work. I still fell into two million pieces. One way or another I've never lived alone. I've always lived with friends, lovers or family.'

By the time Dusty arrived at Heathrow for a press conference to celebrate the release of *It Begins Again* in 1979 she may have looked a very different girl to the one everybody remembered – more 'Hollywood' with her short swept-back hairstyle and subtler make-up – but things hadn't changed that much. From the moment she landed there was trouble. First she was mobbed by press photographers and a scuffle ensued between them and men from the record company; then she was informed that she owed a hefty amount of back tax from six years earlier, a piece of information which, given her not brilliantly healthy bank account, stunned her. But when she turned up at the Savoy Hotel in the Strand, although she was a little subdued, she seemed remarkably composed and, as usual, handled the massed gathering of the press with extraordinary alacrity.

In the huge ballroom overlooking the river some of the people there that day were familiar to Dusty even though she'd been away for six years and, relaxed, she called them by their first names. On their little gilt chairs they and a smattering of well-dressed journalists from the women's magazines looked genuinely pleased to see her. By and large their questions were innocuous and Dusty answered them with the kind of straightforward humour that from the beginning of her career had always charmed reporters. But over the six years she'd been away rumours had begun to filter across from Los Angeles and one male tabloid reporter began to harry her like a terrier with a bone on the subject of men and marriage.

For over ten years the British press had attempted to link her name with a man – any man. Even her gay dancer friend Peppi had been referred to suggestively as her 'constant companion' and very early on there were speculations that she had been having a blazing affair with the singer Eden Kane. At the time neither Vic Billings or their mutual agent Tito Burns had seen any reason to dispel this myth. Obviously she did indeed know Kane, as apart from having the same agent they had often toured together. The tabloid journalist first asked Dusty if there wasn't something missing in her life? 'Do I wish I had a man? Not all the time.' Was there one at the moment? 'No.' Didn't she need a man by her side? 'If you have a hole inside you can't have it filled by somebody else's personality.' The journalist evidently had a picture at home with a caption that said she was engaged to Eden Kane. 'Isn't that amazing. I still see him actually. He works in real estate and is doing very well. He's also married and has two lovely children.'

By now it was obvious to people in the room that Dusty was starting to look slightly panicky and hunted – a look that was to be described by journalists years later as 'wounded'. Before the man could start again two women journalists, from the music paper *Sounds* and feminist magazine *Spare Rib*, decided to intervene by deliberately switching the questions away from her personal life and on to the subject of women in the music industry. From her chair on the platform Dusty smiled and mouthed 'thank you' before she talked about the work she had done, uncredited, on her early albums; it's likely that few people noticed, she segued so successfully.

Of course it didn't always take a newshound desperate for headlines to muddy the waters. Dusty was perfectly capable of doing it herself, as she'd proved in the *Standard* interview before she left for Los Angeles. And she did it again when she returned to Britain in 1979, six months after *It Begins Again* was released. This time round she invented a totally bogus relationship with 'a man called Howard', but he wasn't very successful Dusty sighed, and things got too difficult and it just didn't last.

She was about to begin a nationwide tour – her first anywhere for ten years. It was to culminate with two nights at the Theatre Royal, Drury Lane in London but out-of-town ticket sales were a disaster and the provincial dates were pulled. Dusty, who desperately needed to feel that at least her British fans were behind her, was devastated, although she tried to brave it out by saying that it was probably because she'd been away for so long. Yet *It Begins Again* had, like her other American-made albums, had very mixed reviews. Although she managed to take some very 'hotel-room' cabaret songs such as 'I'd Rather Leave While I'm In Love' and treat them with tenderness rather than taking them by the scruff of the neck, and although she showed that on a classic like 'A Love Like Yours' she could still cut that gospel intonation like no other white singer, the running order of the tracks alternated the mood too much to create the kind of consistent overall 'feel' that had come to be expected from her records.

Nevertheless her London dates sold out within twelve hours and another night was hastily added. London had always been Dusty's mecca and Rod Stewart's manager

Billy Gaff and Harvey Goldsmith, who were promoting the tour, realised that they could have booked a whole week at Drury Lane and sold out every night. Although she had had a terrible row with Barry Krost on the phone to America which led to him pulling out of her management, Dusty managed to cheer up when she was told about the phenomenal ticket sales at Drury Lane. But to make up for the disappointment of the provincial dates she 'needed to be spoiled'. She rang Mike Gill, who by now was working for Billy Gaff, and told him she wanted tea at the Ritz.

At the Ritz Hotel in Piccadilly, sitting under the palm trees in the luxurious hushed surroundings broken only by the chink of bone china teacups, Mike Gill waited for his ex-client to turn up. Fifteen minutes after the agreed time and out of the corner of his eye he saw 'this multicoloured apparition' whizzing down the deep-pile red carpet of the Ritz towards him. It was Dusty – on roller skates. She staggered to a halt in her striped leggings and clomped up the two steps to the 'tea terrace'. Waiters serving from silver salvers nearly dropped their trays, especially when she smiled so winningly at them. 'She's the only person in the world who could have got away with it,' says Gill. 'I know people who did far less and were thrown out of the Ritz.'

And what would madam like? What she really wanted was 'a mandrax and some champagne – but I know I can't have that'. Instead she settled for smoked salmon sandwiches, cut small and with the crusts off, and tiny chocolate eclairs.

If Gill's heart missed a beat at the Ritz it would do so again at every one of the three nights that Dusty roller-skated from one side of the Theatre Royal stage to the other. Dusty was not a proficient skater and each night she was actually pushed from the wings, unsteadily made it across the stage and was caught in the wings the other side before being pushed on again. It was, as the critic Robin Denselow remarked poetically on her opening night, something that contributed to her return to the London stage 'trailing clouds of reputation and the expectation of imminent disaster'. Denselow's review echoed much of the press confusion: the consensus seemed to be that while it wasn't one of her greatest performances it had moments when even the harshest critic was melted by her 'charm and vulnerability'. They were even slightly moved when she broke down in the middle of 'I'll Be Coming Home Again'. But most of all they remarked on her audience.

During her absence in America the one thing that hadn't been quiet was the British lesbian and gay grapevine. As Adam Nattera, the editor of the gay men's magazine *Attitude* told the *Guardian* newspaper: 'After the lost years there was a clever, knowing sense of camp. She was in on the joke, which separated her from traditional gay icons.' Also, when she had come over to promote *It Begins Again* just before the tour, Dusty had given an interview to *Gay News*.

Clearly being encouraged by her record company to reach what they now perceived as a potentially huge audience, Dusty had been uncomfortable and suspicious at the start of the interview, but had warmed up once the conversation moved on to more general attitudes to gay people. Like the *Evening Standard* interview so many years before, the interview again revealed her ambiguous attitude: 'I respect gay people. That doesn't make me one and that doesn't not make me one.' Unlike the *Standard* piece this one quickly did the rounds. The sex lives of the possibly not-that-rich but undeniably famous were becoming far more interesting to newspapers than anything performers might have to say about their craft. Here was Dusty, single at forty when Sandie and Cilla and Lulu had all been married at least once, and under the headline 'Why I Love Gay Folk' she was coyly referred to by the *Daily Mirror* as a 'bachelor girl'.

At Drury Lane what manifested itself was the new climate of sexual politics. What had started with the women's movement in the early seventies and was taken up by the pop world later on, that the personal was political, was now in full flow. Certainly there were plenty of Dusty's regular fans in the stalls, young and old and just as besotted with her now as they had been when she sang 'I Close My Eyes And Count To Ten'. But there were also a great many of Dusty's other fans, those who had grown up with her but had now come out. 'The gay community has been extremely loyal to me as a singer,' Dusty was to say. 'I value that fiercely.' For them Dusty had always been the supreme diva. It was her very 'singleness' that so appealed, the feeling that the emotion she put into a song made it about their lives as much as her own. They loved her for being cosmopolitan and exotic, for recording singles in Italian and French over the years, for knowing about Brazilian music before it was fashionable and for being well travelled, as much as for her 'over-the-top' looks. Most of all they loved her voice and how it combined power with vulnerability.

In 1979, four years before Aids would start to attack the gay community, gays were beginning to enjoy their own visibility. Amongst the straight fans and the large lesbian contingent in Dusty's audience at Drury Lane it was the highly vocal groups of gay men who made the most noise, welcoming Dusty's appearance on stage with a standing ovation and shouting, 'We love you, Dusty!' whenever there was a gap between songs.

Although there was a very slight feeling that the event was as thrilling for the uncertainty of what might happen to the woman up there as for the string of hits she presented – that heady sense of danger – there's no doubt that their enthusiasm buoyed her up on stage. After all, when had she last heard the words 'we love you' coming from an audience? You felt her voice lift along with the smile on her face and didn't worry quite as much that she was going to break an ankle on her rollers.

16

Of all the stars who turned up to Dusty's opening night in October 1980 at the Grand Finale, a small supper club in New York on 70th Street between Broadway and West End, the appearance of Rock Hudson caused the greatest stir.

Hudson, a strikingly tall and handsome man, was one of Hollywood's most famous 'closet' gay actors. Like Dusty he had been forced to endure years of pressure as the press tried to dig up some dirt on his life. The Hollywood studio, terrified that their romantic lead, an actor whose physique and all-American-boy dark-haired looks personified their idea of butch heterosexuality, would be exposed, linked his name off-screen with a string of well-known actresses. But in New York that night, however famous and supportive her audience was, Dusty was two hours late coming on stage.

Despite the success of the Drury Lane concerts and one appearance at the Greek Theatre in Los Angeles, supporting Peter Allen a few months earlier, when the LA *Herald Examiner* noted 'the encores and flurry she generated', Dusty was desperately worried about the New York dates. By now she had recorded the theme track for the film *Norma Rae* in which Sally Field played a union organiser, and the song 'It Goes Like It Goes' had won an

Oscar. She had also released another album, *Living Without Your Love*, with its nod to Motown ('You've Really Got A Hold On Me'), homophobia ('Closet Man'), numbers by new American women songwriters Carole Bayer Sager and Melissa Manchester, and the Drury Lane smash 'I'm Coming Home'. But the album had, once more, not been well received. Critics were still comparing her output to 'the' *Memphis* album and one said that Dusty seemed 'incredibly world-weary' on the new tracks. Not surprisingly then, when she did arrive at the Grand Finale, she was very nervous for the first half of the evening. More so since it was the first time she'd sung on stage in New York for over eight years.

Despite the cream of the city's session men behind her she decided to excuse what she already felt was an under-par performance by announcing not just that New York gave her a cold, but laryngitis: 'But I love it here!' It was what the *New York Times* critic Robert Palmer saw as her typical combination of 'honesty and good public relations' and it was something that had charmed audiences and critics all her life. Vicki remembers her 'sounding pretty rough really, we didn't think she'd get through it. She'd blown her voice at rehearsals, as usual, but the audience were so behind her, they were willing her to be good.'

Having established she was not at her best, Dusty left the male critics to be dismissive of some of her material (most of them always hated Barry Manilow's 'Sandra' from *It Begins Again* which they saw as an exercise in bathos) but were thrilled by her voice, if not on that night then in general. Palmer, who presciently mentioned she would be more effective singing Elvis Costello songs, was still won over by her 'silvery upper register, the warm mid-range, the exceptional intonation and relaxed pacing and dynamics . . . she's really a superb pop singer'. Rock Hudson clearly thought so too. Staying for the whole show he went backstage afterwards. 'When he turned up in the audience we were all gasping and like fans,' says Vicki. 'But when he came back to see Dusty he'd taken his jacket off and he was like a fan himself, very sweet, impressed and the tallest man we'd ever seen. Dusty couldn't get over it. After all, this was a film star and we'd all grown up on Doris Day and Rock Hudson movies.'

The next day Dusty went to the doctor and was given cortisone to get her through the two-week season. Most of the nights she made it on stage and through the set with her voice relatively intact, but off stage Dusty was betraying all those years in AA and rehab by hitting the Grand Marnier ('for my throat') and was also on the anti-depressant Nardil. She was also talking about having Quaalude sandwiches. Quaaludes, which were taken off the market by the late 1980s, were strong barbiturates and Dusty was addicted to them and the euphoric feeling they gave her, along with everything else.

For her two weeks at the Grand Finale Dusty had been booked into the Mayflower Hotel on Central Park West, only a few blocks from the club. With her she had Fred Perry, who was lighting the show, and Susan Shroeder, a tall twenty-year-old whose only brush with the music world had been her long-standing friendship with Gretchen Wyler, star of a host of Broadway musicals. Susan only had a vague idea who Dusty was, but Wyler had shared a dressing-room with Dusty at a Royal Command Performance years earlier. She had never forgotten the moment when Dusty arrived with the biggest bag of make-up she had ever seen and, to her amazement – Wyler was a very neat person – proceeded to tip the entire contents all over the table. Still, the two had got along very well, especially when Dusty discovered that Wyler had set up various animal shelters in New York and Los Angeles.

Knowing that Dusty needed someone with her for the Finale season, Wyler had suggested Shroeder to her and when Susan met Dusty at the Mayflower that autumn she was, like everyone, charmed: 'I thought she was nuts, but a lot of fun'. And Dusty liked Shroeder straight away, in her twinset, pearls and brogues: 'Such sensible shoes,' laughed Dusty and immediately christened her 'Westchester'. This was in honour of the shoes, the part of upstate New York that Shroeder came from and because Dusty always had problems remembering people's names. As Westchester was leaving, Fred Perry took her to one side. 'Whatever you do,' he said, 'don't let her drink.' Shroeder, knowing nothing of Dusty's reputation or the amount of pills she was on, was bemused. After all, her job wasn't to tell this blonde woman what not to do and what's a little drink after all? A few nights later she realised what he meant.

The Mayflower, overlooking Central Park and close to Columbus Circle, is one of the older New York hotels with heavy dark furniture and large table lamps. A constant stream of people go in and out of its lobby where doormen can whistle up a yellow cab with startling precision and where an unsmiling security guard checks your room keys by the lifts. Behind the double-glazed windows and weighty, triple-locked, hinged doors of its suites there is a sudden silence, only broken by the splutter of the air-conditioning or, should you open a window, the low roar of traffic below. Enormous walk-in wardrobes, solid old tiled bathrooms and a fully fitted kitchen hiding behind louvred doors are additions to large bedrooms with unmovable maple beds and an anonymous lounge with dark framed pictures on the walls. It was here, lying on a sofa with her sick cat Moomin transported from LA on her lap, that Dusty would do interviews – having sprayed the room and covered the waste baskets with paper to hide the cigarette ends. For the last year Dusty, who had never had a cigarette near her mouth, had taken to smoking with a vengeance and would often get through three or four packets of menthols a day.

One night after her show Dusty brought back Sharon Redd, one of Bette Midler's backing group, the Harlettes. They were in high spirits, ordered room service and started a food fight. By now Westchester, who had been hired to get Dusty ready to go on stage along with her dresser, and to stake out the dressing-room door and screen after-show visitors, was no longer surprised by anything. At some point in the evening Dusty and Sharon, who had a reputation for being wild, decided the Mayflower's artwork was distinctly dull and Dusty took a picture of a forest off the wall, out of its frame, and they drew animals on it. Much better, Dusty decided. How could you possibly have a forest without creatures in it? The problem was that she couldn't put the picture back on the wall since it would be obvious to the hotel who had scribbled all over it. Instead Dusty opened a window and hurled it out. Far from smashing on to the pavement below, it landed on the hotel awning ten storeys down and was retrieved by less than happy members of the hotel management.

The first time Westchester realised Dusty had a more serious problem than simply pills and drink was one afternoon when she had an argument with Helene. It raged until Helene walked out and Dusty ran into the bathroom. She came out later with blood running down her arms. 'Oh, I did such a crazy thing,' Dusty said. 'I broke a bottle of Scope and look what happened.' It wasn't until some time later that Westchester went into the bathroom and saw that the heavy enamel sink had been smashed into pieces.

Amongst the audience who came to watch Dusty at the Grand Finale that fortnight was Carole Pope, the young, tough-sounding lead singer and songwriter with the highly ranked Canadian band Rough Trade. By 1980 the band, formed round Pope and fellow songwriter and guitarist Kevan Staples as a 'rock and roll version of S&M', were on a roll in Canada. Now a four-strong line-up, their first album *Avoid Freud* had produced two singles, 'Fashion Victim' and the controversial 'High School Confidential'. The group's 'Shakedown' was used as part of the soundtrack for the dark, sexually ambivalent Al Pacino thriller *Cruising* which was seen by gay men as both a fascination with and an indictment of their social milieu. Pope had gone to see Dusty with Vicki who was managing Rough Trade in America. When they came out after the show she stood on the pavement. 'I'd really love to go back and meet her,' she said to Vicki.' But I don't know . . .' Despite her on-stage post-punk persona Carole was basically as shy as Dusty herself.

Not that Westchester got a hint of that when she opened the dressing-room door to find Pope there. Instead what she saw was a slim woman dressed head to toe in black leather with jet-black hair and uncannily blue eyes (Pope often wore blue contact lenses). 'I am not going to say no to this woman,' Westchester muttered to Dusty behind the door. 'I think she'll kill me.' In fact Westchester noticed that, as she came in, Pope behaved much more like a star-struck schoolgirl than a successful rock singer. As usual Dusty flirted madly. 'I remember thinking she was totally not my type,' Pope said later. 'That she was so over the top in what she was wearing. But she was so charming . . .' Pope stayed on in New York longer than she'd meant to.

After the Grand Finale had finished Dusty asked Westchester if she'd hang on for some dates she had at the Sahara Hotel in Lake Tahoe, supporting some old friends from the Gamble and Huff days, the Detroit Spinners. By now, like all the women who came in contact with her, Susan had learned that being around Dusty could often be a lot of fun, certainly compared with her life back in the suburbs.

At the Sahara things ran much as usual. Although there were a few no-shows through throat trouble, when she did appear Dusty was never late on stage. The hotel swimming pool had a few mysterious objects floating in it most mornings and Fred Perry narrowly missed being barricaded in his room by the two women and a giant mattress. Back in her suite Dusty and Westchester indulged in food fights involving the hot fudge sundaes they ordered in the after-show early hours.

By now Dusty and Carole Pope were ringing each other regularly. They decided to meet up in Montreal where Dusty had a show booked. When there was some filming for a TV show in Amsterdam and London, Dusty took Pope with her. It was during these two weeks that the Canadian was brought face to face with what it was like being Dusty Springfield. Carole had been out as a lesbian for years and Rough Trade had always had a large contingent of gay and lesbian fans. Secure in her sexual identity, she had written songs for the band that were sexually upfront – at one point she and Kevan Staples had gone out as the Bullwhip Brothers. Now she was with a woman who was so anxious to look pretty and appealing in front of the cameras, and so insecure about her looks, that she would start putting on her make-up at five in the morning.

As Vicki knew only too well Dusty's routine for facing the cameras would always be the same: first she would put ice on her face to take down the swelling from the few hours' sleep she had managed, then she would put on her full make-up which would take two or three hours, then she would chose what to wear – something that could take another two hours at least. Getting to the studios early was important because she had to sort out her dressing-room and get 'acclimatised'. Then her hair would be done and her make-up 'touched up' before the taping. For Dusty it was normal, for Pope it was an extraordinary performance. 'I realised what a diva she was,' she would tell the lesbian and gay magazine the *Advocate* years later, 'and how out of control she was too.' Even so Pope was 'mesmerised' and they decided that it would make a lot more sense if Dusty left Los Angeles and came to Toronto.

For her move to Toronto Dusty hired a massive twenty-seven-foot-long truck. She rang Westchester who was no longer working for her but was due to go down to LA for Dusty's birthday. Did Westchester know a driver who could get her stuff to Toronto? Westchester, whose work in television had given her a handy list of contacts, could not number amongst them anyone who they could get to drive the truck. Dusty hated to ask but she was desperate: was there any way Westchester could do it? The upstate New Yorker was horrified. Absolutely not. She'd never driven anything that big in her life and anyway it was thousands of miles.

But Westchester's friend, Martha Lee, thought it sounded like a great idea – they would really see America this way and it would be an adventure. Susan and Martha went to pick up the packed truck in LA. The agreement was that they would drive the furniture and personal possessions and meet Dusty in Detroit before they all crossed the border into Canada together. The garage at Dusty's house was so full that Westchester began seriously to wonder if Dusty wasn't so much moving to Toronto to be with Carole but to escape from her collection of junk. With the last few things squeezed into the back of the truck, Westchester and Martha set off, like Thelma and Louise without the guns, leaving Dusty behind.

Dusty's furniture in the huge truck was to travel thousands of miles: across Arizona, Nebraska, Missouri and Illinois. Every so often Westchester would ring LA to find out how Dusty was getting on. She kept getting the same story: Dusty wasn't ready to leave yet. When she called from Chapel, Nebraska, Dusty was shocked that the women had got there so quickly. 'Oh, you're driving much too fast.' Each time they stopped overnight Westchester would ring the house to check and kept being told that she must be doing over ninety miles an hour and she was to slow down. Although Westchester and Martha were seeing a lot more of America than they ever thought they would back on the east coast, life on the road for two young women was proving tiresome.

It wasn't just the driving. Truck stops were exactly that: they could only eat or wash up where other truckers stopped and the men of the road weren't used to having pretty women driving in unless they were 'thumbers'. These were the hookers who worked the routes, picked up by the drivers in one town and dropped off at the next. Conversations in diners were always fraught with these misconceptions and after some days Westchester and Martha stopped finding it funny.

By the time they got to Toledo, outside Detroit, they had to stay for two days waiting for Dusty to fly up from LA. Although Dusty being late was no longer a surprise to anyone, she was obviously having last-minute panic attacks about leaving the city which, despite everything, had been her home for the most part of fifteen years. Finally, in Detroit she climbed up into the cabin of the truck with Westchester and Martha and the three of them crossed the border into Canada.

The Toronto idea was ill-fated. Set on the shores of Lake Michigan, the city's narrow streets proved problematic immediately, particularly since Westchester had never, throughout the entire trip, learned to back up the truck. Worse, if Dusty had felt a failure in Los Angeles, in Toronto she would be practically invisible. It was a city in which Carole Pope had flourished ever since she and Staples had started working the coffee houses and in the eighties she was recognised wherever she and Dusty went. For Dusty it must have been painful being out anywhere with Pope. Dusty was drinking heavily. It was almost as though Dusty, who had always said she had an addictive personality, crowded her worst addictions into those brief six months: hospitalised so many times it's a wonder she and Pope had any time together at all. Although it was a frenetic period, with Kevan Staples's wife Marilyn often having to rush over to Carole's house to avert a major crisis, Pope recalled later that she would sometimes get Dusty to sing to her in bed. 'And that was like – my God – ecstasy.' The song was 'Breakfast In Bed' from *Dusty in Memphis*.

Despite this being one of Dusty's shortest relationships it was during her time with Pope that she started work on what would be her most extraordinary album: *White Heat.*

Put together with the help of Barry Krost's brother Jackie, started in Montreal and finished in LA over the following year, the album was produced by Howard Steele and, for the first time, Dusty shared co-production credits and wrote additional lyrics for the bitter 'Blind Sheep', sung in a much deeper range than she'd ever used before. With a clutch of eighties rock session musicians – British guitarist Caleb Quaye and ex-Rolling Stones pianist Nicky Hopkins, synthesiser player Jean Roussel who contributed English lyrics to the album's one dance track, the suggestively teasing disco number, 'Donnez Moi', and with Dusty and musician and writer Tommy Faragher doing most of the back-up vocals – *White Heat* turned out to be a tough, unforgiving and overtly sexual album.

Although the front cover featured an almost completely bleached-out drawing of Dusty's face, the back cover showed her in what looked like an American football helmet. When the album was released the rumours were that she'd worn the helmet to disguise bruises to her face, yet it's much more likely that it was Dusty's little joke. In Los Angeles she had been a fanatical follower of all-women roller derby teams. This did not feature the kind of beautiful young Billie Holiday look-alike who twirled on her wheels in the video for Gloria Gaynor's 'I Will Survive'. Instead these were big women in helmets who hurled themselves about the rink kicking the hell out of each other, and Dusty knew most of them very well indeed.

Not since her *Memphis* album had Dusty used such a wide range of vocals and such varied pacing. Perhaps

with Palmer's remark in mind from her appearance at
the Grand Finale, on *White Heat* Dusty included an Elvis
Costello song, not one of his more acerbic numbers but the
difficult and melancholic 'Losing You'. She also chose the
emotive ballad 'Time and Time Again'. For someone who
had always complained that producers made her sing 'too
high' 'Time and Time' remains an astounding cut. Whereas
Dusty mixes her voice so far back on some of the other tracks
they become more redolent of hard white rock and of her
desire always to sound like just another instrument, 'Time
and Time' has her close to the mike. The result is that what
could have been a perfectly ordinary 'standard' becomes
a piece of real drama with Dusty pushing her voice up
an octave on the chorus until it sounds like it's about to
crack, and dropping back to a heartbreaking vulnerability
on the verse.

She also cut two Rough Trade numbers: 'I Am Curious',
with its 'melting of two bodies' was a typical Rough Trade
'love' song with Kevan Staples on guitar and clavinet;
and their Bertolt Brecht/Kurt Weill-influenced 'Soft Core'.
When they came to cut 'Soft Core' Staples remembers sitting
at the keyboard in the studio 'kinda warming up and trying
not to be nervous' since only he was playing on it (Tommy
Faragher's percussion was added later), when he heard
the click of women's shoes and Dusty came up behind
him and started to sing. Like everyone she worked with
he was enthralled by her voice and bewildered by her
constant self-criticism. 'It was a very intimate moment
when we cut that,' says Staples. 'That kind of interaction
with a singer is a real highlight in your life and her
voice . . . ! She did everything beautifully but she always
cared too much. All musicians nit-pick, but Dusty would

never just get "close enough", she always felt she could do better.'

Despite the instant appeal of 'Donnez Moi' and 'Time And Time Again', the album was never released in England. Partly it was the result of yet another round of record company takeovers, with *White Heat* finally being released on the American-based Casablanca label, but it may also have been that the British end may have felt that the album was one step too far away from the Dusty they wanted for English audiences. Whatever, 'Soft Core' remains at the heart of *White Heat*'s intrigue. It seems like the height of masochism for Dusty to go into the studio and record a song that Carole Pope could just as well have written about her. 'Soft Core' is a dark song about love and an addiction to a person with 'blood in your eyes' who lives on 'drugs and alibis' and 'a maze of alcohol and neon lies'. If *Memphis* boasted Dusty under the covers, on *White Heat* she was up against the wall. The relationship with Carole, for all its intensity, had burned itself out.

By the summer of 1981 Dusty was back in Los Angeles.

17

Every morning as the sun rises on Los Angeles, a group of down-and-outs gather near the House of Pancakes on the corner of Holloway and Santa Monica Boulevard. Some have dogs, most carry a bottle and the inhabitants of West Hollywood leave their automatic garages and security gates and glide past them in their cars, staring straight ahead. 'I never ended up in the gutter,' Dusty once said when she talked about her final years in Los Angeles, but sometimes she might have been forgiven for feeling it was a close call.

Her return from Toronto was depressing – an empty home, no relationship, no manager, no stage appearances and only AA meetings, when she chose to go to them, to look forward to. When *White Heat* came out it was not, once again, a commercial success, a pattern that had stalked Dusty ever since she'd arrived in Hollywood. Although for the past ten years her work had been in spasmodic bursts, it had kept her going – occasionally emotionally and certainly financially. Now things were beginning to get very tight. Her dabble with cocaine had been an expensive hobby. There was the rent on the house to pay and the pills to buy. Although she had had a two-record advance for *It Begins Again* and *Living Without Your Love* and one for *White Heat*, her recording sessions were so slow and expensive much of the money had been eaten up. There were to be no more impulsive jaunts to Rome or to Rio.

Desperately she sold her fine collection of R&B records to musician Graham Nash. Then her beautiful Jensen Intercepta had to go. She was seeing everything slip away from her. But there were still plenty of people in Los Angeles who wanted to make her feel better: 'Mostly,' says Vicki, 'lesbian groupies who wanted to say they had slept with someone famous.' Dusty herself always pointed out how easy it was to flatter her: 'If someone says they're attracted to me it's like – *wow!* You like me!' Her self-confidence was at an all-time low, and so was her self-respect.

For a while, to make some money, she appeared on stage at gay bars like the Probe on La Brea. For 500 dollars a time, and with her voice shot, Dusty would lip-sync to some of her hits. She would look glamorous; she would look really beautiful in a black jacket and trousers or one of her designer dresses; she would, for ten minutes or so, be adored, but it was poignant and sometimes it was dangerous. Her appearances would be publicised with a run-off handbill, which would circulate the bars. On Halloween 1982, when she was appearing at a bar on Santa Monica Boulevard, there had been no publicity other than 'word of mouth' round the gay community. That night West Hollywood turned out in drag and leather, the crush was enormous and when some people tried to gatecrash the event things turned nasty. Faye, who had turned up to see Dusty, heard a shot ring out and the crowd scattered. In handgun America, where anyone with a grudge can come out firing, any loud noise tends to cause panic. As people ran about the alleys it looked like the evening would end in disaster. But it eventually calmed down before midnight and Dusty, who had arrived incredibly late, luckily knew nothing about it. For Dusty the gay bar circuit was the lowest point in her life.

By now Suzanne Lacefield had moved out of the area and although Dusty still saw her, she had a new sponsor at her AA meetings, an Irish-American woman called Peggy Albrecht. Peggy was older than Dusty, as small, as witty, but an intensely motherly woman who called everyone 'honey' or 'sweetheart' in a soft voice. Kind, but tough, 'a wonderful woman, a steel magnolia' Suzanne called her, Peggy was the only person Dusty ever took real notice of and who, later, helped her to get off drink for good. Peggy was plunged into her sponsorship full-tilt: after the round of boys' clubs and the growing desperation of what her life had become, Dusty coped in the only way she knew how.

One night Fred Perry, who had stayed on in Los Angeles long after Dusty needed him to light her shows, had talked to her on the phone and had become concerned about the state she seemed to be in. He rang Marv Greifinger who had known Dusty since she'd joined the same AA group in 1973. Greifinger was a music-business publicist who was also a friend of Vicki and Labelle and he went over to Dusty's apartment, a condominium on Beechwood Drive – to allay Perry's fears. In the bathroom he found Dusty naked on the floor and covered in blood. Greifinger was as shocked having to cope with a singer he so admired without her clothes on as he was by the fact that she had injured herself. He managed to get Dusty on to the bed and then rang Peggy.

When Peggy found out that Dusty's wounds, although numerous, were relatively superficial she calmly talked him through what to do: get Dusty's pyjamas on, wash her face and arms with cold water, make a large pot of coffee and, after he was sure she was okay, let Dusty sleep it off. Peggy would come by first thing in the morning. The next day she took Dusty off to the Thalians clinic, a mental health and detox centre started by film star Debbie Reynolds. Here they tried to get rid of the poison in Dusty's body by taking her off the pills and the drink. It was hard love. When Faye managed to get in to see her it was the first time she had seen Dusty since one short lunch in Toronto when Dusty was involved with Carole, and Faye thought then she was 'pretty much rock bottom'. Even so she was shattered when she saw her at the clinic: 'She looked gaunt, a shell of a person, and she was shaking badly.'

There's no doubt Dusty gave the Thalians her best efforts for the thirty days it took to detox her, realising how she really did have to change something about her life. When she came out Peggy immediately took her to the Friendly House on Normandy. A halfway house for women with addictions, the Friendly House had been running since the 1950s and had been the subject of a Carol Burnette film. With its front and back gardens and its endless supplies of tea and coffee, the Friendly House was miles away from any institution and felt more like a girls' club than a recovery centre.

Usually there were sixteen resident women at a time, staying between thirty and sixty days, but the house would also host meetings and was run as a 'drop-in' centre for women in the AA programme. Despite its atmosphere the house was run very strictly. There was a curfew for visitors or women attending meetings. Women who stayed there were expected to go to meetings in which they learned to cope with their addictions one hour, one day at a time and functioned as a support group for each other. During their stay residents were not allowed out alone and could only go out on shopping trips if they had qualified by being sober for a length of time. By the time Dusty was going to the house she no longer denied she was an alcoholic, but she still had problems stopping. 'She'd say, "I can't deal with this and I can't do another goddamn album,"' says Suzanne. 'Or it would be, "I'm different, I can't perform without it."'

It wasn't until the summer of 1983, ten years after she had been to her first AA meeting, that Dusty would finally be able to say she was sober.

With a lack of recordings or live work her friends started to think up ways in which Dusty could harness her talents and give herself a sense of direction. For Helene and Suzanne it seemed obvious that, given Dusty's personality and looks and her encyclopaedic knowledge not just of films but of film-making (amongst her books were many about the technical aspects, lighting, structure and framing of films), she should be encouraged to act. It was, after all, what some of the white American solo female singers had turned to in the late seventies when their record market had dried up: Cher, Barbra Streisand, even pretty Michelle Phillips of the Mamas and Papas. Dusty must have been intrigued by the thought, even though she'd never seen herself as a singer in the Cher/Streisand mould. At Tarzana she had met Lilian Chauvin, an acting-coach friend of Helene's and often the three of them would play Dusty's favourite general knowledge game, Trivial Pursuit. Lilian asked Dusty if she fancied sitting in on one of her drama workshops in town and, oddly for her, Dusty had immediately said yes, she'd love to.

In fact Dusty went for a few weeks, even after Lilian

had thrown a script across at her one day and got her to read a part. When Helene asked how Dusty was getting on Lilian was adamant: 'She doesn't need any coaching, she just needs to get a job and start acting. She's an absolute natural.' It was not exactly a surprise to anyone who knew Dusty well. Often they would listen to her on the phone ringing round the doctors she knew would give her the pills she wanted. Sometimes they balked – they'd only just written out a prescription; why did she need more?

At times like this Dusty would burst into tears and sound as if she were on the brink of a nervous breakdown. Directly she got what she wanted she'd put down the telephone and turn to Helene or Suzanne and say in a perfectly normal voice, 'Right, now where are we going?' Dusty had originally wanted to be an actress. She'd only been a singer, she said, because she thought there were so many actresses around it would be more sensible to try a less crowded field. Now, with a string of unsuccessful albums to her name and no recording work, it might have been the perfect answer to her problems, an idea she had toyed with once or twice before. But by now, hardly believing she could do anything successfully, it was an opportunity that she never followed through.

Instead she decided to fill her time working with Martine Collette to campaign for the Wildlife Way Station and against the import and sale of wild animals. Collette had set up the station on over a hundred acres of land in the San Fernando Valley as a refuge for the kind of exotic wild animals sold to millionaire film producers, industrialists and other rich west coast Americans to add a little kudos to their lives. With their claws and fangs removed, the animals were totally reliant on whoever owned them, and often whoever owned them would get bored and simply let them loose.

Dusty, who had always kept tins of catfood and an opener in the boot of her car in case she came across stray felines, would sometimes find tiger cubs or other small beasts wandering near the highways and take them to Martine's. For an animal lover like Dusty it was just another example of what she now saw as not just the grossness of Hollywood, but its lack of compassion. And there was something about not being able to fight back, of the animals' inability to fend for themselves, that got to her too.

One day at an AA meeting Dusty had met a tall, wild-haired singer she was completely fascinated by. Tedda had been in prison on a drink-related charge and with her flamboyant looks seemed incredibly exotic to Dusty, always attracted to the less boring members of the community. Even so, and even given Dusty's penchant for a theatrical event, there was some surprise when only a few months after she and Tedda had moved in together and the relationship was quite obviously turbulent, Dusty announced to her friends that the couple were about to embark on a gay marriage.

By the late 1990s America had recognised lesbian marriages as being 'safeguarded by the Constitution and entitled to the highest level of judicial protection' after an appeal court in Georgia found in favour of Robin Shahar. Shahar had sued the state's Attorney General after she lost her job at the City of Atlanta Department of Law when he found out she was going to marry another woman. By then you could have a gay wedding in Las Vegas if you had a mind to. An 'Alternative Lifestyle Ceremony' run by the Eternal Hope Ministry had participants pledging 'the depth and breadth' of their love.

Back in 1983, however, things were different. But if Dusty was being a revolutionary it was only because she was passionate to the point of obsession about her new partner. And she knew it was not necessarily reciprocal. She always said that her ceremony should have started 'dearly beloved and barely tolerated'. Yet, as usual when there was an occasion, Dusty rose to it wonderfully.

In a gesture of extraordinary generosity, given her love for Dusty, Helene offered Tarzana for the wedding, chickens and all. Dusty had found a lovely old white wedding gown at her local thrift shop. Her 'groom' wore a black velvet suit and gold waistcoat, which looked stunning with her mass of dark hair. Everything on the tables, laid out in the garden, was black including the tablecloth and napkins, and Helene was 'best lady' for Dusty. It seemed like a glorious afternoon and Dusty saw it through stone-cold sober, drifting about in her white dress, and remarking excitedly how 'charming' all her guests looked. The only glitch was that, despite a 'no alcohol' ruling, someone had tied a bottle of whisky to the outside of one of the windows and guests less committed than Dusty had been taking secret swigs of it.

By the time the day was over Dusty and her 'wife/husband/partner' were arguing violently. If Dusty had a model of a marriage from her parents then this was certainly her way of replicating it. Marv Greifinger, who was driving them back to LA in his VW, had the unenviable job of trying to steer as Dusty, in her wedding gown in the front seat, and her partner in the back hurled abuse and hit each other.

Over the next months the relationship deteriorated rapidly. Both women had volatile tempers. One day, during a particularly violent fight over something as mundane as cataloguing Dusty's music, she was hit in the face with a saucepan. It smashed her mouth and knocked her teeth out. For the only time in her life Dusty hit someone. Enraged with pain, she grabbed a skillet and whacked Tedda on the head. Years later when she recounted the story to her closest friends she said what a coward she thought she'd been – because Tedda had her back to her at the time. At Cedar Sinai Hospital Norma arrived from her house in the country and burst into tears when she saw Dusty in bed, her face black and blue, her mouth hugely swollen. For all that Dusty had been playing with fire, living with someone who seemed to be just as unstable as she was seemed like madness. Nobody could believe the damage that had been done to her. Vicki was outraged when Tedda turned up on the ward: 'I remember thinking how weird it was. That this was the woman who had hit her so badly and she walked in as though she was just a regular visitor. Why was she here?'

Dusty's face would never fully recover. Even though Helene lent her the money to have plastic surgery done on her mouth in New York, Dusty chose the cheapest job possible and spent the rest on drugs. From then on her once expressive face looked frozen, and the smile that had enchanted everybody who met her was tight and lopsided. She would sometimes in interviews refer to an 'abusive relationship – the kind many women find themselves in' and she went on to work with Karen Townshend, wife of the Who guitarist, in a charity set up to support battered women.

By 1984 Dusty was staying more and more with Helene at Tarzana. From there she would make weekly sorties to see her one-time 'groom' who was now in Chino's Women's Prison outside LA. Helene would drive and when Dusty would fuss about what she might wear for the visit Helene would cheerfully respond, 'Who's to know, who's to care?'

Indeed it was quite true. By now Dusty had been out of the spotlight for so long nobody knew her when she turned up to prison visits. The only time she was recognised in the street was when she and Helene ran into a coach party of British tourists doing the Hollywood Filmstar Homes tour, and Dusty tried to duck under the seat.

There may have been other reasons for Dusty to make such regular prison visits but the main one was practical: as a non-American she needed Tedda's signature for her food stamps. Dusty was now both on a diet and on welfare. These days she was a long way from the house at Dona Teresa and the swimming pool. Instead she inhabited a series of seedy motels with 'cooking facilities' around the streets of Hollywood and Vine, Los Angeles's answer to New York's Bowery.

That summer she celebrated eleven months of being sober. Despite everything that had happened to her and although there had been the odd slip immediately after the Tedda incident, if Dusty was now hooked on anything it was diet Coke, cigarettes – and her pills. And the pills were a problem in themselves. Although they blurred the lines of her life they made her behave both erratically and, sometimes, irrationally. Nobody ever knew quite what to expect from her and so it might have been better if she had not decided to appear at a charity event for the Friendly House. She was not ready to perform and her appearance was to be the most bizarre she had ever made. A few phrases into her first song Dusty's voice collapsed under the weight of her drug intake. She left the stage to return a few moments later with a Hoover. To the astonishment of the audience Dusty proceeded to hum to herself as she cleaned the stage. She then left, grinning.

A few weeks later she went to New York. Roberta Flack's producer Joel Dorn had rung Vicki up knowing she was in touch with Dusty. He was putting a compilation album together of classic songs sung by a variety of top people. Might Dusty be interested in taking part?

Of all the songs that should have been a breeze for Dusty to sing, the old Shirelles' classic 'Will You Love Me Tomorrow' was an obvious choice. Written back in the early sixties by Carole King and Gerry Goffin it had been one of the classic uptown R&B hits that Dusty loved and had given the black 'all-girl' group their own place in music history. But the all-night sessions with Dorn were disastrous. It was during this visit to New York that her managers Vicki and Jenny Cohen decided to do some straight talking to try and get Dusty back in shape again. A smart, sharp, New Yorker, Cohen had met Dusty through the singer/songwriter S. Pawne Feltington in Los Angeles during 1984. At the time Dusty had just done two spots on the Anne Murray TV show. The Canadian singer, knowing Dusty was having a bad time, had made sure she'd get on the show and get a good fee for her appearances. But Dusty had no manager by now and once she met Jenny she wondered if she felt like managing her alongside her old friend Vicki?

'You can be mutual support for each other,' Dusty had said and Jenny Cohen remembers thinking that she'd never met another artist who seemed so considerate. When Dusty showed her the scars on her arms Jenny was touched by her honesty and told her she certainly wouldn't hold her past against her. It was the combination of Dusty's charm, openness and, as she thought, thoughtfulness that swayed Cohen into accepting the job. 'I had no idea the cutting was still going on. I really did think it was something that was done with,' says Jenny. For Vicki it was impossible to say no to Dusty. It was quite clear she desperately needed someone to take some care of her and take control over things. 'I knew it would be difficult because I'd known her for so long,' says Vicki. 'She could be wonderful and she was such a terrific singer, but there was the other side of her: stubborn, negative and sometimes out of control. She was adorable and she was infuriating. In many respects she was practically impossible to work with, but I knew her well enough to know she needed to have that cushion between her and the outside world.'

Here then were two women committed to Dusty's well-being. But instead of hearing the women say they cared about her but that she needed some kind of professional medical help, all Dusty heard was that they couldn't cope with her any more and that they didn't love her enough to put up with her endless phone calls and incessant panics.

'I always felt that she pushed everyone,' Barry Krost says. 'Like, "How much can you tolerate and still like me? I can't sing, I make you no money and I don't show up – but will you still want to represent me?"' It was after the Dorn sessions and Vicki and Jenny's conversation that Dusty would be rushed to Bellevue from Jeff's apartment and into a straitjacket. Dusty's version of 'Will You Love Me' was unreleasable.

That Christmas Doug Reece was passing through Los Angeles with his wife Wendy and their two children, on their way from Australia to London. Reece had rung Fred Perry and said wouldn't it be like old times if they could all meet up again? When she went to the motel where the Reeces were staying Dusty must have been both pleased and full of trepidation after so much had happened to her. Doug noticed the change straight away. 'She seemed very serious and, in a way, sad. It was like America was taking its toll.' Reece had heard that Dusty was having 'some problems' and, like Pat, always felt that if he could have stayed around he could have helped her. That evening Doug, Wendy, Dusty and the two children went out to dinner together and it was only halfway through the evening that Doug felt 'the old Dusty drifting back'. It was the last time he was to see her.

Dusty was running out of everything. Most of all she was running out of America. After twelve years and a lifetime of experience there were no record companies left who were interested in signing her. She was gloriously talented but she was impossible, she was expensive and she wasn't selling records. They were not, they all seemed to decide, charitable institutions. Meanwhile the people she knew there who cared and would stick with her were getting thinner on the ground. Dusty began to look back to England.

18

In the Star Bar at the Hippodrome Nightclub, Leicester Square, in 1985 Dusty was faced with something that resembled a circus. There was a line of 'Dusty look-alikes' – transvestites in blonde wigs and false eyelashes wearing glittery dresses – there were Persons of Restricted Growth on roller skates wearing gold lamé, there was the 300-pound tattooed man and there was a group of rather bewildered French, Dutch and Italian disc jockeys who had flown in especially for the occasion. This was to be Dusty's big night, her return to British audiences with a new single 'Sometimes Like Butterflies'. With singers Kim Wilde and Jim Diamond and a massive orchestra decked out in Busby Berkeley-style white tuxedos, Dusty was to be the star of 'Live At The Hippodrome', an evening to launch Peter Stringfellow's Hippodrome record label, taped by the BBC and then beamed to television audiences in Britain and across Europe.

Dusty's reputation for being expensive to record had now grown and she was no longer popular enough to bring in a profit. Since the mid-seventies the music business itself had changed. The smaller enthusiastic labels had been swallowed up by the larger corporations and there was a monopoly on distribution. Music was in the hands of the accountants and, in

America, Dusty had used up a lot of goodwill from the people who had always been in her corner. It had been four years since *White Heat* and she desperately needed money. Much of this explains what many people couldn't understand – why she had signed up with Stringfellow.

Entrepreneur and self-publicist Peter Stringfellow had moulded himself as a British Hugh Hefner. Constantly surrounded by young nubile blondes with very little clothing on, with his year-round suntan and long, streaked hair, Stringfellow had very little, if any, of Hefner's savoir-faire. He was a 'lad' to Hefner's more suave-suited business image. In the spring of 2000 he would be given permission to open a lap-dancing club on the site of the failed Fashion Café in Leicester Square which he would call the Passion Café. Meanwhile, in 1985, whilst admitting he knew nothing about the music business, he had started his own Hippodrome record label. Stringfellow may have had a lot of enthusiasm – and he was seriously excited to have netted Dusty – but he had more money than taste and, sadly, his attempts halfway into the 1980s to reproduce what he thought of as the glamorous glitzy days of the Hollywood spectacular with 'Live At The Hippodrome' were looking slightly crazed and very tacky.

It was ironic that Dusty should have been in the Star Bar that night. The Hippodrome was on the site of the old Talk of the Town but these days the plush velvet banquettes were more likely to be the recipients of Stringfellow's 'girls' scantily clad bottoms – his equivalent of Playboy's 'bunnies' – and the décor had changed so much it was practically unrecognisable from the salubrious dinner club of the late sixties. Did Dusty have a moment of nostalgia standing there? If she did it was speedily dispersed when she saw one of her co-stars, Fanny the Trained Dog, peeing up the wall.

Dusty had originally got the Stringfellow deal via her old British manager Vic Billings, but Billings was now busy with other artists. She needed someone with her who could follow through and then handhold her in London, and Jenny Cohen landed the job. In the bar at the Hippodrome Jenny was starting to get a bad feeling about the evening. Before Dusty came to London for the Stringfellow recording, although she had given up drinking, she was heavily into the 'eighties drug' Xanax. An anti-depressant, it actually had the effect of making Dusty very anxious. Jenny had thought London was going to set Dusty on course. Certainly, after the terrible period in LA, there was now more money flying about. Vic had come up trumps for his old client and had negotiated a series of European TV appearances for Dusty. Stringfellow had paid her an astonishing £100,000 for one single and Jenny had won a court case for Dusty over the unauthorised use of her name on advertisements for the Tricot collection by French designer Joseph. She had also negotiated a deal for Dusty to feature in a TV advertisement for Britvic, the soft drinks company, singing 'I Only Want To Be With You'.

It would be the first advert that Dusty had appeared in, as opposed to having her singing voice used on the soundtrack, since her exuberant 1960s appearance on the Mother's Pride bread commercial.

Now able to afford to fly backwards and forwards between London and LA to check on her cats whenever she felt like it, Dusty was also living very comfortably in a spacious rented house in Hampstead, close to the Heath. The one thing Dusty had always had going for her, even when things got bad, was her innate sense of a good song. Jenny Cohen had sent her a mass of demos from America to chose a single from and was completely shattered when Dusty told her that she was going to record 'Sometimes Like Butterflies': 'But, Dusty, that was a Donna Summer "B" side for Christ's sake!' Dusty insisted. She loved the song and it was going to be her single for Hippodrome.

If past recording sessions had been fraught because of Dusty's insistence on perfection, with Stringfellow's lack of musical know-how, Dusty's creakiness after such a long studio absence and the growing realisation that she might have got into something she'd live to regret, the sessions for the single were chaotic. Still on her anti-depressants and, these days, only sleeping for one or two hours a night, Dusty was increasingly tetchy. She and Stringfellow would have blazing rows: 'Peter knows fuck all about the music business. I want to punch him on the nose,' she would tell journalists later. 'But then I'm sure he'd like to punch me on the nose too.' Her backing singer Simon Bell, who was working on the sessions, would say later that he thought they were a bunch of 'amateurs' and didn't have a clue about music.

Jenny Cohen had very little notion of the potential for all this when she arrived in town to be at Dusty's side for the Hippodrome. Dusty had insisted on singing live on the show, even though everyone else was miming. She had done such a great job at the afternoon rehearsal that everyone was very 'up' about the evening performance. If Jenny had rung Vicki at that point she would have been told that far from this being good news it was the worst possible scenario: Dusty would, as usual, have sung herself out for the rehearsal and would have a problem with her voice when it came to the show proper.

All Jenny did know was that she was worried about the

small roller skaters whizzing about, and that Pat Rhodes (formerly Barnett), who had come out of 'retirement' to help out, was already leaving Dusty's dressing-room saying wryly, 'Mmm – time for management I think!' The dressing-room was full of flowers – from friends, fans, and even a bouquet from the House of Lords. The event was being treated as Dusty's 'homecoming' and as a result Dusty was a bag of nerves. When Jenny went in things were flying through the air: 'Having fun are we?' asked Cohen in her New York drawl, reducing Dusty to laughter.

Dusty had entered into the Hippodrome spirit by getting her hair dyed purple and by wearing a silver suit. The result horrified Jenny Cohen and was to be described later in the *Guardian* newspaper as making Dusty look like 'something left over from the NASA space probe'. As Dusty appeared on stage in a flurry of dry ice and flashing lights and opened her mouth to sing, it was obvious that she was hoarse. It seemed everything was going wrong. Jenny Cohen had laid dayglo tape on the floor so that Dusty, with her extreme short-sightedness, could see her way to the stage with the cameras following her. In her high shoes she caught her foot in the tape and tripped up, making her even more edgy. Then, just as Dusty was about to start singing, Jenny caught a flash of gold lamé whizzing past. It was a roller-skating Person of Restricted Growth making for the stage. Knowing that for Dusty this would be the final straw, the tall American flung herself in front of the small figure and stopped him mid-flight, breaking the heel of her best shoes in the process.

When they saw the playback Jenny's worst fears were confirmed. The next day she talked to Stringfellow about Dusty re-recording her vocal and getting it laid on the tape.

If Stringfellow would pay for the sessions the BBC would, unusually, hold the tape and let them add the tracks. Jenny excitedly called Dusty: 'Sweetie, you're gonna be so happy, we're going to go and re-do the vocals.'

'That's great,' Dusty croaked from the other end of the phone. Jenny could hardly hear her. 'I have laryngitis.'

Jenny immediately took Dusty to a Harley Street doctor who was bemused not to see more inflammation in Dusty's throat. As Jenny suspected and Vicki confirmed, Dusty's vocal problems were usually psychosomatic: 'It was like the terror she always felt inside had to be matched by these incredible levels of external anxiety. It wasn't laryngitis, it was all that stress and tension that affected her voice.'

Taking the doctor to one side Jenny suggested taking Dusty to another doctor in Chelsea that Dusty had often talked about and whom she had seen a lot during her days in London. The doctor agreed it might be a good idea to put Dusty's mind at rest and Jenny rang Chelsea to say that all her client needed was some kind of placebo. Instead Dusty was given Ritalin, a form of speed. Used for hyperactive children by treating like with like, it acts to counter their hyperness. But it had a peculiar effect on Dusty and turned her into a 'dry drunk'. After a few hours Jenny was very concerned. It was quite obvious that Dusty was in no shape to re-record anything or, indeed, leave her room. Jenny thought she was 'like a boxer that's had one too many fights' but even with the motherly Peggy Albrecht around Dusty would keep taking the pills. Things were so bad that Jenny rang Vicki in America to get some advice and she put her on to someone in AA in England. The famous British actor, who understood about both addiction and performance stress, finally managed to talk Dusty down and convince her that she didn't need the drugs. By the evening she was calmer, but the Hippodrome show went out: dry ice, trained dogs, NASA suit, bad vocals and all.

Having realised that the Stringfellow association was not going to be the career comeback she'd anticipated and that she'd made an error, Dusty became very low again. Three years later she was to make an even bigger mistake: she agreed to let the *News of the World* take pictures of her working out in the gym in an attempt to lose weight. It seemed at the time to be the most suicidal decision of her career. The Sunday newspaper had a reputation for concentrating its copy on sex and sleaze, while adopting a prurient attitude to both.

Under the strapline 'Pop star fatty books into health farm' Dusty was pictured at Henlow Grange in Bedfordshire and if there was a flattering photograph of her taken that day the *News of the World* certainly chose not to use it. She also talked to the newspaper's reporter, who must have been in seventh heaven, about her alcoholism, her pills and her sex life. Whether her experience of being broke in Los Angeles had so terrified her that, lured by the big sums of money the *News of the World* would have paid, she simply lost judgement, or whether she thought the press would still like her just as they used to, the piece rebounded badly on her: 'I should have known better,' she said later in an interview with the *Daily Telegraph* magazine. 'That was truly dumb. Somebody said I could make some quick money. Didn't I know? Didn't it occur to me?'

In 1985, much to the chagrin of Stringfellow, she did very few interviews to promote 'Butterflies' and refused to do any of the things he tried to set up for her. Instead she stayed in Hampstead, with a succession of American girlfriends coming to visit and a succession of late-night trips to her by now favourite venues – the psychiatric wards of various London hospitals. It was when she was beginning to be successful with the Pet Shop Boys that Stringfellow finally spoke to the *Sun* newspaper. They had rung him when he was on holiday to get a story that was ostensibly two or three years old. It was as though the tabloids had developed a vendetta against Dusty and were trying to rake up as much as they could while presenting it as 'new' information. Stringfellow, not averse to a chat, was rather generous and merely said that Dusty had refused to sing her old hits or record new material for him after 'Butterflies': 'When she started yelling at me I was always going to start yelling back. They were very silly rows. But she was very unhappy in her private life at the time, and that carried over into her public life.'

If there was one place that Dusty was not unhappy it was at Debbie Dannell's house. Debbie, who was Dusty's hairdresser for over ten years, was a straight-talking cockney with bleached blonde hair who lived with her husband Andy, a mechanic, in Borehamwood, Hertfordshire. Although Debbie would often have to sidestep the odd flying hairspray can or brush, Dusty adored her and found being with someone so unaffected therapeutic. It also helped that Debbie drove a truck like a fiend, could dismantle a car engine in a single bound and loved football. Dusty would often turn up at Boreham Wood completely unannounced, hoping to find Debbie or Andy in. If there was a match on TV and Andy's friends were round everyone would sit on the floor drinking beer and smoking. Dusty would often join them, turning up with a case of beer for them, a case of diet Coke for herself and her menthol cigarettes. She was as informed about the game as any of 'the lads' and shouted just as loudly. Often Dusty would get Debbie and Andy tickets for American football at Wembley, sending a driver to pick them up. Dusty would buy popcorn and hot dogs and the three of them would sit in the stands with Dusty debating with Debbie which player she thought had the best backside.

Often she would turn up at Debbie's during the day and let herself in. There in the quiet, unable to be reached by anyone, it was an escape for her. She would make coffee, smoke a couple of cigarettes and then curl up on the front room couch with Debbie's dog Pebbles. Debbie says that every time she came in when Dusty was there, the dog, who would usually rush up to greet its owner, never moved from Dusty's side. Dusty, who had never been able to sleep properly, could sleep on Debbie's couch for hours. When she finally woke up, Debbie would go to the local McDonald's and get her a Big Mac and fries and they would spend the evening talking about very ordinary things like a couple of girlfriends. Because Dusty was so keen on architecture and design – particularly airport buildings which with her obsession for space, planes and getting away fascinated her – sometimes Debbie would tear relevant things out of magazines and keep them to show her.

By 1987 Dusty was back in Los Angeles and at Helene's. Nothing was getting any better.

One day Vicki rang her at Helene's house to say that Allee Willis, whose songs had provided hits for the Pointer Sisters and Earth, Wind and Fire and who knew Vicki was now managing Dusty, had called. Did she know where Dusty was because she'd written a song with Neil Tennant and Chris Lowe 'and the boys love Dusty and want her to do it'. Dusty's initial reaction was no, as it so often was. 'Then there was a pause,' says Vicki.

' "Who are they?" asked Dusty. "You know," I said, "West End Girls".' Oh yes, said Dusty, recollecting who the Pet Shop Boys were and remembering that she really liked that record. 'They're two lads, I think they're gay and you know Allee writes a great song and she's lovely, so why don't you just listen to it and see what you think?' Vicki said. 'Dusty was very good, she listened to it directly it arrived and said yes straight away.'

The song was 'What Have I Done To Deserve This' and it was to give Dusty her first hit for over twenty years.

Neil Tennant and Chris Lowe had been writing songs together since 1981 after they had met in a London record shop. By the end of the eighties they were a highly successful recording team, Lowe's synthesiser music and Tennant's lightly melancholic voice producing a string of hits that crossed from huge success in gay clubs to straight record buyers, giving the duo number one chart positions in England and America. Ironically, 'Go West' had even ended up as a macho roar from the British football terraces as male fans changed the lyrics to 'two [or three or four] nil' in encouragement to their team.

When they wrote 'What Have I Done To Deserve This' with Willis they knew it had to be a duet with Tennant singing along with a female voice. The only singer he had any interest in was Dusty, but the Pet Shop Boys had to fight hard to get her on board. For once it was nothing to do with Dusty herself. When Tennant had put the proposition to EMI Records they weren't keen. She was a bit of a problem wasn't she, not to mention a bit of a 'has-been'? Why didn't they look for someone newer, fresher? Tennant and Lowe were adamant and they were successful enough to get their way.

Although Tennant was slightly nervous because he'd heard Dusty would sometimes sing only one word at a time, the sessions for the single went remarkably smoothly. One reason was that Dusty admired the Pet Shop Boys' finely tuned ear for sound – like Dusty herself Tennant and Lowe had held out against the record company not just because she was their favourite singer but because they knew her vulnerable huskiness would sit well with Tennant's voice. When she arrived at the studios Dusty had asked Tennant and Lowe how they wanted her to sound. 'Like you,' they replied.

The other reason was that for the first time in her life Dusty didn't feel any responsibility for the sessions. In a way they were nothing to do with her. 'All the decisions were taken out of my hands, which I was very relieved about,' she said later. This was Tennant and Lowe's project and if it failed so what? She was, after all, getting used to that.

Dusty was relaxed. She was relatively happy. After all the hardship in Los Angeles she was now staying at the Churchill Hotel in London and drinking so much coffee that room service staff were rushed off their feet. Although, as ever, she fretted over the way she looked on the video for the single – older, bigger, heavier – it was, at least, better than a photograph: 'Much harder to hit a moving target!' In the studio she asked Tennant and Lowe if they thought the record would make number one. 'Do you know I've only had one number one in my life.' She boxed Lowe's ears when he cheekily pointed out that the Pet Shops Boys had had two.

By September she was back in Los Angeles and 'What

Have I Done To Deserve This' was giving her the second biggest hit of her career, getting to number two in both the British and American charts. Suddenly things were looking up in a way she could not have foreseen even six months previously. She began to consider moving back to England but could not contemplate leaving Nicholas and Malaysia, her last two cats, and the draconian British quarantine laws meant they would be locked away for six months. 'Animals are very stabilising,' she told a reporter from the *Daily Mirror*. 'When everything's in chaos you know you have to open a can to feed them or clear up a litter tray.'

Meanwhile the Pet Shop Boys' manager was ringing Vicki. Tennant and Lowe had been asked to write the theme song for a film being made about the Profumo scandal and they wanted Dusty to record it. It would, of course, be the perfect match: Dusty the sixties icon singing about a sixties scandal that had rocked the British government at the time. It was a tale of an MP's indiscretion with a call girl, of a Russian spy and a Harley Street doctor. More, it was the story of a British 'morality' that had not changed since the Victorian era, of sexual prurience and its ultimate result – suicide.

The resulting track, 'Nothing Has Been Proved' with the characters of Mandy Rice-Davies, Christine Keeler, Stephen Ward and John Profumo all given an air-brushing by Dusty's breathy, almost tender, voice, would give her another top five hit and put her firmly back in the headlines herself. From now on her work was clearly destined to be in Britain and the closest she could get with the cats in tow was Holland. She had friends in Amsterdam, she could fly to London from there in less than an hour and the Dutch had no quarantine laws.

19

Herengracht 125 is a huge house overlooking a canal in Amsterdam. Like many of the city's famous ornately roofed and gabled buildings it was originally built in 1635 to accommodate the wealthy (in this case Frans Banning Kok, the central figure in Rembrandt's painting *The Night Watch*), but from the late nineteenth century it had been used for offices and the inside had been pulled apart.

In May 1987 interior designer Pieter van der Zwan and his partner Edwin Prins, a production manager for Dutch TV, took the house over, restoring it to its original glory. Its five-window-wide main rooms overlooked the water and in the summer the sunlight was filtered through the elm trees on the canal. Van der Zwan and Prins created five apartments in the house round a peaceful inner courtyard and lived in the largest, with its eighteenth-century mantelpiece, themselves.

A furry toy animal hopped across the windowsill of Herengracht 125 executing a peculiar little dance from left to right. It was Pieter and Edwin's first startling glimpse of Dusty (or at least her personality). She had been out shopping with her friend Nancy Fox-Martin in the city centre and was now on the way back to her apartment. Fox-Martin, who Dusty originally knew from New York, had been living in the city for a number of years and it was she whom Dusty had phoned when she realised her time in America had run out. Amsterdam was also, despite its bourgeois appearance, an informal city, long associated with being at the vanguard of sensible drug legislation and having a libertarian attitude towards its large lesbian and gay population.

Nancy Fox-Martin had bought the penthouse that Pieter and Edwin left when they took on the house in Herengracht and now she introduced Dusty to the two men who had become her friends. Despite her good post-shopping mood Dusty was still shy meeting the couple and, overawed by both them and the house, she made a beeline for their two cats: cat-talk was always a good way to break the ice. Soon she was dropping into Herengracht for a chat or a cup of tea and when she had to go to London for talks about her work Pieter would go round to her apartment and feed Nicholas and Malaysia.

One day he got a phone call from Dusty. She had flu she said, did he have any vitamin C? 'I feel like I've been run over by a train.' It was typical of Dusty that she would not just be able to ring someone because she was lonely and it's just as likely that she concocted the flu story altogether. Whatever, Pieter went over to her apartment. 'Although it was beautiful and expensively furnished I realised how depressing it was.' At the rear, rather than the canal side, the view from the windows was of the house that Anne Frank and her family had hidden in during the war and from which the Nazis had dragged them to concentration camps. It wasn't surprising that Pieter suddenly found it so depressing; although with her new success Dusty had finally stopped cutting herself it was here that she would play Tchaikovsky records and weep endlessly about the past fifteen years.

Dusty, who by now had fallen in love with the huge light rooms at Herengracht, heard from Nancy that one set of tenants was moving out so one of Pieter and Edwin's apartments would be free to rent. Would Nancy please ask them if she could move in? She couldn't bear to do it herself in case she was being a nuisance or they didn't like to say no. Pieter and Edwin, great admirers of her work and charmed by her personality, were thrilled. In February Dusty arrived at Herengracht with five suitcases and two cats. Settled in her duplex apartment she was completely private, but if she wanted to, she could look down into the courtyard and see from the lights if Pieter was still up. Because he worked from home she would often ring him during the day 'just to talk about very mundane things', sometimes he'd go upstairs for a coffee, and sometimes she'd go down for dinner. Often they would chat until dawn broke.

By now there was talk of the Pet Shop Boys becoming involved in an album project with Dusty and she had decided that the black swirling clothes which hid her late-forties spread had to go. It was time to get back in shape. Although she was smoking heavily, she would now be on bizarre crash diets: cauliflower and ice cream washed down with diet Coke. For the convivial owners of Herengracht this sometimes presented a problem. Keen to introduce Dusty to people they thought would interest her, like Edwin's friend the television documentary-maker Boudewin Buch, they invited them both to dinner. Having cooked a beautiful meal Pieter was not best pleased when Dusty arrived clutching two Tupperware boxes containing her cauliflower and ice cream. They agreed that perhaps it would be better to meet people over coffee or at teatime. 'With other people around,' says Pieter, 'I always noticed how shy she was. When we were alone together we had a lot of fun but she seemed to hide herself in front of people she didn't know well.'

Since the first Amsterdam apartment, Dusty had become increasingly interested in the story of Anne Frank. It was a piece of history she had known about but which she felt, typically, she was not a hundred per cent *au fait* with. One evening Pieter and Edwin invited Miep and Jan Gies for dinner. Miep had been the girl who had helped Anne hide in the attic room and who had kept her famous diary for any survivors after the Nazis dispatched the Frank family to the concentration camps. Dusty had been asked downstairs to join everyone after the meal. At 10 p.m. Pieter's phone rang. It was Dusty: she was really sorry but she couldn't come down because she had a headache. Five minutes later, probably realising that you didn't snub people as brave and important as Miep Gies, she rang back. 'Look,' she said to Pieter, 'I don't have a headache at all, it's just I've never met war heroes before and I'm really nervous.'

It was, in a way, typically Dusty. She always needed someone to put her case for her before she turned up – 'Don't be put off but this girl is very shy' – then she could go in without having to combat anyone's expectations of her. In the event she arrived, ironically, 'like a schoolgirl about to meet a diva'. Pieter got out his videos of Dusty at her Albert Hall concert and an extract from the film of Anne Frank with Mary Steenberg as Miep and played them both as a way of breaking the ice and 'introducing' the women to each other. Dusty sat on the floor with Miep and after the tapes were finished they chatted about their lives as though they had known each other for years.

In many respects Herengracht was, for Dusty, the most suitable place she had lived since Westbourne Terrace over twenty years earlier. As then, she could be alone when she chose to, find company within the house when she felt like it. Better still, Pieter was one of the few people she knew who kept the same mad hours she did: not going to bed until three, four or five in the morning and then sleeping late. But Amsterdam itself was more of a problem. For almost the past two decades she had lived in a country where she could drive to the drugstore at three in the morning and do her shopping. In Holland the shops closed at six at night and nobody living along the canals would think of trying to drive anywhere. Still, she seemed happier than she had done in years, partly because it was almost certain that, despite everything that had happened, it looked as though her career was about to take off again. Within a few months she cheered up even more: she had found the one store in the city that was open all night and she regularly took a taxi there and back to do her shopping.

The success of 'Nothing Has Been Proved' had made Dusty optimistic about life and she was back in London when *Scandal* was opening. She had been invited to the première and had flown Pieter in for the occasion, but on the morning of the opening Dusty said she had a cold. 'I'm not going,' she told him, 'but you certainly are.' Although she'd now had two hit singles in a row she still felt they were really the Pet Shop Boys' work not her own. More, she couldn't face the first-night crowds. She thought they would want to see the sixties Dusty – slim, very blonde, huge black eyes. She doubted if they would be ready to see her as she really was these days, close up and in the flesh, and it's likely she didn't want them to.

When Dusty got back to Amsterdam Madeline Bell was touring with the ill-fated musical *A Night At The Cotton Club*. Pat and her husband Tony came to town for a long weekend and the four old friends met up and went out for a sumptuous meal in one of Amsterdam's best Thai restaurants. Having not seen her since the night in Los Angeles, Madeline was delighted at how well Dusty looked. 'It was wonderful to see her so "up" and nothing like she'd been. She was optimistic and seemed really okay.'

On 16 April 1989 it was Dusty's fiftieth birthday. Pieter and Edwin went upstairs to give her flowers and some beautiful earrings and toasted her with diet Coke. But for the rest of the day Dusty stayed in her apartment. Being fifty was the big one, over halfway through her life. She knew she'd not live as long again and she wasn't taking to the ageing process graciously. Looking in the mirror she saw a woman who had been through a lot – and it was showing. What she needed was a taste of success on her own terms after so long. She couldn't keep commuting from Amsterdam to London and albums took much longer to record than singles ever did. She finally gave up the unequal fight and decided that the cats would have to be locked away in England for a while if she was ever to get on with her life.

Wellbank was the closest house to the quarantine cattery near Heathrow Dusty could buy. Fairly new and rather nondescript, it was at least near enough to Maidenhead in Berkshire for Dusty to be able to do her shopping easily. Although she could move in without needing builders or decorators, there turned out to be one major problem with the house: the garage was so small that she could not put her car in. The first time she tried to drive in she found that, once parked, she couldn't open the car doors far enough to squeeze out. After two attempts, and realising that it had nothing to do with putting on weight, she gave up and backed the car out again – cursing that measuring the width of the garage was the one thing she'd forgotten to do in her hurry to find a house.

Still, here, back in the English countryside where she had not lived since she was a child, and now on her own, she led what seemed to be a relatively calm life after the chaos of the last few years. She even dutifully trotted off to meetings of the local residents association. When Pieter arrived in Oxford to be with Edwin who was working on a new television show, Dusty went up in her new car and took her ex-landlord off to see Blenheim Palace before they went for tea in Woodstock, a pretty old village in the Cotswolds. It was getting late by the time Dusty drove Pieter back to his hotel in Oxford and they had to stop when she realised that she had run out of shampoo. When Dusty came out of the shop everyone rushed to the shop window to watch her get back into the car.

After all the years of being largely ignored in America, being back in England must have been a delight for Dusty who had always thrived on the attention of her fans. When Helene came over for a visit she remarked that she found English shopping habits peculiar: why did everyone at the supermarket in Maidenhead wheel their trolleys round in a line, following each other bumper to bumper? It was only later she realised that this was unusual, even for the peculiar British. The shoppers were following Dusty round the store, watching to see what she was putting into her basket.

The same spring Dusty went into the studio to record *Reputation*. Of the album's ten tracks at least eight could have been released as successful singles. Dusty had not produced such a commercially viable album since the 1960s and *A Girl Called Dusty*. If her choice of material usually reflected her state of mind and emotions, then *Reputation* was interesting in that it reflected the dichotomy between the public and the private. It was with A&R director Tristram Penna that Dusty would spend long hours at the EMI offices in Manchester Square working out the songs. For years in America one of the things that had always upset Dusty so much was the constant changes of personnel that accompanied each switch of record labels or each 'buy-out' of one record company by another just as her tracks were about to be released. To keep herself steady and feeling a little more confident she needed to construct some kind of emotional tie with the people she worked with. Penna confirmed the habit Dusty had started in the sixties but had never been able to construct in America – of having someone young, male, smart and gay close to her and her work. During the course of *Reputation* the pair became friends, Dusty regularly visiting Tris in hospital when he was suddenly taken ill and, when he was fit and healthy, leaving him notes on his desk at EMI ironically noting that fame is 'so fleeting'.

The Pet Shop Boys produced five of the tracks, including their own 'Daydreaming', a painful exposé of a fated relationship, and, with Julian Mendelsohn, a version of Goffin and King's 'Just Want To Stay Here' which took the cuddly, slow original and turned it into a fast, playful

Dear Tris,
    Came by — please
could I have some posters for "Reputation"
single + album and do you have anything
left on "In Private" like the one on the door
(2 doors down) — I have nothing egotistical
to put on my walls and fame is so
fleeting — where are the things I'm supposed
to sign — will be in town again next
Thursday for Kraut press.
                Love
                    Dust

dance track. Some of the other songs were produced by Dan Hartman. Hartman, a good-looking young American, had already been responsible for bringing some of America's finest black singers back into the charts after a dearth of hits, including Tina Turner and James Brown, and Dusty already knew him from his friendship with Vicki and Nona Hendryx.

The Hartman tracks were produced at his Multi Level Studios, a rambling riverside house in Connecticut that was also his home. Dusty and Helene stayed there during the sessions which were only slow this time because Hartman was as fussy as Dusty about her vocals, and stopped and started her over and over again. The combination worked particularly well on Allee Willis's second song for Dusty, the sexy, driving 'Send It To Me' written with Lauren Wood. Yet the hardest track to listen to on the album was produced by Paul O'Duffy. Dusty is at her most heartbreaking on the Rupert Hine/Janet Obstoj song of supplication, 'Arrested By You'.

Reputation produced Dusty's third hit single in a row, 'In Private', and a return to newspaper column inches. The album was, said the critics, 'an inspired deployment of Dusty's voice and aura as sixties icon'; her most 'potent work in decades'; 'a satisfying renaissance'; she took on a new round of interviews in a positive frame of mind. She was, she said, very grateful to the Pet Shop Boys for her recent successes and she felt that the album, with its mixture of producers, had started to give her confidence and 'allow me a little more freedom'.

Although when 'Arrested By You' was released as a fourth single and did not do so well, mainly because it was not a dance track, suddenly Dusty was hot again. It

Jenny Cohen's nightmare:
Dusty in her 'NASA space suit'
and trying to do her bit for
Peter Stringfellow in 1985.

Always an animal lover, Dusty
(above) at the Los Angeles
Wildlife Way Station where
she was campaigning for a halt
in the import of exotic animals
as pets.

With Chris Lowe and Neil
Tennant of the Pet Shop Boys
for a triumphant return to hit
records in 1989.

1989 / 21642 COPYRIGHT EMI RECORDS (UK)— PHOTOGRAPHER: PAUL RIDER

DUSTY SPRINGFIELD

Fame again in her 50s: Dusty's inimitable remarks on the contact sheets for her CD with the Pet Shop Boys.

(*Left*) Dusty in good shape and in high spirits during a shoot for her Nashville album cover. A week later she was diagnosed with breast cancer.

(*Below*) In remission, Dusty undertakes a gruelling round of promotion for the album.

(*Left*) The accidental tourist: Dusty during a trip to Blenheim Palace with Pieter van der Zwan.

(*Below*) Friend and healer Lee Everett-Alkin at Henley with Dusty's cat Nicholas.

(*Below*) Henley, Christmas, 1997: Dusty, fighting cancer, opens her 'Boxing Nun' Christmas present from singer Nona Hendryx.

must have been an extraordinary feeling, like the climb to the top of a rollercoaster. Now it was easier to get a deal with a record company for a new album. The cats were out of quarantine and Dusty was out of trouble. Even when Malaysia was run over by a car in the countryside Dusty was philosophical. The cat, she said, had gone to 'the great litter tray in the sky'.

20

The first intimation that Dusty might be seriously ill came in 1994 at the Bennett House studio when she was cutting *A Very Fine Love* for Columbia. Nashville was experiencing its worst ice storm for a decade. When it started Dusty was thrilled with the snow. She and Pat stood outside the studios, huddled up in thick jackets and scarves against the cold, smoking cigarettes and watching how, beautiful but deadly, the snow immediately iced over the leaves on the trees until they glinted a hard crystalline in the late afternoon sun.

Despite the success of *Reputation* the Nashville sessions were not going well. Dusty would usually turn up at four in the afternoon and work into the night but, as so often happened these days, her voice would give up on her. Although Nashville was firmly placed in the record-buying psyche as the home of country music, particularly those good ole girls with tortured hair, it also had a place in the annals of soul music. It was the base for Monument Records where Ella Washington and Joe Simon had recorded in the late 1960s and early 1970s and for other labels and studios, which gave Joe Tex and Esther Phillips hits – records Dusty had been a fan of directly they were released.

Dusty remained fascinated by the history of the place and

had read up as much as she could on Nashville's environs. When she had a day off she would drive Pat round the area to look at old graveyards. Here she would give Pat a lecture on the American civil war. 'She knew everything – dates, places. She had this amazing facility to learn and remember. She just soaked it all up.'

Nashville had an added attraction for Dusty. Now into her fifties and no longer the slim young thing she'd been at the height of her success, she began to regret not having stayed on back in the early 1960s when the Springfields had gone there. It seemed to her that her career would have been very different there with its history of sad singing women who battled against the odds such as Patsy Cline. Audiences in Nashville were loyal to these women no matter if they put on weight and wore outrageous clothes. All that counted to them was the authenticity of the experience, usually expressed in their bruised voices.

For her old American manager Barry Krost, who considered Dusty's hair to be 'a lethal weapon', country music had been the obvious answer to Dusty's lack of direction, but when he suggested it to her in Los Angeles she was still desperate to rekindle her past success as a white soul singer and couldn't see how she could turn that around. Although the original plan for the album had been to call it *Dusty In Nashville* after the success of the Memphis sessions, Columbia decided against it in the belief that it would lead audiences mistakenly to expect a country album.

By the second day of the storm trees were down, tumbling over from the weight of the ice and crashing through the power lines. The lights had gone out in Ernest Tubbs's record store and the Grand Ole Opry was to fight with its generator for days. With recording impossible, the sessions were postponed. Dusty and Pat, holed up in a motel nearby, had no heat, no light and not a torch between them. 'I took Dust up the one and only candle they had in the place because we had to just go to our beds, it was the only place to keep warm.' That night Pat, back in her room, had to take her make-up off by the flame of her cigarette lighter.

Although the power was out, the telephones were still working. Dusty, who had been expecting Faye to come down from LA, rang her. 'You can't come – there's no light, no heat and no food.' The next morning she and Pat decided to set out the sixty miles to the next town where they had generators in case of an emergency such as this. It was a terrifying, icy drive with the storm still raging and the car sliding across the roads, but at least eventually they had food and warmth. The storm lasted for five days and when Dusty got back into the studios one of the musicians returned with the sad news that his entire tank of tropical fish had frozen into a solid block of ice.

The six-week Nashville sessions were turning into twelve weeks and Dusty's voice was still sore and playing up, but she put it down to the cold weather. Finally it went completely and, probably to convince the record company it wasn't Dusty being her infamous self, Pat dragged her to a top throat specialist at Nashville's main hospital. 'There didn't seem much he could do but he gave her a very thorough examination and then he looked at her very hard and said, "When you go home please promise me that you'll go and get checked out over there." He had a reputation for curing everyone, but he couldn't fix her and I think he knew that there was cancer in her body.'

Dusty had only been back from America for four days when she discovered a lump in her breast and rang Vicki who was in London. 'Typically she didn't tell me until way into the phone call. We'd been talking about promotion for the album and she just slipped it in.' Vicki asked her what the doctors had said about the lump. 'Oh,' said Dusty, 'I don't have a doctor, you know I don't go to doctors.' Vicki immediately got off the phone and called her own doctor, arranged an appointment and rang Dusty back. 'It's just not convenient, Vicki I've got all these things to do . . .' It was very rare for Vicki to lose her temper but this time she did. 'I said, "Just shut the fuck up." Luckily the fact that the doctor was a woman and in Harley Street probably made a difference.'

Dusty was now living at Frogmill, a house that Lee Everett had found for her, close to the one that Lee shared with her second husband John Alkin, in Berkshire. It was in Hurley, a village where the church and some of the pale stone houses had been built in the seventeenth century. In the cloisters of the church the walkways had been bricked in and turned into beautiful rambling old houses, some of which still had secret passages next to the vast open fireplaces. Through these the Cavaliers had escaped into the surrounding countryside when Cromwell's Roundheads came galloping into the village looking for traitors – all fascinating stuff for our amateur historian.

Over the years Hurley had grown, first as the rural idyll for retired colonels and their families and then, much to the chagrin of the locals, as an overspill for council tenants in nearby Maidenhead. Frogmill lay somewhere in between the old and the boxed new. Dusty's house was one in a series of newly converted barns built in a semicircle. Although the downstairs rooms tended to be dark, the lounge upstairs had Dusty's favourite almost double-height ceilings that she'd had at Dona Teresa. It went into the rafters and had a panoramic view of the Thames bending its way through the English countryside. There were ducks and swans and coots' nests on the bank, and in the summer busy river traffic to watch. Built round a huge communal garden the house had enough trees and space to keep Nicholas the cat happy for a lifetime.

The Harley Street doctor had immediately rung the Royal Marsden Hospital in Chelsea to make Dusty an appointment. As they came out of the surgery Dusty turned to Pat and Vicki. She knew the Royal Marsden was the best cancer hospital in London. 'It doesn't look good, does it?' The pair tried to encourage her although they were worried themselves. 'Well, we just don't know – let's wait and see what the specialist says.'

Dusty went back into the studios to finish off her side of a 'duet' with Darryl Hall, Diane Warren's 'Wherever Would I Be' from the film *While You Were Sleeping* (as was often the case with her duets Dusty and Hall actually recorded their tracks separately). A few days later the Marsden confirmed what Vicki's doctor had suspected, that the lump was not benign and Dusty had cancer. The diagnostic specialist and Dusty had been talking about their cats. 'She had a cat called Moses,' Dusty recalled later to *Woman* magazine 'and she was looking at the results of my cells on a screen and I saw her face change and I thought, Hell, that's it, and eventually she said, "I'm afraid it's a tumour and one we just don't want."'

Even though Dusty had been worried when she came out of Harley Street she couldn't believe the worst was actually happening. It seemed more than life giving her a sideswipe. Her work with the Pet Shop Boys had made her a success all over again. Now Quentin Tarantino had used her 'Son Of A Preacher Man' in the cult film *Pulp Fiction* and there was a whole new audience of teenagers in dark suits who wanted to know all about her. Bad timing. The specialist suggested a course of chemotherapy followed by surgery to remove the lump and any other tissue they were worried about, then radiotherapy. Only human, Dusty had a good cry but she was also Dusty; she'd taken enough people with her to suggest that now, she, Vicki, Pat, and a newly concerned Tom, back in touch with his sister, all went out to lunch. Over twenty years Tom had had very little contact, if any, with Dusty. Peggy Albrecht was always bewildered that when she and Dusty were in London, staying in Chelsea below Tom's flat, they had never seen him, not even to say hello to. Dusty's description of their relationship as 'ambivalent' seemed something of an understatement.

It was obvious to Vicki that the chemo would make it impossible for Dusty to promote the new album and Dusty asked her to tell the record company. Vicki also knew that there was a chance Columbia might decide not to put the album out at all, but when she met record executive Kip Krones he suggested that they simply put it on 'hold' until Dusty had recovered from the treatment and was feeling better. It was the first piece of good news they'd had and it made Dusty feel more optimistic about her chances of recovery.

When she was 'clean' and off drink and drugs, Dusty could often be an essentially very private person. Her backing singer Simon Bell would find that whenever he'd driven her around, and despite the fact that he'd been with her most of the day, when they got back to Frogmill Dusty wanted to be on her own. 'I expect you'll want to go up the road now,' she'd say. 'She never wanted you to stay and watch TV or have a coffee,' says Simon. 'And whether that was because she didn't want you there or because she couldn't believe you'd possibly want to be with her for the evening . . .'

Bell had been a Dusty fan all his life. As a teenager in Glasgow his bedroom walls had been covered with two images: one was *Dr Kildare*'s Richard Chamberlain, the other was Dusty in a variety of sparkling dresses and dramatic arms-up poses. Dusty had first met him when he was singing back-up for Madeline in 1978. When she'd come over from America for the *It Begins Again* album promotion she'd needed backing singers. Madeline had suggested Simon because she knew that he was so besotted he could sing every Dusty song practically backwards.

In fact Dusty had originally met him in 1964, though she had no recollection of it. Some time before he had realised he was gay, he had screamed over the balcony at her on stage, chased her car through the streets and got her to autograph his wrist. We're talking serious fandom here and it's likely that, once she found out, Dusty found it amusing that he was now working for her. She liked the fact that he was musically on the ball. More, she was enamoured by his enthusiasm to be her stand-in. When she had to do lighting and sound checks at Drury Lane, Simon, roughly the same height and build, would be only too happy to do them for her: 'waving my arms about and everything – very sad!'

Although she had used Simon for back-up on a few singles and the odd concert, when her first illness was diagnosed he came to take on more of the driving. They would go on shopping trips together and sometimes she'd say, 'Let's go through Ealing and I'll show you where I used to live,' even though her old house was no longer there. Sometimes she'd ask him to drive through High Wycombe and do the same thing. Often he would be dispatched to undertake 'mercy visits' that she couldn't make herself: it was Simon who turned up at the Cavendish Hotel in the spring of 1992. Pieter van der Zwan had come in from Holland and had been due to visit Dusty down at Frogmill but had collapsed with a stomach virus. When he rang to tell her he couldn't make it she informed him a rescue package would be on the way. Within an hour Simon had arrived with Dusty's parcel: flowers, some fruit, a thermometer and a copy of the camp book on Hollywood's major 1950s stars Bette Davis and Joan Crawford, *The Divine Feud.*

Before she was ill and when she was in remission, Dusty would revert to an old habit. On Sunday mornings she would drive herself to Heathrow airport to pick up the early newspapers. Once there she would stay for a couple of hours on her own watching the planes take off. Why did she do it? 'Oh, to watch them go up in the sky and think of where I'd been in my life and where I might go.' She was living alone and she was liking it. 'This is a period in my life I've been given to concentrate on what I'm supposed to be – a singer,' she told the *Daily Mirror* and added that relationships and her didn't really go together, mainly because 'I fall in love about three times a day.'

Equally, when she found out she was ill she only rang a few friends to tell them, and even then she slipped it into the middle of the conversation, almost as an after-thought. Norma and Faye had stayed in fairly regular contact with her for years, now they would talk more often and Dusty read up on everything she could find to do with breast cancer, from self-help books to medical journals. 'She became an expert,' says Vicki. 'She would check out all the treatments, she knew exactly everything the doctors were suggesting and what effect the treatment would have, she even knew all the medical terms.'

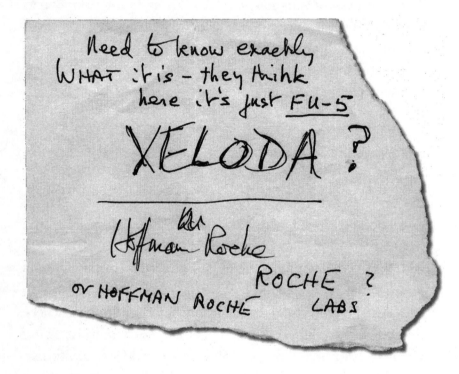

Most of all Dusty kept a constant watch on the American medical journals and anything Simon could pull off the Internet about new treatments, scribbling to Vicki to find out anything she could about the latest American cancer-treating drug.

One day Tedda rang from America but Dusty refused to talk to her. It wasn't that she hated her for the past, much more that she was still besotted by the singer and terrified she would get drawn back into a relationship which, surely, would not just end in tears but the very real possibility of something far worse. She would confide in Helene that she wished she had spoken to Tedda because, 'I do love her, you know, but . . . our relationship was always impossible.'

Because she'd beaten so many other things in her life Dusty always believed she could beat the breast cancer. It was an odd thing about her that friends noticed – how she'd make the same crisis out of the cleaners losing a pair of her trousers as she would about an opening night. Now here was a real enemy invading her body, not the demons she'd summoned up for so long, and she faced her illness in an almost sanguine mood. It was much the same attitude she'd had the day in LA when Helene had taken her out on a day pass from the psychiatric ward at the hospital at Redondo Beach.

That day, on the way back they were three hours late, partly because Dusty had wanted to go first to LAX to watch the planes and then drive into the mountains. The two women had drawn up at a stop sign in downtown Los Angeles and Dusty was fumbling about in her handbag when her car door was wrenched open, a man's arm went round her neck and he started to pull her out from the passenger seat. Dusty tried to fight him off as Helene jumped out of the car and screamed at him. With other cars now pulling up behind them the man suddenly let Dusty go and ran off with her bag.

'You should have locked your door – what do you think you were doing with your damn door unlocked!' Helene screamed as Dusty shook herself off and got back in the car.

'Well,' said Dusty calmly, 'all the time I've been in LA this has never happened to me before. Anyway,' she laughed, 'all my medication's under the seat and he didn't get anything worth while – unless of course he's a drag queen, because he's got all my make-up. So, no harm done.'

By the autumn of 1995 Dusty had finished her treatment at the Marsden and, although often very tired from the effects of the radio- and chemotherapy, she and Vicki had given Columbia the go-ahead to put out *A Very Fine Love*. Produced by Tom Shapiro, the album was a step away from the gay sensibility of *Reputation*. Instead it was a tight, narrative package opening on the philosophical optimism of the anthemic Will Jennings/Martee LeBow 'Roll Away', with its nod at the Impressions' 'People Get Ready'. It closed with the raunchy gospel-tinged K.T. Oslin/Jerry Gillespie number 'Where Is A Woman To Go?' with K.T. and Mary Chapin-Carpenter on back-up (the answer, ironically, given that Dusty had been 'dry' for ten years, was to the nearest bar). In between it would take a genius to guess the struggle the sessions had been – particularly on Dusty's lived-in vocals on 'All I Have To Offer You Is Love' and the potently sexy yearning of her voice on 'Go Easy On Me'.

'I stumbled through the record,' she would say in her promotional interviews for the album. 'I'd work ten minutes, we'd take a half-hour break.'

All the journalists who interviewed Dusty during her promotion for *A Very Fine Love* wrote long profile pieces in which Dusty was as honest as she could be about her past, her current life and her future. They were all flattering (most journalists were always completely enamoured of her) and rather touching. Most skirted round the issue of her sexuality. For the *Sunday Telegraph* she was 'quite simply the best female pop singer Britain has ever produced';

for *The Times* she remained unique 'so ingrained in our national consciousness that it's hard for us to think of her as anything but the arch-diva of sixties pop'. When she flew to New York for American promotion the press coverage was equally adulatory. With her hair now short and silver Dusty wore black with turquoise jewellery. 'She looked like a very beautiful lady golfer,' wrote the *Village Voice*'s Stacey D'Erasmo, a woman clearly smitten, and she noted, amongst other things, how short Dusty was; for the *New York Times* Dusty could 'with a mere vocal wink still go places that aren't in the repertory of their [other younger singers] imaginations'.

One journalist in London noticed that there was rather a lot of canned cat food piled up in Dusty's Churchill Hotel suite, used while she was promoting her record. Indeed there was. Dusty had now been convinced by Vicki to get a fax machine at the house. Her first fax was typically Dusty: 'Mission accomplished – GRRR. Please send me a nice fax IMMEDIATELY! to test my new machine. Yours kicking and screaming into the 90s.' After that she had spent many happy hours faxing her manager on the subject of American cat food for Nicholas. This was Gerber's baby food and since Nicholas was now eating so much she needed two hundred cartons. Was it coming by ship or on a truck? Did it have to be protected from freezing or should it actually be frozen? Over less than a month there were as many faxes on the subject of cat food as there were about money, the many offers of beer commercials, large-scale TV specials, and a Three Divas tour on the lines of Three Tenors – this time with Dusty, Dionne Warwick and Petula Clark (she was tempted by the diva idea but it came to nothing). Vicki was starting to regret having suggested the machine to Dusty except that there would occasionally be one to make her laugh: 'Furthermore,' faxed Dusty, after a lengthy discussion about why she felt like 'a performing dog', 'Nicholas just threw up on my Harrods account bill, so that just about says it all.'

In all her interviews Dusty talked about her cancer treatment. As usual she made it part serious/part joke: how her body had responded so well because after all the years of drink and drugs 'it still liked poison. It was saying "Yes! Give me some poison"'; how the illness had been 'a learning curve'; how 'I never expected to live this long, so all of this is uncharted territory'. But journalist Louise Harding noticed that despite how Dusty looked she was obviously weak: 'She lost the thread of our conversation several times towards the end. She began to weep for the slightest reason.'

The promotional tour was, indeed, exhausting, culminating in a party Sony threw in Manhattan, but Dusty knew it was the least she could do for Columbia given their patience and understanding, and now she was back on her feet she also knew that you had to stay in the public consciousness to sell records. Neither 'Roll Away', the single, nor the album sold spectacularly because, said Kip Krones, it was hard to get thirty-year-old radio programmers to play it. But Columbia got reasonable figures and Dusty got a lot of magazine cover lines in a period when Aretha Franklin was having to rely on singing commercials.

Whether British DJs were any kinder on her than the Americans is debatable but at least she had a different kind of status in Britain, particularly amongst other musicians who themselves had spent half their lives listening to her voice. Dusty was booked for a series of TV appearances, which resulted in a rash of faxes to Vicki about dresses, make-up, numbers and the minutiae of a Dusty appearance: 'Will have to be in make-up to go into make-up!' And Dusty did two important TV shows in 1996. One was the profile *Dusty – Full Circle* where she was such a 'natural' in front of the camera talking about her life that the original idea of having comediennes Jennifer Saunders and Dawn French do a spoof interview was dropped after the first ten minutes of editing.

The other was on Jools Holland's highly rated late-night BBC TV music programme *Later*. With Alison Moyet and Sinéad O'Connor doing back-up, Holland on piano and a gospel choir, Dusty gave a superb performance of 'Where Is A Woman To Go'. Nearly three decades after her Ronettes intonations she proved she had never lost the quality she had been born with, as her entreaty to make it 'bettah' showed.

It was to be Dusty's last TV appearance. *A Very Fine Love* would be her last album.

During the recording for the album a *Radio Times* journalist had turned up in Nashville to take her to lunch and write a piece to go with the broadcast of *Dusty – Full Circle* on British TV. Dusty made the *RT* man promise not to make her sound 'politically incorrect' – because she was smoking so much 'and eating meat and drinking diet Coke – a totally wanton woman!' As far as the Nashville recordings went, 'I'd been offered a lot of rent-a-diva type dance stuff and I'd have felt dumb promoting them. I'm a woman of a certain age and I'm comfortable with music that reflects my age.'

And the future? 'I haven't a clue. That's one of the wonderful things. Imagine how awful it would be to know the ending . . .'

21

To celebrate getting a clean bill of health from the Marsden, and having done the promotion for *A Very Fine Love,* Dusty decided to take a couple of weeks off and drive round Ireland with Helene. Whenever she made this kind of trip Dusty would plan everything in meticulous detail. Out would come the maps, the notebook, the pen and she would make a list of every tiny village on the route.

She loved the maps, always had. Unlike most musicians whose touring pattern consists of almost total alienation from their surroundings, whenever Dusty was off on the road – and particularly if she was touring in other countries – she pored over atlases, working out the exact relationship between where she was going to appear and the rest of the country. After they'd separated, when Faye was on a cruise round the Dalmatian coast, she would sometimes ring Dusty to tell her where she was, 'And she'd say, "right, well then you'll be going round here and then on to there, and oh this will be good because you'll see so-and-so." It was as though she was on the boat herself.' Once, when Dusty decided to take Helene to see Stonehenge she spent three days researching the most interesting route while Helene sat in her room tracing Druid history. 'So she'd be lost somewhere in the countryside and I'd be lost somewhere in 2000 BC and between us we researched enough to start on a trip.'

What was less certain was whether anyone driving with Dusty would live long enough to enjoy any of this careful planning.

Her eyesight was terrible. Once in Los Angeles on their way to a party Dusty had made Helene wear her glasses. As her friend staggered up the stairs into the room where the party was being held she practically reached out in front of herself: 'Dusty, I can't see a thing.'

'Now you know,' said the singer firmly. 'That's my vision all of the time. See, people think I'm standoffish or I ignore them, but I seriously can't see people until their faces are so close to mine that they're practically on top of me.' None the less such lack of vision did nothing to dampen her love of speed.

From the moment Dusty got her first car in Baker Street her driving terrified everyone. Friends thought it was amazing that large parts of London had not been decimated, given Dusty was behind the wheel of her car. Pat recalls that Dusty would often drive with a block of wood over the brake – being small it meant she could get more pressure, faster, when she needed to stop. 'When she got the sports car she decided to give me a ride in it and we tore up Baker Street with me sitting on Tom's lap and her zipping in and out of the traffic. I just sat there shaking thinking, oh shit, oh shit. Then she whizzed round the corner, stopped and grinned. "How was that?" and I fell out and couldn't answer.' In 1966 Dusty was taken to court and fined over £2,000 for knocking down the owner of a Mayfair boutique while she was driving down South Audley Street. Although the woman was not seriously injured the judge pointed out that the singer had been wearing dark glasses at night and driving too fast. In those days the fine was not a small amount, particularly since Dusty's car insurance was useless because the company, Fire, Auto and Marine, had collapsed.

Dusty desperately wanted to get back to Ireland. Somehow, since the chaos of America and the shock of her illness, she had been trying harder to define herself and find some roots. 'I am,' she said in many of the interviews she gave around the promotion of *A Very Fine Love*, 'Irish, not English, remember.' 'My name is O'Brien and I'm glad it is,' she told *Mojo* magazine around the same time. 'I'm glad my name is Mary Isobel Catherine Bernadette and I can weep at *Riverdance* and it makes me laugh.'

Six months before her trip she had made a video with cinematographer Seamus McGarvey and director Sean O'Hagan to go with 'Roll Away', a track from the album. McGarvey and O'Hagan had minor success with a couple of agit-prop videos, one with Sinéad O'Connor, and the idea for Dusty was to emphasise her Irish roots by filming on the windswept west coast of southern Ireland. Needless to say the shoot did not go according to plan. Dusty was insistent on having a huge American Winnebago truck to take her from the hotel to the beach location. When the wind got to her – her hair being blown in any direction was enough to stop her lip-syncing to the record mid-phrase – she suggested they might be able to construct a windbreak. 'We explained that, save for a Christo-style wrapping of the entire coastline, there was sod-all we could do about the wind,' recalled O'Hagan in an article for the *Observer* Sunday newspaper. 'We shambled along on the verge of panic.'

Dusty had broken down in tears during that afternoon and so O'Hagan and McGarvey sat up with her that night until the early hours of the morning talking to her about her life. The next day Dusty did a perfect shoot, wind or no wind. Although O'Hagan put it down to her behaviour as 'ever the diva, waiting until the eleventh hour then performing faultlessly, passionately, for the camera', it's just as likely that Dusty, exhausted from her hospital treatment and even more self-conscious than usual about her on-screen image, had actually made contact with her film-makers on a different level. Once she realised how much they admired her, she trusted them more behind the camera, and with her usual charm she bought the crew champagne to celebrate the end of filming.

During work for the video Dusty had stayed at Cregg Castle, once a Celtic stronghold, now a hotel on the wild western coast north of Galway, and had become friendly with the owners, Annemarie and her husband, nicknamed the Bog Man ostensibly because he came from a little way south. Dusty had rung Helene from Cregg saying it was 'just like Tarzana' and that she'd love it, it was exactly her kind of place: 'There are Irish wolfhounds and the ponies and sheep come into the house, all the animals.' Now she was determined they'd go there together. She mapped the route through tiny towns and villages with names in Gaelic and English and her handwritten instructions were most precise: 'go two and three-quarter miles then turn right . . .'

She drove, and Helene was in charge of directions. Within seconds they were arguing. Helene remembers they used to call themselves Laurel and Hardy until Jennifer Saunders and Joanna Lumley made *Absolutely Fabulous* such a huge hit on television. Then, with Helene being so tall and Dusty only five foot three, they became Lumley's 'Patsy' and Saunders's 'Edina'. Since Dusty refused to drive at less than eighty miles an hour around tiny country lanes full of hedge-lined blind corners, Helene could not bear to look out of the front window. 'I do have good peripheral vision and it was so frightening in case something was coming round that hedge. We argued through every village because her instructions always gave you multiple choices and I was usually too terrified to concentrate.' Sometimes they would pass so close to the walls of houses that Helene, with her side window down, would have curtains from passing kitchens flapping in her face.

They got lost, drove round the same villages three times and fought. 'Suddenly I'd see her hand go up and realise that she was steering with one hand and looking at her nail varnish – we should never have been let loose.' Once, as they tore through a town, there was a loud metallic click.

'What was that?' asked Dusty.

'It was your side view mirror hitting the side view mirror of the other car.'

'Well – he was going too fast.'

'Dusty, he was parked. It was a parked car we hit.'

Helen knew as soon as she said it that it was a mistake. Dusty scowled at her.

'Are you saying I'm driving too close?'

'I'm not saying you're driving too close, I'm just describing the events and the sound that was produced as a result. You can draw your own conclusions.'

Furious with this carefully chosen phrasing and the implied criticism, Dusty lost her temper. 'My driving's been fine with you up until now. You haven't said anything. If you don't like the way I drive – walk.'

This squabbling continued all day long. Yet by the evening they would laugh about it. 'On the road together was a comedy,' says Helene. 'It was hell, but in an odd way we travelled well together so it would always be the same and I always said yes to another trip.'

The drive up the western coast of Ireland was both spectacular and melancholic. The Atlantic Ocean remorselessly battered the cliffs and there was nothing to see through the fine sea spray and the heavy mist except the foam-topped waves hurling themselves at the shore and, occasionally, the rocky outline of Great Skellig ten miles offshore, once the home of Celtic monks. Somewhere, thousands of miles away, lay the eastern coast of America, where starving Irish families had desperately made the perilous journey to escape the great famine at home. Tiny campions and long tough sea grass clung to the cliffs and, away from the wind, wild pink and purple fuchsia smothered the hedgerows.

On the way to Cregg, Dusty and Helene passed Celtic sacred stones, crofters' cottages deserted and ruined, without roofs, their walls tumbling into the black earth of the peat bogs. When they eventually got to the castle Dusty was thrilled to hear Helene's stories of how the Celts fought off the Romans right there on their chariots. Most of all she loved to hear how the women had stood on top of the castle walls beating drums. In the evening Annemarie, her husband, Dusty and Helene would gather round a huge log fire. Annemarie would play the drum and Bog Man would play the complex Irish pipes and there would be singing from the pure voice of their thirteen-year-old daughter. Dusty would sit by the fire and listen very quietly. 'She was always looking for the ideal place, one that didn't really exist,' says Helene. 'But I saw her complete happiness in Ireland and it was not, as it turned out, destined to be a completely happy trip.'

One day Dusty decided that Helene had to go and see the Tor – a great ring of sacred stones. As usual Dusty did not get out of the car. It was the same wherever she took Helene – Stonehenge, the Ring of Kerry near to where Kay had been born – it was 'the getting there, not the arrival, she loved'. Dusty would sit inside with the windows up and watch as her friend leaped about these historic sites, or listen to Helene talk about the ancient history associated with the great stones. It was much as her father would have done. Once in New York Dusty got Norma to take OB on a tour bus round the sights. At each one they stopped at OB would be too busy talking and being curious to actually go into any of the buildings. Finally they got to the Empire State and Norma said, 'OB, we really ought to go up here you know.' 'Yes, yes,' said OB, 'but just tell me – do you think it was right when Truman dropped the bomb on Hiroshima?'

It was a long trip from Galway to Sheen Falls in the south-west and when she and Helene left Cregg it was, as usual, later than they planned. Dusty rang ahead to the hotel and said could they hold the reservation as they might be a bit late. The trip was argumentative but they did a detour so that Dusty could show Helene 'the wonderful way'. This happened to be over mountains, through passes, stuck on roads full of obstinate sheep and past waterfalls. Then they hit a storm. The drive became more and more hazardous with torrential rain and mist and then darkness. By the time they got to the hotel they were four hours late but Dusty was exhilarated. 'She just swept into the lobby like a Celtic queen, for God's sake,' says Helene. '"Terribly, terribly sorry for being so late," she said in her best English accent, "but there was a bit of a storm on the mountain."'

Her remark caused consternation amongst the hotel staff.

Didn't Miss Springfield know that the pass was closed off at this time of the year because it was so dangerous? Nobody, not even locals, drove that way for at least six months.

Earlier, when she and Helene had stopped on the cliff edge that morning, driving down from Galway and they'd looked down at the roaring Atlantic, Dusty had said, 'You know, when I die, this is where I'd like my ashes scattered.' It could have been a depressing moment there on the windy bluff looking out at infinity, but Dusty had laughed. 'I would like you to do it, Helene, but I'd prefer to have my ashes scattered and not your body, so maybe Tom should do it.' Helene was touched, since she was as aware as anybody that, given her vagueness and a mind usually deep in ruins and history, she would have been first over the clifftop before she could get the lid off the urn.

In fact the remark wasn't as out of the blue as it might have seemed. Although Dusty seemed to have beaten the breast cancer, she'd had a cough before she went to Ireland and it got worse during the trip, as did a strange pain in her collarbone. Helene's father had been a doctor and with Dusty's mother Kay having died of lung cancer Helene's first thought was that Dusty's period of remission was over. Dusty, not wanting to spoil the holiday or have a fuss, told Helene she thought she'd probably got a touch of bronchitis but she rang Vicki. 'I don't think this is good news do you?' she said. 'But I'm having such a good time I'm going to stay on an extra week.'

At Cregg Castle Helene, who thought Dusty had no idea she might be seriously ill again, approached her and said that since there was a pneumonia epidemic might it be a good idea to get her lungs checked? 'No,' Dusty had replied, 'I've had enough of that, I'm well now.'

Still worried, Helene confided in Annemarie and they concocted a plan: Annemarie would say she was having to take her daughter to the doctor's and, since the young girl liked Dusty so much, maybe she'd go along with them and Helene would get the doctor to x-ray Dusty. It's highly unlikely that Dusty was fooled by any of this, more that she felt that perhaps she ought to know after all rather than be so unnerved by the pain.

The x-rays were sent directly from Ireland to the Marsden. Helene called Pat in London and told her to make an appointment for Dusty the day she got back. 'Oh,' said Pat, 'she won't go anywhere the day after you get back here.' But she rang the specialist at the Marsden and made the appointment even though both she and Helene were crying.

The news was bad. The cancer had gone into Dusty's bones.

That week Dusty went back to the Marsden for more chemotherapy. It was a pattern she would keep up for the next two years – going in for doses of chemo – even though the doctors had warned her that, at best, they were only holding things at bay. At one point there was a discussion about a possible bone marrow transplant and Tom had gone in to be tested. Like many troubled people, having created endless crises in her life, when she was hit with a real one not of her own making Dusty rose to the battle magnificently. She ordered screeds of medical journals from America and talked constantly to anybody she thought might have a new idea about how to beat the disease.

Meanwhile, being Dusty, her first appearance back at the Marsden was not exactly plain sailing. After the breast cancer she had grown very familiar with the place and saw the staff as an extension of her friends, particularly since they had allowed her to ring them any time, day or night, if she was worried or upset. Now the Marsden became her own hospital and, like a hotel, she expected to have her old room back. When she walked in there was a very ill patient in the bed, and Dusty demanded to know what he was doing in 'her' room. When it was pointed out that she was somewhere else and this man was much sicker than she was Dusty retorted, 'And I've had more hit records than he has,' before flouncing out. 'Of course she regretted it instantly afterwards,' says Vicki, 'and went back and apologised – as usual.'

It was a side of Dusty, this mortification after she'd let something nasty slip out, that her neighbours at Frogmill were familiar with. It was to Lorna and Gib Hancock, who lived next door to her, that Dusty would always run when she thought she had done something unspeakably rude – losing her temper and flaring up at people who were, by and large, only trying to help her. 'You'll never guess what I just said,' she'd say in their kitchen. 'I feel terrible, I really shouldn't have done it.' In some respects, while she was at Frogmill and even afterwards, the Hancocks – even though they were much younger than Dusty's own parents – somehow became substitute parental figures.

A middle-class, and middle-England, couple, they had lived in Europe travelling extensively through Gib's job with ICI. Gib now wrote books in his spare time and was fond of cricket and football. He says he was always amazed that Dusty seemed to know who was in and out of the England team and who had beaten who in the League. Lorna, like Kay, was a slim, vivacious woman although she wore tailored expensive clothes and jewellery – quite a way from

Kay's equally neat but far less fashionable turnout. While Gib, like OB, was meticulous to the point of being pedantic, Lorna, like Dusty – and Kay had she had the money – loved shopping. The Dusty they met was an interesting neighbour: warm, gregarious, with an infectious laugh and a strong sense of right and wrong. 'Sometimes she would say things to me and they were so moral I'd be surprised,' says Lorna. 'I'd think, good heavens, that's the kind of thing I'd say! I just didn't expect it from someone who was in that music world.' Chameleon-like, it was almost as though Dusty had gone back to Ealing as a middle aged woman, without the intervening turbulent years, or the feeling that she had to succeed at any cost.

Often the Hancocks would visit Dusty in hospital if she was in for a long bout of treatment. And Dusty got on particularly well with Lorna who, apart from being smart, was kind and would often run in with meals for Dusty when she was back home feeling worn out from the chemotherapy. Many times she and Gib would have to prop up Simon Bell, upset after a particularly tense row with Dusty next door.

When Dusty was told the cancer was back some people were surprised that she didn't ask how much time she might have left or plan to go off round the world – particularly as travelling had been her passion for as long as she could remember. Instead she seemed to withdraw into herself as though she were building up her resources to fight. It was as though the woman who had blithely shrugged off any disaster – at least when she had her bravura front on – with the remark, 'There's always another motel up the road', had run out of places to move on to. Dusty had decided to stay put.

22

In fact Dusty did have to move on. The house at Frogmill was under siege. Word had got out that Dusty was now facing a potentially terminal illness and although Vicki had tried to keep the press at bay, issuing statements that Dusty was 'in good spirits', the tabloids had tracked her down. Now they were there, rattling Dusty's letterbox, shouting her name and trying to get pictures of her through her windows.

She moved out for a week to the Churchill Hotel to try and shake them off. The Churchill, slap in the middle of the West End by Portman Square, had always been her favourite. It wasn't just the pastel icing colours round its ornate interior, the huge chandeliers and the big sofas in the lobby, it was also the fact that they had a twenty-four-hour breakfast menu, offering a refined version of the truck-stop food Dusty had loved so much in the States. She had always tried to stay there whenever she'd had a couple of TV appearances to do. 'Suddenly,' says Vicki, 'Nicholas would be fine by himself and all those other minor things that stopped her working would disappear.' With her odd hours – even when she was ill she still hardly slept – Dusty could order eggs and bacon, toast and mushrooms whenever she wanted to and have it brought up, with a white starched tablecloth and heavy silver cutlery, to her room. It was here that she liked to do her interviews and she had stayed there, courtesy of the record company, when she was doing her promotional interviews for *A Very Fine Love* a year earlier when she thought she had beaten the cancer.

There was always a routine arriving at the hotel suite before facing the press. Debbie Dannell would empty the minibar of alcohol and fill it instead with Dusty's diet Coke. Then, since her hair was much thinner due to the effects of the chemotherapy and because Debbie had cut it close to her head, Dusty would decide what wig she would wear. Would it be 'Doris', or would it be 'Mavis'? Although she was still weak from the cancer treatment and sometimes appeared to magazine journalists as if she might suddenly burst into tears, she retained her bizarre sense of humour. Just as she had named her wigs at *Ready, Steady, Go!*, nearly thirty years later she was still imbuing them with a life force of their own: Maeve, for instance, was a bad lot, the one who might get into a hotel minibar *before* Debbie had cleared it.

Dusty usually felt reasonably relaxed with writers from magazines, who she knew would be writing long profiles rather than three-paragraph headline grabbers. She always saw them as less salacious and potentially less unkind than those from the tabloid newspapers. Yet if any of them, during that first day of interviews, had wondered why she stayed seated throughout the long conversations, or why Debbie or Dusty's make-up girl Phyllis flew round the table every five minutes to light Dusty's cigarette, they would have put it down, not unreasonably, to her still feeling weak after her illness. In fact just before the first interview was due to start Dusty had split a nail. Such imperfections, likely, she imagined, to be noted by a sharp-eyed reporter and mentioned, caused Dusty disproportionate panic. Debbie and Phyllis got out the superglue but, since the first reporter was at the hotel door, they were in such a rush to mend the nail that Dusty found that her left hand had been glued to the table and refused to budge. It wasn't until three interviews in that Debbie had time to use the remover and release the offending finger from its spot.

One day, back at Frogmill, she was on the phone to Pieter van der Zwan talking, as ever, about fairly mundane things like Nicholas needing an injection and the new kitchen she wanted, when she suddenly said, 'Pieter, I have cancer.' Van der Zwan was still in shock when Dusty got particularly businesslike. 'I just want to discuss all this with people who are knowledgeable.' She knew that Pieter's mother had died of breast cancer just before she had gone to live at Herengracht and that when Edwin had been diagnosed with Non Hodgkin's Lymphoma in 1990 he had undergone extensive chemotherapy and a bone marrow transplant. Halfway through the conversation she became irritable and told Pieter to hold on. 'I've just had to pull the curtains because there's someone with a camera outside the window,' she said when she came back on the phone.

When the first cancer was discovered Dusty had rung Lee Everett-Alkin. In the years since Los Angeles Lee had not only remarried but also taken a new direction and become a practising healer. Could she consult Lee professionally? Although she had long since abandoned the Catholic Church Dusty still believed in some force, something spiritually bigger than she was. Dusty would often go to Lee's house for healing. On days when she felt weak, particularly after another round of chemo, Lee would go to Frogmill. For a while she had shingles and stayed away in case Dusty, with her much-lowered immune system, would be infected. When she finally went back she found that the house had changed. 'I can't believe how dark this house has got,' she told Dusty. 'It's like wading through a huge dark cloud to get to your bedroom and it feels full of weeping.' It was this, and the almost constant presence of the national press outside, that convinced Lee that Dusty would have to move.

By 1998 Lee and Vicki were in daily contact. With Vicki in New York they decided that it would be Lee who would find Dusty somewhere more suitable to live. Knowing that she had run out of what little money was left and was worrying that she could no longer work or record, Vicki had suggested to Dusty that the one thing she had left to sell and so finance the move, were the royalties from her back catalogue. That way, Vicki thought, but did not tell her friend, Dusty could at least live out what was left of her life in some comfort.

The Prudential did the deal. Although the press reported that it was the back catalogue, and that it had been sold for six million dollars, in fact the deal was for only the projected future royalties on her records and the real amount was less than £750,000. It may have seemed very little for a lifetime of music and a decade of hit records, and Dusty knew it, but it was enough to give her a new home – somewhere the press couldn't reach her.

The house was close to Henley in Oxfordshire and behind a five-bar gate marked 'Private Property'. Old and rambling, it had six bedrooms, nearly as many bathrooms and a massive garden that rolled down to the grassy edges of a golf course. Dusty loved it immediately, particularly since it was in a place called Harpsden Bottom, which she found highly amusing. Getting her there, however, proved difficult. As Pat had found many times to her cost, moving Dusty was not to be undertaken with a faint heart. Yes, she'd go tomorrow. No, she couldn't possibly; she hadn't started packing yet. This went on for weeks with Lee ringing Vicki in frustration. Finally Vicki flew in and the two women decided the only thing they could do was get Dusty into a car, take her to Harpsden and get her possessions sorted out at Frogmill in her absence.

Yet Dusty protested to the last nanosecond. She had grown to be unhappy at the Frogmill house, which she'd never really thought of as home, but she was equally reluctant to leave. It was an upheaval to move even if you were well and she was not keen to leave the Hancocks. She had come to rely upon their presence.

Decades earlier, when Dusty was touring, she had always insisted on packing up her own dresses and make-up bag when she'd come off stage, even though Pat was competent to do it. It would take Dusty two or more hours, talking most of the time and so it would be nearly two in the morning before she and Pat would leave the venue. 'It got to the point,' says Vicki, 'that although it was terrific going to the shows I used to do a runner straight afterwards. Going backstage and waiting for Dust was excruciating. She would obsessionally put things in exactly the right spot in her make-up bag and once you were in the dressing room you were trapped.' With the thought that moving Dusty from one house to another with her 'things' would be an even worse re-run than the dressing-room saga, Vicki and Lee finally did what they laughingly referred to as 'a kidnap raid' and got Dusty to Harpsden.

Once Dusty was in the new house with her things

ferried across from Frogmill she was much happier. In her cinema-loving way she called it her 'Tara', a reference to Vivien Leigh's love affair with the estate in the deep south that ruled her emotions in David O. Selznick's *Gone With The Wind*. Lee was convinced that moving to the new house gave Dusty at least another year of life.

Bone cancer is a particularly nasty disease and by March Vicki and Lee, knowing that Dusty would often feel debilitated or worse, decided that she would have to have a housekeeper. Eileen Hurley, who had only recently nursed her dying husband and who knew Lee, was the perfect choice. Reliable and sturdy, she was also Irish. When she was told about Eileen, Dusty sent Vicki a fax saying she hoped Mrs Hurley wasn't 'too grand' for her. 'After all there won't be Twinkies to help her,' she scrawled – referring to the young housemaids in Victorian upper-class homes who were actually called 'tweenies'. 'She sounds GREAT . . . I'm actually quite terrified of her. I'm no good with staff – they try to convert me to strange cults! All very promising though. Hare Krishna or something.' In fact Eileen found favour with Dusty immediately – not easy given Dusty's natural inclination not to want anyone around full-time.

It was also obvious that as the illness progressed she'd need someone more or less permanently with her and able to drive her around. With Vicki in America, Lee married and Pat with a husband and son, Simon Bell was the one person who had no prior commitments. It was decided that he would move into Harpsden for the duration, do any shopping Dusty wanted, run errands and be around for her. As with most of the gay men she knew Dusty's relationship with Bell was volatile and they would often fall out. By spring Dusty was going backwards and forwards to the Marsden for courses of chemotherapy. She still believed she could beat the cancer just as she had beaten the booze and the pills and the arm cutting. After all, as she pointed out to journalists when she was promoting *A Very Fine Love*, given what she'd done in America she had no right still to be alive. Now she fought to try and hold the cancer at bay.

23

By that summer, however, she was enjoying the relative peace of the new house and was feeling stronger. Faye, on her way to Europe for a film festival, was staying at the Ritz Hotel and had rung Dusty on the off-chance. Although they had been in contact by phone over the past ten years, when the cancer was diagnosed Dusty had been firm – there were to be 'no deathbed scenes' she had told Faye, so she was only to come to the house when Dusty was feeling okay. 'Anyway,' says Faye, 'it didn't surprise me. You couldn't call her and make a date even when she was well. It alarmed her to make that kind of commitment.'

Dusty sent Simon to the Ritz to pick Faye up but when she got to the house Dusty was upstairs making-up. She must have been nervous. It had been nearly twenty years since she and Faye had lived together. Faye, left roaming downstairs, got a jolt when she saw many of the things that Dusty had had when they'd shared the Hollywood houses. She wandered into the garden, down the rolling lawn and turned around to see Dusty standing outside the windows, 'looking beautiful, wearing blue and white. She looked just like the woman I'd met in the early seventies. I went back up the hill towards her and – it was both amazing and like a bad TV commercial really.'

As usual when Dusty was nervous she stood in front of Faye looking at her feet and shuffling. 'It was very difficult for us both,' says Faye. 'We hadn't seen each other for years, and we knew we weren't going to see each other again.' They played with Nicholas, talked about Faye's mother and her work. After a while it was obvious that Dusty was tiring but before Faye left she went upstairs and came back with a Harrods bag. Inside were a pair of bright cerise high-heeled ankle boots: 'I want you to have something that will always remind you of me,' she said, smiling. She knew Faye would think they were outrageous and never wear them. In fact, later, Faye sometimes wore them around the house since they turned out to be very comfortable, but the only time they made a public appearance was at the funeral of Dusty's old Hollywood agent Howard Portugais. Faye, wittily, took them in a see-through plastic bag as a token of Dusty's presence. Dusty's original American manager Alan Bernard recognised them immediately: 'Dusty's shoes!' he yelped.

By 1998 everyone knew that Dusty was now fighting cancer full on. Amazingly, in a world so full of gossip, the recurrence of her illness had remained a relative secret. In February Dusty had been due on stage at the Brit Music Awards. Instead, comedian Ben Elton announced that she was too ill to turn up and the public was given the first hint that Dusty's life might be on the line.

Meanwhile Dusty replaced her reliance on drink and drugs, her addictions, with a different kind of obsessiveness. Just as recording always became obsessive, just as any TV appearance where she had to talk became a nightmare for the sound people because of miking up her clothes – 'God forbid her lapel should be half a millimetre out,' says Vicki – so Tara became the focus of Dusty's perfectionism. Or rather wrapped in it. There were plastic runners in the hall for muddy feet and Nicholas's paws; there were plastic covers on the chairs.

Certainly covering everything up and making a fuss until things were in their right place was so untypical of the old Dusty, yet in a way, unable to stop the cancer however much she put her body through, it may well have been her only way of controlling what she thought of as the ultimate disruption. A wet cup was never allowed on the stainless-steel kitchen sink in case it left a watermark and tea parties came to resemble the very atmosphere that had so driven Dusty crazy at Westbourne Grove, with cup and plate whisked from under your nose directly you put them down.

And there were epic tea parties at the house, with a groaning table of cakes and scones, enough to feed at least twenty people. Dusty would dispatch Simon or Eileen to the local Tesco supermarket and, in an effort to appear to be sensible, insist that everything they bought was practically fat-free. When Tom would make a rare appearance, or Vicki and Nona were coming, this array included defrosted Swiss rolls with ice cream in the middle. In a strange way these events were like children's tea parties and of course half the food would be wasted. Dusty, who had always loved this kind of carbohydrate high, would be left to munch her way through as much as she could cope with. Even so the progression of the illness meant she underwent an enormous weight loss. She tried to make light of it by saying to Lee that it was wonderful because now she might even get into her Versace suit.

Dusty still avidly studied the clothes catalogues. 'Don't you think this is nice?' she'd ask Lee, showing her an expensive woolly hat and scarf and carefully turning down the corner of the page. 'For God's sake, Dust,' Lee said, 'the only time you go out is when you go to and from hospital in an ambulance. When are you going to wear a hat and scarf?' Still Dusty kept the page turned down and on various occasions coming back home from the Marsden would insist on stopping the ambulance so that she and Lee could stagger into Divertimenti, the serious cooks' shop in Fulham Road, to buy gleaming stainless-steel draining racks, juicers and food mixers – top-of-the-range kitchen kit for meals she would never eat . . .

That autumn Suzanne Lacefield and her partner Barbara went to Tara for four days. They had been to London when Dusty's first cancer had appeared and had met her at the Churchill. In between there had been phone calls, but this was the first time they had stayed with her for any length of time. Before they arrived it was chaos in the house with Dusty running about laying out clean towels and bedding. 'It was kind and generous of her but we kept telling her not to worry about it,' says Suzanne. 'She would insist there was lots of soap and lots of flowers and we said, "But you don't have to take care of us. We're here to see you and tell you we love you and take care of you."'

There were, of course, the inevitable teas and quite a few tears to boot. On one occasion Dusty drew Suzanne to one side: 'You don't know how grateful I am to you for saving my life,' she said quietly. 'You gave me another twenty years.' One evening during the visit Suzanne, Barbara, Nona and Vicki, Lee and her husband John, Simon and Eileen were all sitting round the kitchen table laughing and Dusty stood in the doorway watching. 'It's what I've always wanted,' she said wistfully. 'To have everybody round the table having a good time and now – here you all are.' She went in and out of the kitchen a few times, almost to check that the image she'd seen stayed the same.

Just before Christmas 1998 Dusty was spending more and more time on the sofa in the huge front room where she could look out of the window at the animals and watch Nicholas trying to hunt the birds. By now she had deliberately broken one arm of her glasses so that they'd be more comfortable when she turned her head to watch the television and she would wear her Brazil football T-shirt when she watched football matches. That Christmas Tom sent Dusty a Christmas card and Dusty was incredibly excited, opening it over and over again to read what it said. Lee couldn't work out why she was making such a fuss; after all, she would say to Dusty, it was only a card. 'I know,' Dusty would answer, her eyes shining. 'But it's the first one Tom's ever sent me.'

Every Christmas for five years Dusty and Faye had spoken on the phone and sung a rousing rendition of 'Angels We Have Heard On High' long-distance, with Faye singing the lead and Dusty doing descants and at least thirty different chorus fills. This Christmas was different. After years of 'Angels' Dusty left Faye a message on her machine. She was crying: 'I'm sorry, I don't think I can sing it this year. I can't sing at all.' Faye faxed her the lyrics instead.

Just before Christmas Dusty was back at the Marsden. Although she knew there wasn't much else the doctors could do for her, she remained in reasonable spirits. She was a big favourite with the other patients because she always remembered where they were on their course of treatments and would chat to them to cheer them up: they seemed to have put on a bit of weight; oh, they were looking so much better! By now most of her friends knew that if they wanted to talk to her, ringing her in hospital was their best chance. Once she was back home their hopes of getting through to her were negligible. Faye was amazed when she rang her room one day and, knowing she wouldn't want a serious conversation about her health, started 'prattling about these two Turkish men I'd met who sold rugs and how I was getting them started up in LA'. Despite everything Dusty was both in a protective and funny mood: 'Beware of men in light suits and shiny glasses with lots of Ns in their name,' she said to Faye and laughed.

The Marsden doctors were doing everything possible to keep Dusty going, including full blood transfusions to battle against the white blood cells. Most days the only people who could get into her room regularly without having to wait were Vicki and Debbie – neither of whom ever stayed long and didn't get upset in front of her. One day Dusty rang Debbie with, 'Deb, I've got to be in my coffin as a blonde, please come as soon as you can.' That evening, armed with her hairdresser's equipment and a large bottle of bleach, Debbie turned up to the Marsden to be faced with a client attached to a transfusion drip. Hobbling between the bathroom and the smoking area, wheeling the drip with them, Debbie and Dusty giggled and smoked their way through a packet of cigarettes and an entire lightening process. Occasionally the Marsden's doctors and nurses popped their heads round the door only to recoil in consternation. By one thirty in the morning Dusty was a pretty soft blonde and was happy. 'Now,' she said, smiling, 'I can have an open-topped box.'

Although she would also often joke with Simon about his upcoming James Last tour – 'Well, I'd better be gone by then' – she was now, understandably, far less likely to be ready with a *bon mot*. One night she had rung Los Angeles in a panic: 'I'm going to die,' she said to Faye, 'and I don't know how to do it – I've never done it before.' It was as though her fear of what she might appear to be like at the end was as overwhelming to her as her fear that the orchestra notes would be wrong when she got on stage. It was the Catholic Faye and the spiritualist Lee who would calm her: Lee by convincing her that they'd still be able to contact each other; Faye by inventing a heaven in which Bette Davis was furious because there was no smoking and where Sammy Davis took rousing gospel services each morning.

It had taken her friends six long months in 1998 to convince Dusty to make a will. If anything had brought Dusty to tears over the last few years it was concern over the fate of her cat. When she had had the first news from the Marsden she said she had gone back to Nicholas and hugged him. Sitting in the hall she'd wailed, 'Who's going to look after you when I'm gone?' In truth, although Nicholas had doubtless been a highly appealing kitten and a great ball of fluff, he had grown into a rather unfriendly and supercilious cat who wouldn't let anyone but Dusty stroke him or pick him up. Only Lee, whose love of animals matched Dusty's own, could go within a yard of this long-haired grey mat on legs. Securing the future of her last remaining cat was the one thing that made Dusty finally sort out what was left of her finances, and it was to Lee that Dusty left Nicholas – to keep him in the manner to which he had become accustomed.

Although Dusty kept changing her mind – and the levels of bequests – by October 1998 a will was in place. Gib and

Lorna Hancock and a solicitor would oversee her estate and take on what Lorna describes as 'the not inconsiderable task of administering her affairs'. Helene would be contacted to translate Dusty's rather daffy instructions over the sums involved when she wrote that someone should get 'a little' and someone else 'a lot'. By then Helene was the only person Dusty really seemed to trust fully and she had given Helene the keys to her lock-up in Los Angeles where she had stored the things from her past. Later when Helene unlocked it she found that, amongst the possessions, Dusty had kept all her teenage film magazines from the 1950s.

By January 1999 word had come through that Dusty was to be given a place in the Rock and Roll Hall of Fame in the middle of March that year. Dusty had smiled when Vicki told her. Finally America was going to recognise her. Ironic really. The Hall of Fame, in Cleveland Ohio, was started in 1986 to be a research base and permanent exhibition centre for 'rock's true pioneers', artists who had been involved with music for at least twenty-five years and who had made what was judged a remarkable contribution to their art. Dusty was to join the list of the great and good which included the Rolling Stones, the Beatles, Otis Redding and Stevie Wonder.

At least Dusty knew that, whatever else, she would always have her place in history, and in the event it would be Elton John who would accept the award on Dusty's behalf at the ceremony at the Waldorf Astoria in Manhattan in March: 'I think she was the greatest white singer there has ever been,' he said that night. 'Every song she sang, she claimed as her own.'

That January Dusty had been named in the New Year Honours List for an Order of the British Empire. The list is drawn up annually by the Queen and the government of the day and although Dusty was pleased to be getting some recognition after all the years, she was also cynical enough to suspect that she was only getting the award because she was terminally ill. Vicki, who was in London, rang St James's Palace and talked to them about exactly how a seriously ill Dusty was going to get her medal. She was told there were three different things that could be organised. The first was that they could arrange a wheelchair and special access to the investiture so that Dusty could receive the award directly from the Queen; the second was to send an official to the hospital so that he could 'bestow' it on her; the third was for Vicki to pick it up and take it to her.

Since Vicki knew Dusty was too exhausted to make a journey out of the hospital and then sit about for hours in public, option one was out of the question; since it was likely that, ill though she was, Dusty would have had a giggling fit if anything had been 'bestowed' on her, the second option seemed fraught with risks. Vicki therefore went to the grandly named Central Chancery of the Orders of Knighthood at St James's Palace, dressed in her regulation black clothes and being her usual cheerful self: 'And they were very sweet. They were disappointed Dust wasn't going – they'd got all her albums there, waiting for her to autograph them.'

The OBE was in a little case; a letter and a large plaque went with it. Vicki wondered, had they got a bag she could put everything in? The palace staff rifled in the cupboard and flourished a Fortnum and Mason's bag. Dusty's favourite shop. Vicki thought it was all too perfect.

Back at the hospital Dusty was initially more thrilled at the sight of the bag than she was at the OBE. 'Isn't this the award they give to cleaners?' she asked Vicki and she thought the ribbon attached to the medal looked 'a bit frayed'. Vicki had decided that the event should not pass unmarked and had invited everyone on the other wards to come to Dusty's room later. 'At first, of course, she threw an absolute wobbler. "I can't see anyone, I'm not well enough, now they're all going to hate me." So we looked at the OBE and I said, "Look I'll just tell everyone to go away, it's no big deal for me to do that." And she said, "No, no, no."'

Just as she had pulled out the stops at the last minute, right the way through her career, Dusty got up, did her hair, put on her dressing-gown and pink slippers and went round the hospital. Everyone at the Royal Marsden, on the wards, in private rooms, the patients, doctors, nurses and visitors, were thrilled as Dusty did the rounds with her OBE. 'It was extraordinary in a way,' says Vicki. 'There she was with no make-up on and she was genuinely excited getting the OBE and at everyone's reaction, and they were genuinely thrilled to bits for her.'

By February Dusty was back at Tara. She was still refusing to have morphine IV, where a controlled amount of pain-killer would have been fed through an attached line directly into her bloodstream. Instead she was taking the morphine in tablet form. Lee would go and get the prescriptions for her and she and Dusty would joke that, for the first time in her life Dusty now had a 'habit' that was legal. Still, there wasn't much joking going around that month.

One day towards the end of February Pat rang Lee in a panic. For months Pat had not been near the house. She couldn't bear to see Dusty so ill and so weak and she had been sick herself. Now Simon and Eileen had gone out shopping and Pat was alone with Dusty. 'Lee, you've got to come over here quickly, please. I think Dusty's dying. I think she's going to die any minute.'

When Lee arrived twenty minutes later Pat was shaking all over. 'I told her to go and have a cup of tea and that I'd go straight in to see Dusty,' says Lee. 'Dust was there on the sofa and I must say I thought, oh God, she's gone, and then she moved and opened her eyes and looked at me.'

Realising that Dusty knew she was there, Lee gave her some healing and then sat in a chair close to her as she always did. After a while Dusty sat up. 'Is there,' she whispered, a very slight smile on her lips, 'any more of that cake left in the fridge?'

24

March is usually a miserable month in England, full of bluster and noise. High cold winds can nip off the heads of daffodils, grey sleety rain can fall like a curtain, holding out the sun and turning the grass into a tangle of brown mud. Yet Friday, 12 March 1999 dawned with a surprisingly mild airstream as though it were early summer, a kind of lazy morning with only the lightest touch of drizzle falling on to the river at Henley.

Dusty's funeral at the twelfth-century parish church of St Mary the Virgin was due to start at twelve thirty, but from dawn people had been pressing behind the barriers outside. St Mary's towered in the town centre, surprisingly large, with the solemnity of a cathedral rather than the intimacy of a local church. Because of its position, on a curve, swept by the main road through town, it was impossible to see it if you were walking up the river towpath from the station.

It seemed like such an incongruous place to hold the funeral of a woman who was the greatest soul singer Britain has ever produced. Almost as incongruous as Ealing had been as a place for that same woman to grow up. Henley is middle England at its finest and bleached white. Once a year it hosts the Regatta, now as well known as Ascot for bringing out the upper classes in their hats and with their picnic baskets loaded with smoked salmon and champagne. Its position on the Thames riverbank gives it a rural feeling and the centre of town resembles a picture that looks as if it has hardly changed for a century.

Yet Dusty had perhaps been more contented here, fighting a real battle against real odds, than she'd been anywhere for years.

For a few minutes it seemed as though it were just any old Friday morning in semi-rural England: the bustle of locals at the butchers and greengrocers with their shopping baskets, the smell of fresh-baked bread, fruit and herbs wafting through open shop doorways. So it was a shock to turn the corner and suddenly to hear nothing, except the tolling of the church bell and the palpable silence of hundreds of people who were now patiently standing in the drizzle, behind the metal barriers on the pavement. For a moment it brought back pictures of that other funeral only rather more than a year before. There was the same expression on these faces: as though someone they had known with enormous intimacy had died. And in a way, like Diana, they had and they hadn't.

Dusty had died at her home on 2 March, a few weeks before her sixtieth birthday – the one she had probably never wanted to face. For Dusty, so associated with youth, her sixtieth would have marked a particular psychological impasse: too old, she would have thought, for people to find her attractive; not old enough to wear purple and be truly eccentric or wise.

It was also the day, had she been well, she would have gone to her investiture at Buckingham Palace to receive her OBE from the Queen. As a 'civilian' she would have been expected to wear 'Day Dress, Morning Dress or Lounge

Suit' – a list that would have caused consternation and hours of delay while she dragged everything she owned out of the wardrobe. Would she have ever got there between ten and ten thirty that morning? And if she had would the Queen have remembered that she was about to give a medal to a woman who, years earlier, had been told to apologise for taking her name in vain?

In 1978, after her Drury Lane concerts, Dusty had appeared at the Royal Albert Hall for a special concert for the Invalid Children's Aid Association. Princess Margaret had been in the royal box and, again, Dusty's audience had a hefty sprinkling of gay men and lesbians. At one point in her set, when a couple of rows of boys got over-excited, Dusty had laughed: 'I'm glad to see,' she had said teasingly, 'that royalty isn't confined to the box.' Whether it was simply that the Princess had a sense of humour failure and was stuffily outraged at the 'family firm' being compared to hoi polloi in the stalls, or whether there was a lot of lateral thinking going on between the word association 'royalty' with 'queens', who knows? After the show Dusty, stuck in the line-up to be greeted by the Princess, was cut dead. A few days later she received a letter from the Palace demanding that she sign the attached: a letter of apology to Her Majesty.

Dusty had died at eleven at night; she had, at least, been spared her demonic two hours between 12 and 2 a.m. Once the news was released on the wires, the next twenty-four hours were frantic. Her death was an item on every news TV programme and took up three or four pages in every national newspaper. It was marked in Australia, South Africa, across America and Europe, with, on radio and TV, ten-minute profiles of Dusty the artist and her music.

In Ireland it seemed like an unofficial day of mourning, with her records played constantly on the radio.

It was, said one newspaper, 'the day the music died'. Women journalists who normally wrote pieces to prick your social conscience remembered how, when they were teenagers, they would enter talent contests miming to her songs; an American journalist hoped he'd meet Dusty in heaven.

Like a teenager who wants to know that there will be a good turnout of friends at their funeral, as though somehow they'd be there to see it, Dusty had planned some aspects of her funeral before she died. She wanted the traffic stopped in Henley, so yellow-jacketed police outriders stood next to their bikes, hands clasped in front of them. Incurably romantic, she had also asked for black horses with plumes to pull the glass hearse. The arrival of her coffin was thus preceded by the sound of hooves on the cobbled road and the sniffling of the crowds into their handkerchiefs. Even though an enormous wreath, spelling out 'Dusty' in white flowers, lay against the side of the coffin, like the ones that read 'Mum' or 'Dad' from the solid working-class families of the East End of London, for a second the scene, with its carriage and horses, was like something out of a Russian novel.

Except, of course, that the massed banks of press photo-graphers were out in force too. Camera bulbs flashed in unison, as though, in some bizarre way, the elegantly suited Neil Tennant with Chris Lowe at his side, Lulu in her dark glasses, brother Tom, a surprisingly tender-looking Elvis Costello, Nona Hendryx a vision in black fur trim, all of whom were to recall Dusty during the service, were like stars attending a film première. Inside the church Madeline

Bell was telling her mother to take her dark glasses off. 'I keep telling you, nobody's going to recognise you, Mother!' Designer Jasper Conran and his friends resolutely refused to pray when everyone kneeled down; Julie Felix with her long dark hair looked startlingly similar to the way she had when she swung around in Dusty's hanging chair in Kensington so long ago.

Hundreds of bouquets of flowers were tiered inside the nave, like a star's dressing room on opening night: from Elton John on tour in America; Rod Stewart, Cilla Black, Lulu, Tom Jones, Sandie; from a plethora of record company executives, including the founders of Atlantic; from the Rolling Stones; from Dusty's favourite American songwriters, and from 'Paul McCartney and kids' who was glad that he had been able to tell her, when they had exchanged phone calls before Linda died, how great she was.

Yet standing there in that dignified church 'saying goodbye to our sister Dusty', something seemed to be missing. Yes, she was 'fab', she had a voice 'that was full of longing and demanded your attention' and in that huge vaulted space you could bear witness to this as a succession of her greatest records were played, and yes she had also been a revolutionary in the music world she inhabited. With her strong personality and her forceful musical opinions, she had made it possible for other women musicians after her to take control of their careers – even if she hadn't been able to herself. But, just as importantly, Dusty the private woman had the most terrific sense of humour. At times it had been her salvation.

Amongst the flowers, on the cold flagstone floor, someone had left a small custard tart in memory of just that side of her personality. It was, as it happened, Red Nose Day in Britain, when comedians and celebrities appear in TV marathons to raise money for charity and people wander around with plastic red noses on. It is an event that has been successfully running for years. If Dusty had known the date of her funeral in advance there's little doubt she would have insisted that red noses would have been *de rigueur* for everyone at St Mary the Virgin that Friday.

Dusty's funeral was her final show and Vicki and Simon Bell had worked on which of her songs to include in the service. Dusty's coffin was carried in, sadly closed despite her last minute hairdo, to her recording of 'You Don't Have To Say You Love Me'. Her version of Carole King's brilliant and elegaic 'Going Back' coming through the speakers was the perfect finale. As her coffin left the church it was greeted by the extraordinary spectacle of the crowd and the mourners bursting into applause – as though she had just come off stage.

And in a way she had. Because her records were played throughout the service you could close your eyes and, if not count to ten, at least envisage that half smile, the arms going up and the head tilting to one side. With the latest hi-tech system, you thought how happy she would have been with the sound. In that massive space it finally gave her the echo she'd always wanted.

Most of all, appropriately, Dusty's voice was the thread that held the service together. It was a voice that had sometimes let her down and had sometimes been abused, but when she died music critics compared her, not to her white peers but to the great black American singers such as Al Green, Aretha, Gladys Knight. And to her audience in the Henley streets that Friday Dusty represented more than just a great singer who seemed to have had a tough life.

In a way she was like a film star to many of them, the closest Britain in the sixties had ever got to producing a talented bottle blonde who was as charismatic as Marilyn Monroe – stronger for sure, less sensual, but with that same beguiling mix of child/woman vulnerability. They had grown up with Dusty's singing, they had romanced and danced to her music, they could probably have told you where they were the day they first heard 'You Don't Have To Say You Love Me'. For them her death represented the passing of their own history as much as hers.

The spectre of two other women singers had always haunted Dusty. One was Judy Garland, the other was Florence Ballard. Garland had married a succession of gay men and died at the age of forty-seven from barbiturate poisoning. Ballard had formed the Supremes but started drinking when Berry Gordy pushed Diana Ross into the limelight. Involved in an abusive marriage she had died, penniless, at the age of thirty-three. Dusty had once invoked both Garland and Ballard's names in interviews quite early in her career. When things got bad for her in America it looked as though she were on the path to a self-fulfilling prophecy. Yet, in the end, she had not only lived longer than either of them but had, in her late fifties, started to experience success again.

'What a marvellous life,' Dusty had once said in one of her less self-flagellating moods. 'To be able to sing and to enjoy it.'

Index

Credits

Photo Credits

Lyric Credits

SIMPLY DUSTY

4 CD BOXSET

The Definitive Dusty Springfield collection.
A Musical Anthology spanning her entire career, from her earliest
recordings with the Lana Sisters through to her celebrated
comeback with Pet Shop Boys and final recording
"Someone To Watch Over Me"

•

Over 90 Digitally Remastered tracks, many hard to
find & previously unavailable.

•

48 Page colour booklet includes rare & unseen
photos & Dusty memorabilia

•

Includes tributes from Carole King, Annie Lennox &
Sir Elton John amongst others.

•

Features 19 Top 20 Singles, including I Only Wanna Be With You, I
Just Don't Know What to Do With Myself; Son of A Preacher
Man, The Look of Love, What Have I Done To Deserve This (with
Pet Shop Boys)...

Available now on Mercury Records.